SHOCKiNG WHiSTLE-BLOWER TESTiMONY

"Those bodies—the Roswell bodies—they weren't aliens. The government could care less about stories about alien bodies found at Roswell, except to hide the truth. Those bodies were Japanese people. I should have spoken about this years ago. I should have said something.

"The Japanese and the Nazis had done unspeakable things to these people. Well, it was probably inevitable that someone is going to realize that there is a huge research value to looking at the way in which people and bodies have been used . . . in high-altitude experimentation, pressurization tests, injecting of plagues and viruses, chemicals, and—later, here—exposure to radiation.

"Word came down that this was to be a highly-classified project: 'If it helps us get an edge on the Russians, do what you have to do with these people, but you keep it classified and you commit nothing to paper.' They knew, we all knew, that this was going to be damned and dirty. Everyone had their own pet projects with these people . . . And the desert was big enough for everyone to have their slice."

OTHER BOOKS BY NiCK REDFERN

BODY SNATCHERS iN THE DESERT

THE HORRiBLE TRUTH AT THE HEART OF THE ROSWELL STORY

NiCK REDFERN

PARAVIEW POCKET BOOKS

NEW YORK LONDON TORONTO SYDNEY

PARAVIEW
191 Seventh Avenue, New York, NY 10011

POCKETBOOKS, a division of Simon & Schuster, Inc.
1230 Avenue of the Americas, New York, NY 10020

ISBN: 978-0-7434-9753-4

First Paraview Pocket Books trade paperback edition June 2005

10 9 8 7 6 5 4 3 2 1

Designed by Jaime Putorti

For information regarding special discounts for bulk purchases,
please contact Simon & Schuster Special Sales at 1-800-456-6798
or business@simonandschuster.com.

CONTENTS

INTRODUCTION

In the summer of 1947, *something* crashed to earth in the blisteringly hot and barren deserts of New Mexico. The event has been the subject of many books, official investigations undertaken by both the government and the military, numerous television documentaries, a movie, intense media coverage and speculation, and has left in its wake a legacy of controversy and a web of intrigue that continue to reverberate nearly sixty years later. It has come to be known as the Roswell Incident.

It is a matter of record that in early July 1947, the then Army Air Forces announced that it had recovered the remains of a "flying disc" that had been found on a ranch near the town of Roswell, New Mexico. The intense media frenzy that followed was only brought to a swift and conclusive halt when the AAF hastily retracted its statement: the flying disk story was a huge mistake and the crash "remains" were actually nothing more than a weather balloon. Today, the United States Air Force tells a different story: that the debris found at Roswell came from a top-secret balloon project designed to monitor Soviet nuclear tests and that claims of unusual-looking or "alien" bodies found at the site were, in reality, based upon witnesses remembering having seen "crash-test dummies" utilized in parachute experiments.

Those who champion the idea that something truly anomalous occurred at Roswell scoff at the ever-mutating assertions of the Pentagon and maintain that a conspiracy of truly cosmic proportions exists at the highest level to hide the out-of-this-world truth of the affair and its alien origins.

But what if there was another, distinctly darker explanation behind the Roswell legend—one that summarily dismissed the balloon and crash-test dummy claims but that also laid to rest the theories that extraterrestrials met their deaths in the New Mexico desert? From 1996 to 2004, I spoke with a number of military and intelligence whistle-blowers, all of whom related to me the details of a series of shocking post–World War II experiments undertaken on American soil. I confess that I did not initially pay much attention to the claims. But as time progressed and additional and corroborative data and testimony began to surface, the horrible truth behind the legend of Roswell became apparent. This controversial body of data and never-before-revealed testimony forms the crux of *Body Snatchers in the Desert*.

ONE

THE OAK RiDGE SECRET

It is a fact of life that people can't keep secrets. They wait for the right moment and the right person to tell their secrets to. As a full-time investigative author and journalist who has spent more than twenty years delving deeply into the murky world of official secrecy and probing the innermost workings of the intelligence community, I have often been that person. But never have I been told anything as shocking as what an elderly lady told me after a speaking engagement in Los Angeles in July 2001.

Because she does not want her identity revealed, for reasons that will shortly become apparent, I will refer to her as the Black Widow. When I met her, she was nearly eighty years of age. From the mid-1940s to the early 1950s, she had been assigned to the Oak Ridge National Laboratory, Tennessee, and she said she had firsthand knowledge of the Roswell mystery that I "might find interesting." I had heard many Roswell revelations before, but what she was about to tell me was unlike anything I had ever heard.

A sprightly character, the Black Widow smiled and laughed a lot as she spoke. But behind that facade I detected a distinct air of anxiety, and she possessed the sad and somewhat sunken eyes of a person with the weight of the world on her shoulders. She was clearly looking for someone to speak with; but equally, she was very concerned about the ramifications of doing so, "if the government finds out."

I reassured her that since the government and military asserted strenuously that nothing more unusual than a balloon crashed to earth in New Mexico in 1947, they were hardly in a position to take action against her for what they claimed was largely a nonevent. She smiled, nodded, and a look of relief spread across her face—momentarily, at least. We agreed to meet the following morning for breakfast at a nearby diner. And so it was that she revealed her dark and disturbing tale.[1]

Spread out along broad valleys cut by the Clinch River and framed by the foothills of the Appalachian Mountains, Oak Ridge seems an unlikely setting for events that changed the course of history. In early 1942, the Army Corps of Engineers designated a 59,000-acre swatch of land between Black Oak Ridge to the north and the Clinch River to the south as a federal reserve to serve as one of three sites nationwide for the development of the atomic bomb.

No fewer than 3,000 residents received court orders to vacate—within a matter of weeks—the homes that their families had occupied for generations. Thousands of scientists, engineers, and workers swarmed into Oak Ridge to build and operate three huge facilities that would change the history of the region and the world forever. On the reservation's western edge rose the gaseous diffusion plant, designated "K-25," a warehouselike building covering a larger area than any structure ever built up to that time.

Completed at a cost of $500 million and operated by 12,000 workers, the K-25 plant separated uranium-235 from uranium-238. On its northern edge rose the workers' city, named Oak Ridge; south of the city, the Y-12 plant, where an electromagnetic method was used to separate uranium-235, was erected. Built for $427 million, the Y-12 plant employed 22,000 workers. Near the reservation's southwest corner, about ten miles from Y-12, was the third plant, X-10.

During the war, X-10 was called Clinton Laboratories, named after the nearby county seat of rural Anderson County; and in 1948, Clinton Laboratories became Oak Ridge National Laboratory. Today the laboratory, which celebrated its fiftieth anniversary in 1993, has evolved from a war emergency pilot plant, which operated under an overwhelming cloak of secrecy, into one of the nation's outstanding centers for energy, environmental, and basic scientific research and technology development. It currently employs about 4,500 people, including many scientists recognized internationally as experts in their fields. Laboratory endeavors range from studies of nuclear chemistry and physics to inquiries into global warming, energy conservation, high-temperature superconductivity, and new materials. Its institutional roots, however, lie with the awesome power released by the splitting of the atom. But in the mid to late 1940s, said the Black Widow, Oak Ridge held a far more awesome— and horrific—secret than anyone could possibly have imagined.[2]

As we sat and ate, the Black Widow told me what her job at Oak Ridge had involved. It was her duty to assist in research that was being conducted at the time to determine the effects of radiation and high-altitude exposure on the human body. Much of the research, she explained, was related to experiments that had been undertaken both at Oak Ridge and Los Alamos after 1946 and that specifically centered upon the military's then-fledgling plans to build and fly a nuclear-powered, prototype aircraft as part of the Nuclear Energy for Propulsion of Aircraft (NEPA) project—and later, Oak Ridge's own Aircraft Nuclear Program (ANP). Although much, if indeed not all, of the research was still at the drawing-board stage in the period 1946–47, of paramount concern to the military, she expounded, was the possible effect that such a power source might have on the physical health of the aircraft's crew when matters progressed to actual test flights.

The Army Air Forces had other concerns as well as it ventured into the fields of truly futuristic aircraft designs and technologies. There were, she explained, "cosmic ray worries, pressurization experiments, human ejector research [and] health worries that might be found from very high altitude flying for long periods."

She stopped speaking at that point and said nothing for a long while. Finally she said, "I am really thinking whether or not I should tell you this." Anxious not to lose her trust, I nodded and said that I understood her delicate position.

I detected a long, audible breath and the Black Widow began to reveal a story she had obviously kept to herself for decades. On three occasions from May to August 1947, she told me, "horrible-looking bodies were brought to Clinton in trucks." The bodies arrived in a "preserved" condition and in three batches of five, she said. The Black Widow added that she personally viewed three of the bodies and had seen black-and-white photographs of several more.

All of the bodies, she stated, were "Oriental" and around five feet in height. Some "looked like normal Japanese people, but injured as if from an accident," and several exhibited signs of severe physical handicaps—such as oversized heads and malformed faces and hands—while others had "slightly larger and protruding eyes." Some of the bodies were relatively intact; others displayed the types of devastating injuries that one would expect to find following an aircraft crash; and the remaining ones were characterized by intense burns to their bodies and heads.

"How many bodies in total are you aware of that were brought to Oak Ridge?" I asked.

"I knew of fifteen and saw three," she replied, "but those were later sent to Los Alamos, where other studies were made of them."

"Do you know where they came from?" I asked.

She breathed deeply and her face took on a concerned expression that was a mixture of fear and intense stress. "Those bodies—the Roswell bodies—they weren't aliens," she said quietly. "The government could care less about stories about alien bodies found at Roswell—except to hide the truth. Those bodies were Japanese people."

"How do you know this?" I asked, anxious to keep her talking.

"From working there, from the people I spoke with, and the things I saw with my own eyes." The Black Widow said that research into "atomic issues" was undertaken at Oak Ridge, Los Alamos, the White Sands Proving Ground, and the University of Chicago in the 1940s and "these people, these bodies, were seen as expendable and were used in tests and experiments."

"What sort of experiments exactly?" I asked.

"In balloon tests," she said quietly and with a slight quiver in her voice, "high-altitude balloon tests; experimental aircraft flights that the Air Force and the nuclear aircraft people were interested in for their work; and in atomic and biological warfare tests to measure and understand radioactive contamination in people."

The Black Widow then began to divulge even more startling information. From what she learned at Oak Ridge, the government had first acquired some of these "people and bodies" in early 1945 after a battle between American and Japanese troops on a small island in the Pacific. She explained that after the Japanese unit had been overrun, a small medical laboratory where Japanese doctors and scientists were conducting all manner of atrocities on both physically and mentally handicapped people was discovered on the island.

Experiments were conducted, she elaborated, to determine the effects of temperature extremes on people—some had arms and legs missing as a result of being exposed to freezing conditions. Others had been deliberately infected with virulent diseases and toxins, and the remainder had been subjected to a range of truly bizarre (and always fatal) experiments that involved the grafting of limbs from one patient to another. For the most part, she related, the "surviving people of the experiments," although severely traumatized and scarred, "looked normal."

Some, however, most definitely did not look normal. "No one

seemed to know where these other people came from, and no one at Oak Ridge knew, either, I think," she explained. "But there was no doubt that they were human—handicapped humans—and from Japan or China, I would say to you. Some were obviously the result of inbreeding and some showed characteristics of larger heads, some what I now know to be progeria, six fingers—all kinds of syndromes.

"I don't know anything at all about how these people were brought [to the United States], but I heard at Oak Ridge that some of them were in the States in late 1945 and brought over with Japanese doctors and Nazi doctors who had been doing similar experiments. That's when some of this began."

"When some of what began?" I asked her.

"All [of] this . . . this research." She paused for a moment and then continued. "I should have spoken about this years ago. I should have said something. Do you have any idea what was happening? My government was doing experiments on handicapped people."

And Roswell?

"That was all a part of this. There were never any aliens found at Roswell. Never. Some of those Roswell . . . those desert stories . . . come from the wreckage of a balloon and a capsule that was advanced and that included research into understanding high-altitude flight and exposure on the human body for the military [and] how that tied in with the crews in plans NEPA would have to one day build nuclear aircraft that would be able to fly at high altitudes—*very* high altitudes, for long periods.

"After the war we had access to advanced balloon plans that the Japanese had to attack us with—very futuristic balloons for flights across the Pacific—and we used this technology and their people for our work and used these balloons with the high-altitude work. And these were the main things: high-altitude exposure and understanding it and how it affects the human body and also rapid-decompression experiments and learning from that. Others were test flights with balloons for biological warfare, for delivering biological substances onto an enemy." [3]

I later confirmed that the military, in the immediate postwar era, *was* looking at ways of better understanding the nature of the upper atmosphere and how aircrews might be affected by extended and repeated exposure to it. For instance, a May 1946 Army Air Forces memorandum makes references to planned flights of "manned balloons" to heights of 125,000 feet for the specific purpose of obtaining "upper atmosphere" data.[4] Further evidence comes from a letter dated September 27, 1946, from Maj. Gen. Curtis LeMay, then deputy chief of air staff for research and development, to the commanding general, Air Transport Command, Washington, D.C.: "The use of jet-propelled aircraft and the increased operation of aircraft at high altitude makes imperative the establishment of a program to provide sufficient and accurate upper air information to all AAF units. This should include synoptic observations and forecasts of meteorological phenomena into the stratosphere."[5]

The Black Widow continued: "You see, some people were really forward thinking at the time, and I met a lot of the NEPA and ANP people at Oak Ridge as this really interested me: future aircraft and what we might be doing in the future. There was the idea to use the understanding from human biology experiments, altitude experiments, cosmic ray tests, high-altitude balloon tests and apply that to what problems a crew might face if we decide to have a high-flying nuclear-powered plane that could fly for truly long periods at a fantastic height and attack Russia—atomic bombs.

"People were thinking: Can we expose our men to a very higher [*sic*] altitude? The thought was to someday build an aircraft that would fly very high and for an extreme amount of time. But how will [the crew] be affected? And if we can really do all this—and even though it might be years and probably even decades ahead—can we develop a unique type of nuclear aircraft and engine that can fly very high and if necessary stay up there for an extreme period of time? And if we don't have the nuclear aircraft flying now, in 1947, can we do a simulation flight that might replicate a real situation?

"So you had them doing biological work at Los Alamos and Oak Ridge on bodies and people to understand how they might be affected with altitudes, radiation and cosmic ray exposure and to work with the technology that was there back when, and others working on some very strange aircraft ideas at Oak Ridge and White Sands, and the two crossed paths and merged—to an extent."

The Black Widow was telling me an unbelievable story. "But surely you're not saying that these people—if they were physically and mentally handicapped—piloted this capsule you referred to?" I asked her.

"No," she replied quickly. "These were balloons—several balloon tests—with what I would call 'gondola capsules,' that were designed to reach an extremely high height. These were designed for tests with animals and later with dummies. But you had certain people in government splitting this off and sharing it with people we brought over from Japan and Germany after the war: scientists, doctors, balloon experts, aircraft experts. The two were combined and so there were these balloons flown from White Sands, on a part of the range that had been secretly planned for this—Tularosa—and that was well out of the way to the people there that weren't cleared to know. Very classified.

"The people were there as expendable to see how they responded to the upper altitudes, radiation contamination in a simulated nuclear aircraft environment, space biology, cosmic rays, pressures, upper atmosphere problems. Remember that this was 1946 and 1947 and no one was really sure what we might discover in near space or very high altitude with health hazards to us for extended times. Also, although the plans were to build nuclear aircraft that would fly very high, we weren't in a position to build anything like that back then, as this was a long ways ahead, and so they worked with simulations, with the technology that was available back then, limited as it was."

"And these bodies were then brought to Oak Ridge?"

She looked me squarely in the face. "I don't know all of the details and don't know much about what happened at White Sands or all the wartime things, but I *do* know that these bodies were brought to Oak Ridge in 1947 because I saw them with my own eyes. It was just horrible. Horrible.

"The [bodies] that I saw were *very* badly damaged from one of several crashes at White Sands. I was told that there were, I think, three classified balloon flights in May, June and July 1947 and at least two were disasters. There may have been more and they may have all failed badly. This would involve balloons reaching very high altitudes, with an anesthetized crew of these handicapped people kept in a small compartment, kind of a rounded gondola. Sometimes there would be experimental shielding in a radiation experiment and the people would be separated—some having shielding, pressurization, and some not, depending on the experiment. That way it gave better results if we were able to see how one person would be more affected than another. Or worse: died. Although I don't think that *crew* is the right word to use because guinea pigs would be better. We were told that on board each flight was a pilot who had undergone intense high-altitude training and who was protected from any hazards by a modified pressure suit.

"It was his job, when the balloon [array] reached a certain altitude, to release the capsule from the balloons, and it would fall back to earth, with its own parachutes slowing the descent like a parachutist. But the other people, the poor people, were dressed casually in normal flight suits and just the minimum safety that offered no real protection to whatever might be encountered. But this was what the experimenters wanted. They wanted to know how we might be affected—biologically and cell mutation—by exposure to cosmic rays and high altitudes. There were even nuclear aircraft simulation tests with loading radioactive materials on board to see how a person might be affected or protected by new radiation-shielding materials that were planned—plastics, metals. They didn't care how they got results. These were German and Japanese scientists [and] doctors and they had far too much power. My Lord, these were Nazis and Japanese. Nazis! Getting paid to carry on what the war was supposed to stop—and in America.

"With the bodies I saw, this [capsule] had crashed just outside White Sands after its parachutes failed to open properly, and I believe this was early June 1947. The pilot was killed and two of the other bodies had lost limbs and were very, very severely damaged. These were all Japanese, about five feet tall, shaved heads, and two had slightly large heads, and there is no doubt, [were] very deformed and handicapped from birth. It was shocking to see them. Shocking. Others, I heard, from one other successful landing, had hardly a scratch on them and died in the gondola after something went wrong and the capsule blew out or something while still in the air. These are your crashed UFO legends, absolutely.

"I wasn't involved in the autopsies, but several of my colleagues were, and I know that files were written on all of these bodies [that were] brought to us. But after August [1947], we never had any more of these people brought to Oak Ridge. We heard later that when certain people—elected people—in government heard what was happening, all of this was stopped. The bodies were destroyed, people lost their jobs, and documents were destroyed, and other things, too, to hide the story. Scarier things with people dying, suicides that I never thought were true and that I won't talk about with you."

"So the trail is cold, you mean, now?" I asked.

"Well, maybe cold. But there are still a lot of people like me that know the truth about White Sands and the bodies," she responded. "We're not all dead, you know. Some of us would like to tell our story—the real story, those of us that are left, about this."[6]

DARKNESS iN THE DESERT

The Black Widow's story forces us to take a closer look at both post-war American history and the Roswell controversy—and the subsequent cover-up in particular—in a totally new and alarming light. Can the Black Widow's story be validated? Does recorded history support her claims? Over the last few years, I have been able to uncover sources that validate and support the Black Widow's story. A large and astonishing body of corroborative evidence and documentation has been staring at us in the face all these years; only we've been looking at the material from the wrong perspective. Now, for the first time, with the Black Widow's story in mind, all the details of the Roswell story—even its inconsistencies—begin to make sense.

It all began with that now famous headline on the front page of the *Roswell (N.M.) Daily Record* on July 8, 1947: "RAAF Captures Flying Saucer On Ranch in Roswell Region." This was not some fanciful story concocted by an enterprising hoaxer. Rather, the newspaper caption was based upon an officially sanctioned press release issued by 2nd Lt. Walter Haut, the press information officer at the nearby Roswell Army Air Field:

The many rumors regarding the flying disc became a reality yesterday when the intelligence office of the 509th Bomb Group of the Eighth Air Force, Roswell Army Air Field, was fortunate enough to gain possession of a disc through the cooperation of one of the local ranchers and the sheriff's office of Chaves County.

The flying object landed on a ranch near Roswell sometime last week. Not having phone facilities, the rancher stored the disc until such time as he was able to contact the sheriff's office, who in turn notified Maj. Jesse A. Marcel of the 509th Bomb Group Intelligence Office.

Action was immediately taken and the disc was picked up at the rancher's home. It was inspected at the Roswell Army Air Field and subsequently loaned by Major Marcel to higher headquarters.[1]

Shortly after this astonishing news had spread quite literally around the world, the Army Air Forces made another announcement: the whole thing had been a false alarm. What had in fact been recovered was the radar reflector from an errant weather balloon. To bolster this explanation, Brig. Gen. Roger Ramey of the Eighth Air Force at Fort Worth, Texas, allowed press photographers to take shots of the debris from the stricken balloon, which had been laid out on the floor of a small office at the base.

Despite the decidedly unimpressive-looking nature of the wreckage on display for the photographers, the media apparently chose not to express its incredulity that anyone could confuse what was obviously weather balloon–borne debris with something potentially more exotic. The official explanation was accepted and, at a stroke, interest in the story dwindled, and the entire matter was laid to rest. That situation remained practically unchanged for thirty years.

Until January 20, 1978, to be precise. On that date Stanton T. Friedman was in Baton Rouge to give a lecture at Louisiana State University. Friedman had obtained his Master of Science in Physics at the University of Chicago in 1956 and, for the next fourteen years, had worked as a nuclear physicist for a variety of organizations, including General Electric, Aerojet General, Westinghouse, and General Motors. During that time he developed an intense interest in UFOs and, in 1970, began to lecture on the subject on a full-time basis.[2] While in Baton Rouge for his lecture, he agreed to take part in a number of media interviews. One such interview took place at a local television station. During a break Friedman was introduced to the station manager, who, as luck would have it, was a friend of Jesse Marcel. Marcel had been the intelligence officer for the 509th Bomb Group at Roswell Army Air Field in 1947, and basic details of the Roswell incident were imparted to Friedman. Acting on this information, he wasted no time in contacting Marcel, who had a most interesting story to tell concerning what happened back in 1947.[3]

"I saw a lot of wreckage but no complete machine," said the retired Marcel, explaining that whatever the object was, it must have exploded in the air. "It had disintegrated before it hit the ground. The wreckage was scattered over an area about three quarters of a mile long and several hundred feet wide.

"I was pretty well acquainted with most everything that was in the air at that time, both ours and foreign," Marcel continued. "I was also acquainted with virtually every type of weather-observation or radar-tracking device being used by either the civilians or the military."

Marcel added that in his opinion the debris was not from a weather-tracking device, nor was it from an aircraft or a missile. "What it was we didn't know. We just picked up the fragments." Marcel was certain, however, that the debris was unlike anything he had ever seen before or since, and that "it certainly wasn't anything built by us."[4]

During the course of his investigations Friedman hooked up with William Moore, a writer and researcher who expressed an interest in pursuing the case and who had his own leads that seemed to support Marcel's account. As a result of their inquiries, Friedman and Moore were able to confirm where the unusual debris had been found: the Foster Ranch, a remote piece of land located in an area some seventy-five miles north of the town of Roswell, New Mexico, and worked by one William Ware "Mack" Brazel. Regrettably, Brazel had long since passed away; however, his friends and family, some of whom still lived in the vicinity, recalled the incident well.

Commenting on the strange material found on the ranch, Brazel's son, Bill, stated that it was " . . . something on the order of tinfoil except that [it] wouldn't tear. . . . You could wrinkle it and lay it back down and it immediately resumed its original shape. [It was] quite pliable, but you couldn't crease or bend it like ordinary metal. Almost like a plastic, but definitely metallic in nature. Dad once said that the Army had once told him it was not anything made by us."[5]

Jesse Marcel also elaborated on the extraordinary properties present in the material that he recovered: "[It] could not be bent or broken . . . or even dented by a sixteen-pound sledge hammer. Almost weightless . . . like a metal with plastic properties."[6]

Another lead came from Vern and Jean Maltais, who stated that a friend of theirs, Grady Barnett, a field engineer with the Soil Conservation Service, had confided to them that he had come across a grounded object ("a kind of disk [that] looked like dirty stainless steel") in the New Mexico desert in the vicinity of the Plains of San Augustin, around which were a number of small, and quite dead, bodies of an unusual nature. All were small in stature, with large, pear-shaped heads, "oddly spaced eyes," skinny arms and legs and completely hairless. Needless to say, the military arrived quickly on the scene and assumed control of the situation.[7]

As the 1970s drew to a close, enough data had been gathered to warrant the publication of a full-length book on the case: *The Roswell Incident*, coauthored by Moore and the late Charles Berlitz, published in 1980.[8] By 1985, research had uncovered almost a hundred people who had knowledge of the events at Roswell in some capacity. The official "weather balloon" explanation was crumbling fast.

In July 1985, Moore gave a presentation at the annual symposium of the Mutual UFO Network (MUFON) at St. Louis, Missouri. During the course of his lecture, he revealed what had occurred when Friedman brought up the matter of the unusual bodies with Lewis "Bill" Rickett, a former Counter Intelligence Corps (CIC) officer stationed at Roswell at the time of the incident. The following is Friedman's own assessment of the interview: "When I mentioned bodies, Rickett clearly reacted and indicated that this was an area he couldn't talk about. He indicated there were different levels of security about this work—that a directive had come down placing this at a high level. He went on to say that certain subjects were discussed only in rooms that couldn't be bugged."[9] Rickett has been identified as one of at least two men (the other being Rickett's superior with the CIC, Sheridan Ware Cavitt, about whom more later) who accompanied Major Marcel back to the Foster Ranch to inspect the mysterious debris.

Further information on the Roswell incident surfaced in the late 1980s and 1990s from the investigative team of Kevin Randle and Don Schmitt. Randle, a captain in the Air Force Reserve, and Schmitt cowrote two books on the Roswell controversy suggesting that on the night of July 4, 1947, an extraterrestrial spacecraft crashed to earth some miles from the town of Roswell, having already deposited a sizable amount of debris on the Foster Ranch. In contrast to the accepted wisdom, the vehicle, their sources asserted, was rather narrow with a batlike wing and no longer than thirty feet in length—this point having been insisted upon by CIC man Lewis Rickett.[10] Similarly, Thomas Gonzalez, who was stationed at Roswell Army Air Field on returning to the States after the end of World War II, described the vehicle as an "airfoil"; Johnny McBoyle, reporter and part owner of the KSWS radio station in Roswell, recalled seeing a "big crumpled dishpan"; and Frank Kauffman referred to the object as being "heel-shaped."[11]

According to Lewis Rickett, he became deeply embroiled in the Roswell affair in September 1947, when he spent time working with Dr. Lincoln La Paz of the University of New Mexico. La Paz was a mathematician whose interests shifted from ballistics during World War II to the study of meteorites. At a time when meteorites were widely viewed as curiosities, La Paz had the vision to recognize their scientific significance, established the Institute of Meteoritics at the University of New Mexico, and described numerous new meteorites, many of which he had personally recovered for the outstanding meteorite collection at the university.[12]

According to Rickett, he and La Paz were given an assignment to determine "the speed and trajectory" of the object that impacted near Roswell. Rickett further claimed that he and La Paz had discovered a "possible touchdown point" about five miles northwest of the debris field located by rancher Brazel. Not only did they retrieve material identical to that which Rickett had handled before at the Foster Ranch, they were startled to find that the sand in the high-desert terrain had crystallized, apparently as a result of exposure to tremendous heat.

Rickett and La Paz reportedly spent a total of three weeks interviewing witnesses and making their calculations, which were contained in an official report prepared by La Paz. Although Rickett never had a chance to see the document, which was delivered directly to the Pentagon, the professor confided to Rickett that, in his opinion and based on all of the physical evidence they had collected and tested, the object was an "unmanned interplanetary probe."[13]

As far as the story of bodies found at the crash site is concerned, Randle and Schmitt's sources informed them that up to five were found in the vicinity of the crash, one of which, incredibly, survived the initial impact. Among those who were willing to speak on the subject—albeit in a fragmented and cryptic fashion—were Edwin Easley, the provost marshal at Roswell, who made brief allusions to "the creatures"; Sgt. Melvin E. Brown, who stated that, "They looked Asian but had larger heads and no hair. They looked a yellow color"; and the aforementioned Thomas Gonzalez, who described them as "little men."[14]

Other accounts abound, including that of Dr. La June Foster, a renowned authority on the human spinal cord, who had held a security clearance and had worked undercover for the FBI during World War II. Foster, according to the research of Schmitt and Randle, was flown to Washington, D.C., following the crash, where she was asked to examine the spinal structures of the retrieved bodies and reported that it was possible one had survived the initial impact, albeit in a critically injured state. Foster also described the bodies as being short, with oversized heads. Most disturbing of all, Foster was told that if she talked, she would be killed.[15]

Frankie Rowe, whose father was attached to the Roswell Fire Department in 1947, heard a somewhat similar death threat. Rowe reports that her father confided in the family that he had seen both debris and bodies, including one live being: "[T]he one that was walking was about the size of a 10 year old child, and it didn't have any hair . . . it seemed so scared and lost and afraid." Several days later, claims Rowe, three military policemen came to the family home and said that if anyone talked, "they might just take us out to the middle of the desert and shoot all of us and nobody would ever find us."[16]

A similar account comes from Glenn Dennis, a mortician at Ballard's Funeral Home in Roswell, who claims to have received a strange telephone call from the mortuary officer at the base: "He was inquiring about what size, what type of caskets, and how small [were the] caskets that we could furnish that could be hermetically sealed," said Dennis.

Dennis also signed a sworn affidavit confirming that a nurse friend at the base had admitted to him that a preliminary autopsy of the bodies had been conducted at Roswell Army Air Field: "[S]he went into this room to get some supplies and saw two doctors in there with a gurney and these small bodies that were in a rubber sheet or body pouch.

Two of the bodies had been very badly mangled, like maybe the pred-ators had been eating on them . . . one of the hands was severed from the body, and when they flipped it over, there were little tiny suction cups on the inside of the fingers. . . . The heads were large, eyes were set in. The skulls were soft like a newborn baby's; they were pliable. The ears, instead of one canal, had two canals, no lobes or anything, just a little flap over each canal. The mouths were just very small slits. Their faces and noses were concave." [17]

Many pro-UFO researchers are now suspicious of Dennis's story, but accounts like his abound. In 1947, Lydia Sleppy was employed as a Teletype operator at the KSWS radio station in Roswell. When reporter Johnny McBoyle telephoned her to say he had seen a "big crumpled dishpan" out on the Foster Ranch at 4:00 P.M. on Mon-day, July 7, 1947, she recognized that this was a "pretty big story." In-deed it was. According to Sleppy's recollections, McBoyle added excitedly: "The Army is there and they are going to pick it up. And get this—they're saying something about little men being on board." Fifty years after the events in question, McBoyle steadfastly declined to elaborate on what it was that he saw on the Foster Ranch.[18]

On the day following Johnny McBoyle's experience—July 8, 1947—the FBI office at Dallas, Texas, forwarded a Teletype mes-sage to FBI director J. Edgar Hoover concerning the events at Roswell. This is one of the few officially declassified documents on the case that have surfaced under the terms of the Freedom of In-formation Act:

Major Edwin E. Kirton, headquarters Eighth Air Force, tele-phonically advised this office that an object purporting to be a flying disc was recovered near Roswell, New Mexico, this date. The disc is hexagonal in shape and was suspended from a bal-loon by cable, which balloon was approximately twenty feet in diameter. Major Kirton further advised that the object found resembles a high altitude weather balloon with a radar reflector, but that telephonic conversation between their office and Wright Field had not borne out this belief. Disc and balloon being transported to Wright Field by special plane for examination. Information provided this office because of national interest in case and fact that National Broadcasting Company, Associated Press, and others attempting to break story of location of disc today. Major Kirton advised would request Wright Field to advise Cincinnati Office results of examination. No further investigation being conducted.[19]

It is obvious from the document that the FBI only possessed part of the story: that part had been supplied sometime previously by Major Edwin M. Kirton of Army Air Force Intelligence at Fort Worth. Indeed, it seems even the FBI was fed the story that the "disc" recovered at Roswell was probably a weather balloon and was being forwarded to Wright Field for further examination as part of a concerted effort to confirm this hypothesis.

An intriguing footnote to the story of the FBI's involvement in the Roswell controversy occurred in 1981, when researcher William Moore succeeded in tracking down the by-then-retired FBI agent who transmitted the Teletype. The agent refused to discuss the incident in any shape or form, however. In a July 1988 lecture Moore graphically recalled the agent's words to him: "I have had no unexplained fires in my garage, and I have had no men in dark suits at my doorstep. I'm enjoying my retirement and I want to keep it that way, Mr. Moore. I have nothing to say to you." An unusual comment, particularly if all that was recovered at Roswell was a weather balloon.[20]

Almost three decades after the late Maj. Jesse Marcel resurfaced with his story of what occurred at Roswell, similar accounts and testimony continue to circulate and mutate. In fact, the case generated such interest that in the mid-1990s, after nearly fifty years of deafening silence, the United States Air Force was finally forced to confront the controversy head-on.

THREE

THE SECOND COVER-UP

In the spring of 1993, New Mexico Congressman Steven Schiff began to make inquiries of the Department of Defense in an attempt to determine the truth surrounding certain aspects of the Roswell controversy. In a letter to Les Aspin, who was then Secretary of Defense, dated March 11, Schiff wrote:

Last fall I became aware of a strange series of events beginning in New Mexico over 45 years ago and involving personnel of what was then the Army Air Force. I have since reviewed the facts in some detail, and I am writing to request your assistance in arriving at a definitive explanation of what transpired and why.

In brief, according to contemporary newspaper, wire service, national radio newscast, and numerous eyewitness accounts, on or about July 3, 1947, rancher William W. [Mack] Brazel found a large amount of unusual debris on property he managed northwest of Roswell, New Mexico, near the town of Corona. He brought his find to the attention of Chaves County

Sheriff George Wilcox, who then contacted the Roswell Army Air Field, home of the 509th Bomb Group (Atomic) commanded by Colonel William H. Blanchard. . . . According to testimony of the group intelligence officer, Major Jesse A. Marcel, he and the Counter Intelligence Corps officer in charge at the field, Captain Sheridan W. Cavitt, then accompanied Mr. Brazel to the discovery site.

Marcel testified that he and Cavitt found an area measuring about three-quarters of a mile long by 200 to 300 feet wide densely strewn with a large amount of extremely lightweight, extremely strong materials neither could identify. Samples of these materials were flown to Eighth Air Force Headquarters in Fort Worth, Texas. . . .

A few hours later, Eighth Air Force Commanding General Roger M. Ramey told reporters in Fort Worth that what had been found in New Mexico were the initially misidentified remains of a weather balloon and its Rawin radar target. Recently, in written and videotaped depositions, Brigadier General Thomas J. DuBose, USAF(ret.), General Ramey's chief of staff at the time of the incident, testified that the balloon explanation was a cover story. . . .

The inconsistency between repeated official denials and the public record and testimony of those involved has led to a great deal of sensational speculation and called into question the credibility of the Departments of Defense, Army, and the Air Force. . . .

Therefore, Mr. Secretary, I respectfully request that you direct such a review be undertaken on a priority basis and that a representative or representatives of the Department of Defense and the responsible Military Departments promptly arrange to brief and provide me with a written report providing a current, complete, and detailed description and explanation of both the nature of what was recovered and all official actions taken on the matter. . . .

Schiff received a reply to his letter on March 31, 1993. It came not from Aspin, but from Col. Larry G. Shockley, USAF, director, plans and operations, who said, "I have referred this matter to the National Archives and Records Administration for direct reply to you." Rudy deLeon, special assistant, Office of the Secretary of Defense, also contacted Schiff a week later and recommended that he "contact the National Archives for additional information."

Schiff realized he was getting the runaround and quickly sent a follow-up letter to Secretary of Defense Aspin:

I realize that, after almost 46 years, it is a virtual certainty that all or most of the records concerning this incident have been archived. However, my staff and several independent investigators have conclusively established they are not in any of the unclassified, including previously classified, holdings of the National Archives. Moreover, it is my understanding that it is highly unlikely they reside in any of the classified files in the custody of the Archives.

Wherever the documents may be, what is at issue is my request for a personal briefing and a written report on a matter involving actions taken by officials of the U.S. Army and U.S. Air Force, agencies under your purview. I realize the research required to uncover the relevant documents and related materials will take time and considerable effort, and I am prepared to wait a reasonable amount of time for this to be accomplished. However I expect the job to be done and my request to be addressed. . . .

On May 20, 1993, the National Archives replied to Schiff's original letter to Aspin:

The U.S. Air Force has retired to our custody its records on Project BLUE BOOK relating to the investigations of unidentified flying objects. Project BLUE BOOK has been declassified and the records are available for examination in our research room. The project closed in 1969 and we have no information after that date. We have received numerous requests concerning records relating to the Roswell incident among these records. We have not located any documentation relating to this event in Project BLUE BOOK records, or in any other pertinent Defense Department records in our custody.

Interpreting the fact that he was being passed back and forth from the Defense Department to the National Archives as stonewalling, Schiff once again determined to resolve the matter once and for all with Secretary Aspin in a letter on May 10, 1993:

While I realize that the Department of Defense, and you, Mr. Secretary, have been very busy in areas throughout the world, while also concerned with proposed changes in policy within the Department, I must insist on the courtesy of a reply to my letter, which is now three months old. To reiterate, while I am prepared to wait a reasonable length of time for the briefing I requested, I do insist that the Department do the research on my inquiry and report the findings to me. I also must insist on having my letters to the Department of Defense acknowledged and acted upon. I look forward to your response to my letters, and to the scheduled briefing. . . .

When Schiff did not get his wish, he contacted the General Accounting Office, the investigative arm of Congress, in a concerted effort to bring the Roswell controversy to rest once and for all.

In January 1994, the *Washington Post* reported:

GAO spokeswoman Laura A. Kopelson said the office's investigation . . . stemmed from a meeting in October between Schiff and GAO Controller General Charles A Bowsher. Schiff com-

plained then that the Defense Department had been "unre-
sponsive" to his inquiries about the 1947 incident. . . .

"I was getting pretty upset at all the running around," Schiff
said, adding that at his meeting with GAO officials, "they made
an offer to help.

"Generally, I'm a skeptic on UFOs and alien beings, but there
are indications from the run-around that I got that whatever it
was, it wasn't a balloon. Apparently, it's another government
cover-up," Schiff said.

He called the Defense Department's lack of response "as-
tounding," and said government accountability was an issue
"even larger than UFOs."

. . . He added, "If the Defense Department had been responsive, it wouldn't have come to this." [1]

The GAO duly launched its investigation and on July 28, 1995, a
report on its results surfaced from its National Security and International Affairs Division. Commenting on an Air Force report on
Roswell that had been published in the interim, in July 1994, the
GAO informed Schiff that while it now seemed unlikely that the
weather balloon explanation was correct, the Air Force had come to
yet *another* conclusion in its attempt to lay the mystery of Roswell to
rest:

DOD informed us that the U.S. Air Force report of July 1994,
entitled [sic] *Report of Air Force Research Regarding the
Roswell Incident,* represents the extent of DOD records or information concerning the Roswell crash. The Air Force report
concluded that there was no dispute that something happened
near Roswell in July 1947 and that all available official materials indicated the most likely source of the wreckage recovered was one of the project MOGUL balloon trains. At the time
of the Roswell crash, project MOGUL was a highly classified
U.S. effort to determine the state of Soviet nuclear weapons re-

search using balloons that carried radar reflectors and acoustic sensors.

The Mogul explanation is one that the Air Force would champion for years to come, despite the fact that no documentation ever surfaced conclusively linking the incident at Roswell with the crash of a Mogul balloon. Indeed, on the issue of whether or not there was actually any data in evidence to support the notion that something—Mogul balloon, UFO, aircraft or something else—crashed near Roswell, New Mexico, in early July 1947, the GAO advised Congressman Schiff:

According to an Army records management official, in 1947 Army regulations required that air accident reports be maintained permanently. An Air Force official said there was no similar requirement to report a weather balloon crash. According to an Air Force official who has worked in the records management field since the mid-1940s, air accident reports prepared in July 1947 under Army regulations should have been transferred to Air Force custody in September 1947, when the Air Force was established as a separate service. The Air Force Safety Agency is responsible for maintaining reports of air accidents. We examined its microfilm records to determine whether any air accidents had been reported in New Mexico during July 1947. We identified four air accidents during this time period. All of the accidents involved military fighter or cargo aircraft and occurred after July 8, 1947—the date the RAAF public information office first reported the crash and recovery of a "flying disc" near Roswell. According to the Army Air Forces' Report of Major Accident, these four accidents occurred at or near the towns of Hobbs, Albuquerque, Carrizozo, and Alamogordo, New Mexico. Only one of the four accidents resulted in a fatality. The pilot died when the aircraft crashed during an attempted take-off.

While the GAO investigation was useful in at least ruling out any of these four particular aerial accidents as being related to the Roswell affair, it still failed to answer conclusively the question of what did or indeed did not occur at Roswell. There was, however, a genuinely intriguing surprise in store for GAO investigators when they began to search for records in an effort to try and better understand what had taken place: the *entire* group of outgoing messages from Roswell Army Air Field generated between October 1946 and December 1949 had been destroyed—under circumstances that could not be fully determined, no less.

Congressman Schiff, who described the GAO report as "professional, conscientious and thorough," remained troubled by the apparent disappearance of years of outgoing documentation from Roswell Army Air Field: "It is my understanding that these outgoing messages were permanent records, which should never have been destroyed. The GAO could not identify who destroyed the messages, or why."

While the GAO investigation certainly did not uncover any smoking guns or firmly resolve the Roswell affair to everyone's satisfaction—if anything, the inexplicably missing RAAF files of 1946–1949 only intensified the debate—it did at least prompt the Air Force to present its *third* explanation for what occurred at Roswell, the crash landing of a highly secret Project Mogul balloon train.

To which Schiff commented: "At least this effort caused the Air Force to acknowledge that the crashed vehicle was no weather balloon. That explanation never fit the fact of high military security used at the time." But did the presence of that aforementioned "high military security" support the Mogul explanation?[2] The answer to that question lies in what the Air Force admitted about Project Mogul—and what it failed to reveal.

Before revealing the Mogul explanation, however, the July 1994 *Report of Air Force Research Regarding the Roswell Incident*, authored by Col. Richard L. Weaver, USAF, director, security and special program oversight, turned its attention to firmly laying to rest the issue of "What the Roswell Incident Was Not." In a section of the report titled "An Airplane Crash," it stated:

Of all the things that are documented and tracked within the Air Force, among the most detailed and scrupulous are airplane crashes. In fact, records of air crashes go back to the first years of military flight. Safety records and reports are available for all crashes that involved serious damage, injury, death, or a combination of these factors. These records also include incidents involving experimental or classified aircraft. USAF records showed that between June 24, 1947, and July 28, 1947, there were five crashes in New Mexico alone, involving A-26C, P-5 IN, C-82A, P-80A and PQ-14B aircraft; however, none of these were on the date(s) in question nor in the area(s) in question.

If not an aircraft, could the Roswell debris have originated with a classified missile launch, especially considering the sheer scale of work that was being undertaken at the nearby White Sands Proving Ground, New Mexico, at the time? According to the Air Force:

A crashed or errant missile, usually described as a captured German V-2 or one of its variants, is sometimes set forth as a possible explanation for the debris recovered near Roswell. Since much of this testing done at nearby White Sands was secret at the time, it would be logical to assume that the government would handle any missile mishap under tight security, particularly if the mishap occurred on private land. From the records reviewed by the Air Force, however, there was nothing located to suggest that this was the case. Although the bulk of remaining testing records are under the control of the U.S. Army, the subject has also been very well documented over the years within Air Force records. There would be no reason to keep such information classified today. The USAF found no indicators or even hints that a missile was involved in this matter.

And what of the possibility of a nuclear accident? The Air Force considered that, too:

This was a logical area of concern since the 509th Bomb Group was the only military unit in the world at the time that had access to nuclear weapons. Again, reviews of available records gave no indication that this was the case. A number of records still classified TOP SECRET and SECRET—RESTRICTED DATA having to do with nuclear weapons were located in the Federal Records Center in St. Louis, MO. These records, which pertained to the 509th, had nothing to do with any activities that could have been misinterpreted as the "Roswell Incident." Also, any records of a nuclear related incident would have been inherited by the Department of Energy (DOE), and, had one occurred, it is likely DOE would have publicly reported it as part of its recent declassification and public release efforts. There were no ancillary records in Air Force files to indicate the potential existence of such records within DOE channels, however.

The Air Force then turned its attention to dismissing what remains to this day the most controversial explanation for the Roswell case: an extraterrestrial spacecraft.

The Air Force research found absolutely no indication that what happened near Roswell in 1947 involved any type of extraterrestrial spacecraft. This, of course, is the crux of this entire matter. "Pro-UFO" persons who obtain a copy of this report, at this point, most probably begin the "cover-up is still on" claims. Nevertheless, the research indicated absolutely no evidence of any kind that a spaceship crashed near Roswell or that any alien occupants were recovered therefrom, in some secret military operation or otherwise. . . .

Likewise, the researchers found no indication of heightened activity anywhere else in the military hierarchy in the July, 1947, message traffic or orders (to include classified traffic). There were no indications and warnings, notice of alerts, or a higher tempo of operational activity reported that would be logically generated if an alien craft, whose intentions were un-known, entered U.S. territory. . . .

To bolster its down-to-earth hypothesis, Colonel Weaver then fo-cused on one of the most controversial characters in the whole Roswell mystery, Lt. Col. Sheridan W. Cavitt, USAF, who—it is unanimously accepted by both the Air Force and UFO researchers and authors—was one of the first to have direct hands-on access to the Roswell debris:

Cavitt is credited in all claims of having accompanied Major Marcel to the ranch to recover the debris, sometimes along with his Counter Intelligence Corps (CIC) subordinate, William Rickett, who, like Marcel, is deceased. Although there does not appear to be much dispute that Cavitt was involved in the ma-terial recovery, other claims about him prevail in the popular literature. He is sometimes portrayed as a closed-mouth (or sometimes even sinister) conspirator who was one of the early individuals who kept the "secret of Roswell" from getting out. Other things about him have been alleged, including the claim that he wrote a report of the incident at the time that has never surfaced.

Since Lt. Col. Cavitt, who had first-hand knowledge, was still alive, a decision was made to interview him and get a signed sworn statement from him about his version of the events. . . .

In this interview, Cavitt related that he had been contacted on numerous occasions by UFO researchers and had willingly talked with many of them; however, he felt that he had oftentimes been misrepresented or had his comments taken out of context so that their true meaning was changed. He stated unequivocally, however, that the material he recovered consisted of a reflective sort of material like aluminum foil, and some thin, bamboo-like sticks. He thought at the time, and continued to do so today, that what he found was a weather balloon and has told other private researchers that. He also remembered finding a small "black box" type of instrument, which he thought at the time was probably a radiosonde. . . . He did not even know the incident was claimed to be anything unusual until he was interviewed in the early 1980s.[3]

That is not the story Cavitt told UFO researchers, as Tom Carey and Don Schmitt reveal:

When Sheridan Cavitt . . . was located by Roswell researchers in the early 1990s, he at first denied that he had ever been stationed at Roswell AAF. When confronted with documented evidence to the contrary, he admitted that, yes, he had been stationed there in the late 1940s, but only after the time of the Roswell Incident. Confronted again with documentary evidence that he had arrived in Roswell prior to the famous incident, Cavitt resorted to the "I can't remember . . . I don't recall" routine used by so many witnesses who wish to neither speak the truth nor tell outright lies.

. . . While Cavitt was still telling this tale to civilian Roswell investigators, he was telling a different story to U.S. Air Force investigators, who were commissioned by the GAO in 1993 to look into the Roswell case. "Yes," he remembered it, he told them but it was "a solitary, mundane weather balloon" that he and Rickett—and, perhaps, Marcel—had found. That was it.

There was no sheep rancher and no strange wreckage. End of story.[4]

There is an interesting footnote to the controversy surrounding Sheridan Cavitt. In 1991, Counter Intelligence Corps operative Bill Rickett received an enigmatic telephone call from Cavitt, according to researchers Schmitt and Carey, who described the curious episode:

> "Happy birthday, Bill," said the voice on the other end of the phone. "It's 'Cav,' your old boss."
>
> After exchanging niceties, Cavitt queried, "Have you been talking to anyone about what happened back in 1947?" Rickett identified one specific investigator, who Cavitt knew as well.
>
> "What have you been telling him?" pried Cavitt. "We both know what really happened out there, don't we, Bill?"
>
> "We sure do," Rickett responded.
>
> After a short pause Cavitt snapped back, "Well, maybe someday. Goodbye, Bill."
>
> Rickett passed away in October 1993, never hearing from Cavitt again.[5]

In any case, after dismissing the extraterrestrial explanation, the Air Force report turned to the possibility that a balloon may have been responsible for the Roswell story:

> As early as February 28, 1994, the . . . research team found references to balloon tests taking place at Alamogordo AAF (now Holloman AFB) and White Sands during June and July 1947, testing "constant level balloons" and a New York University (NYU)/Watson Labs effort that used " . . . meteorological devices . . . suspected for detecting shock waves generated by Soviet nuclear explosions,"—a possible indication of a cover story associated with the NYU balloon project. Subsequently, a

1946 HQ AMC memorandum was surfaced, describing the constant altitude balloon project and specified that the scientific data be classified TOP SECRET Priority IA. Its name was Project Mogul.

. . . [E]fforts also revealed that some of the individuals involved in Project Mogul were still living. These persons included the NYU constant altitude balloon Director of Research, Dr. Athelstan F. Spilhaus; the Project Engineer, Professor Charles B. Moore; and the military Project Officer, Colonel Albert C. Trakowski.

All of these persons were subsequently interviewed and signed sworn statements about their activities. These interviews confirmed that Project Mogul was a compartmented, sensitive effort. The NYU group was responsible for developing constant level balloons and telemetering equipment that would remain at specified altitudes (within the acoustic duct) while a group from Columbia was to develop acoustic sensors. Doctor Spilhaus, Professor Moore, and certain others of the group were aware of the actual purpose of the project, but they did not know of the project nickname at the time. They handled casual inquiries and/or scientific inquiries/papers in terms of "unclassified meteorological or balloon research." Newly hired employees were not made aware that there was anything special or classified about their work; they were told only that their work dealt with meteorological equipment.

An advance ground team, led by Albert P. Crary, preceded the NYU group to Alamogordo AAF, New Mexico, setting up ground sensors and obtaining facilities for the NYU group. Upon their arrival, Professor Moore and his team experimented with various configurations of neoprene balloons; development of balloon "trains"; automatic ballast systems and use of Naval sonobuoys (as the Watson Lab acoustical sensors had not yet arrived). They also launched what they called "service flights." These "service flights" were not logged nor fully accounted for in the published Technical Reports generated as a result of the contract between NYU and Watson Labs. According to Professor Moore, the "service flights" were composed of balloons, radar reflectors and payloads specifically designed to test acoustic sensors (both early sonobuoys and the later Watson Labs devices). The "payload equipment" was expendable and some carried no "REWARD" or "RETURN TO . . ." tags because there was to be no association between these flights and the logged constant altitude flights which were fully acknowledged. The NYU balloon flights were listed sequentially in their reports (i.e. A, B, 1, 5, 6, 7, 8, 10 . . .) yet gaps existed for Flights 2-4 and Flight 9. The interview with Professor Moore indicated that these gaps were the unlogged "service flights."

 . . . According to the log summary of the NYU group, Flight A through Flight 7 (November 20, 1946–July 2, 1947) were made with neoprene meteorological balloons (as opposed to the later flights made with polyethylene balloons). Professor Moore stated that the neoprene balloons were susceptible to degradation in the sunlight, turning from a milky white to a dark brown. He described finding remains of balloon trains with reflectors and payloads that had landed in the desert: the ruptured and shredded neoprene would "almost look like dark gray or black flakes or ashes after exposure to the sun for only a few days. The plasticizers and antioxidants in the neoprene would emit a peculiar acrid odor and the balloon material and radar target material would be scattered after returning to earth depending on the surface winds." Upon review of the local newspaper photographs from General Ramey's press conference in 1947 and descriptions in popular books by individuals who supposedly handled the debris recovered on the ranch, Professor Moore opined that the material was most likely the shredded remains of a multi-neoprene balloon train with multiple radar reflectors. The material and a "black box," described by Cavitt, was, in Moore's scientific opinion, most probably from Flight 4, a "service flight" that included a cylindrical metal sonobuoy and portions of a weather instrument housed in a box, which was unlike typical weather radiosondes which were made of cardboard. Additionally, a copy of a professional journal maintained at the time by A.P. Crary, provided to the Air Force by his widow, showed that Flight 4 was launched on June 4, 1947, but was not recovered by the NYU group. It is very probable that this TOP SECRET project balloon train (Flight 4), made up of unclassified components, came to rest some miles northwest of Roswell, NM, became shredded in the surface winds and was ultimately found by the rancher, Brazel, ten days later.

But if Mogul was indeed the culprit, was there any evidence to suggest that the flying disk and weather balloon explanations had been officially utilized as convenient cover stories to hide the truth of what was certainly a legitimate Cold War secret project? Or were those explanations simply erroneous ones based upon the inability of trained personnel to identify balloon-borne debris? According to the Air Force:

Concerning the initial announcement, "RAAF Captures Flying Disc," research failed to locate any documented evidence as to why that statement was made. However, on July 10, 1947, following the Ramey press conference, the *Alamogordo News* published an article with photographs demonstrating multiple balloons and targets at the same location as the NYU group operated from at Alamogordo AAF. Professor Moore expressed surprise at seeing this since his was the only balloon test group in the area. He stated, "It appears that there was some type of umbrella cover story to protect our work with Mogul."

Although the Air Force did not find documented evidence that Gen. Ramey was directed to espouse a weather balloon in his press conference, he may have done so because he was either aware of Project Mogul and was trying to deflect interest from it, or he readily perceived the material to be a weather balloon based on the identification from his weather officer, Irving Newton. In either case, the materials recovered by the AAF in July, 1947, were not readily recognizable as anything special (only the purpose was special) and the recovered debris itself was unclassified. Additionally, the press dropped its interest in the matter as quickly as they had jumped on it. Hence, there would be no particular reason to further document what quickly became a "non-event."

. . . Additionally, the researchers obtained from the Archives of the University of Texas Arlington (UTA), a set of original (i.e. first generation) prints of the photographs taken at the time by the *Fort Worth Star-Telegram*, that depicted Ramey and Marcel with the wreckage. A close review of these photos (and a set of first generation negatives also subsequently obtained from UTA) revealed several observations. First, although in some of the literature cited above, Marcel allegedly stated that he had his photo taken with the "real" UFO wreckage and then it was subsequently removed and the weather balloon wreckage substituted for it, a comparison shows that the same wreckage appeared in the photos of Marcel and Ramey. The photos also depicted that this material was lying on what appeared to be some sort of wrapping paper.

It was also noted that in the two photos of Ramey he had a piece of paper in his hand. In one, it was folded over so nothing could be seen. In the second, however, there appears to be text printed on the paper. In an attempt to read this text to determine if it could shed any further light on locating documents relating to this matter, the photo was sent to a national level organization for digitizing and subsequent photo interpretation and analysis. This organization was also asked to scrutinize the digitized photos for any indication of the flowered tape (or "hieroglyphics," depending on the point of view) that were reputed to be visible to some of the persons who observed the wreckage prior to it getting to Fort Worth. This organization reported on July 20, 1994, that even after digitizing, the photos were of insufficient quality to visualize either of the details sought for analysis. . . . [6]

Eight years later the issue of what could be determined from digitizing and analyzing the Fort Worth photographs was taken to a whole new level by David Rudiak, who has a bachelor's in physics and a doctorate in optometry from Berkeley and is a dedicated researcher into the many and varied complexities of the Roswell story. While most of the Ramey memo remains indecipherable even upon detailed examination, Rudiak's research has shown that one specific line of the memo appears to make a reference to the "victims of the wreck." Needless to say, any reference to "victims" effectively rules out the possibility that the Roswell event was the result of nothing more than the crash of a Mogul balloon.[7] So convincing is Rudiak's finding that one wonders precisely why the "national level organization" that analyzed the memo for the Air Force was unable to make a similar identification.

Nevertheless, thus was born Roswell explanation number *three* from the Air Force: Project Mogul. There are, however, two key and troubling issues regarding the recovered debris in the Mogul scenario. Why should such overwhelming secrecy accompany the retrieval of the materials found at Roswell? And why would the civilians involved be threatened, as some have alleged?

Some have answered these questions by pointing out, quite logically, that given the very real military threat posed to the Western world by the former Soviet Union in the late 1940s, the crash of a Mogul balloon at Roswell had simply prompted an overinflated degree of "Cold War nerves" response on the part of the Army Air Forces, which in turn led to the issuing of rash warnings to those with intimate knowledge of what occurred at Roswell. This particular hypothesis is not without merit. But unfortunately, it is totally belied by the facts.

A document from the archives of the FBI provides some illuminating insights into the security constraints that surrounded the containment of suspected Mogul crash sites and the retrieval of fallen fragments. On September 23, 1947, the FBI drew up a one-page memorandum concerning its acquisition of an "Instrument found on farm near Danforth, Illinois." The similarities between the events at Roswell and those at Danforth are, at the *very* least, striking. For example, both "objects" were found on ranch land, both were initially suspected of being flying saucer debris, and in the same way that the Air Force tried to lay the Roswell controversy to rest with its Mogul hypothesis, the material evidence in the Danforth case was also suspected by some within the military of originating with a Mogul balloon array.

According to the FBI's records, the strange find was handed over after its discovery to a Mrs. Whedon of the Army Engineers, who postulated that "the instrument had been used by the Air Forces on tests which were classified as 'Top Secret.'"

Special Agent S. W. Reynolds of the FBI's Liaison Section made additional inquiries and contacted the Intelligence Division of the Air Force, which informed him: "Mrs. Whedon alluded that the instrument was used in 'Operation Mogul.'"

Moreover, deeper inquiries revealed that the entire matter was in reality nothing but a hoax, and that the "object" was actually part of an old-style radio loudspeaker. Initially, however, and based chiefly upon telephonic descriptions of the material, it *was* believed to have been Mogul-based debris. And when faced with the possibility that debris from a top-secret military balloon-based project had come down on an Illinois ranch (and under circumstances practically identical to those at the Foster Ranch near Roswell), what did the Air Force do? Did it issue stark threats of death? Did it cordon off the area? No. The material was simply forwarded with the minimum of fuss to Wright Field for inspection, and it was Wright Field's staff that concluded, despite the initial assertion from the Army Engineers, that the debris was unconnected to Mogul.

For proponents of the theory that the object found at Roswell was a Mogul balloon, this presents a major problem. We have two incidents, one in New Mexico, one in Illinois, both on ranch land and both tied to flying saucers and to Mogul. In the first instance, the Air Force asserts that a Mogul balloon was most likely recovered, and in the second instance, Mogul was suspected by the military itself, no less. Yet the procedures undertaken to deal with the recovery and analysis of both objects were entirely different. More important, the overwhelming secrecy afforded the Roswell case at the Foster Ranch was absent in the incident at Illinois.

Had the two events occured in different time frames—say, over the space of two or three years—it could be argued that the secrecy surrounding Mogul had been downgraded. Yet the Roswell and Danforth events took place *only weeks apart.*

While the Air Force report on Roswell authored by Colonel Weaver delved deeply into the world of Project Mogul, most noticeable by its stark absence was any serious attempt to address the statements of those witnesses who claimed to have seen unusual bodies at the Roswell site. This aspect of the controversy received only a brief dismissive statement from Weaver: "It should also be noted here that there was little mentioned in this report about the recovery of the so-called 'alien bodies.' [T]he recovered wreckage was from a Project Mogul balloon. There were no 'alien' passengers therein." [8]

Three years after Colonel Weaver's report was published, however, the Air Force made a surprising acknowledgment that the reported sightings of strange bodies at Roswell *did* have a basis in fact. So compelled was the Air Force now to address the "bodies" issue that it authorized the release of yet *another* report on Roswell. The final word was apparently not the final word after all.

Titled *The Roswell Report: Case Closed*, the Air Force's second report on the New Mexico events of 1947, was published in 1997 and marked the 50th anniversary of the incident at Roswell. The report did little to dampen the notoriety surrounding the case, however. Indeed, the question of *why* the Air Force had concluded that there was a pressing need on its part to explain the reports of unusual bodies found in New Mexico, when it could have summarily dismissed them as hoaxes or modern-day folklore, arguably only heightened the interest in what did or did not occur.

The second Air Force report on Roswell was written by Capt. James McAndrew, an intelligence applications officer assigned to the Secretary of the Air Force Declassification and Review Team at the Pentagon who had served special tours of duty with the Drug Enforcement Administration. The report, which focused practically all of its 231 pages on the alleged recovery of the strange bodies, essentially concluded:

"Aliens" observed in the New Mexico desert were probably anthropomorphic test dummies that were carried aloft by U.S. Air Force high altitude balloons for scientific research. The "unusual" military activities in the New Mexico desert were high altitude research balloon launch and recovery operations. The reports of military units that always seemed to arrive shortly after the crash of a flying saucer to retrieve the saucer and "crew" were actually accurate descriptions of Air Force personnel engaged in anthropomorphic dummy recovery operations.

The historical record shows that the Air Force did indeed conduct a wide array of tests using crash test dummies in New Mexico and that at least some of these tests *did* occur in the vicinities of both the White Sands Proving Ground and the town of Roswell. But were those same tests responsible—either in part or in whole—for the stories concerning highly unusual-looking bodies recovered by the military during the summer of 1947?

During World War I, extensive research into the development of parachutes for the military was conducted at McCook Field, Ohio. To test the parachutes, engineers experimented with a number of different dummies, finally settling on a model constructed of three-inch hemp rope and sandbags with the approximate proportions of a medium-sized man. Known by the nickname "Dummy Joe," the model made more than five thousand "jumps" between 1918 and 1924.

By 1924, parachutes were routinely required on military aircraft, with their serviceability tested by dummies dropped from aircraft. This practice would continue until the early stages of World War II, when, due to both increased reliability and large numbers of parachutes in service, this routine practice was discontinued. Nevertheless, test dummies were still used frequently by the Parachute Branch of the Air Materiel Command (AMC) at Wright Field, Ohio, to test new parachute designs. But it was as a result of research into ejection seat development that the crash test dummy came to the fore in the postwar era.

The ejection seat had been developed and used successfully by the German Luftwaffe during the latter stages of World War II, and was recognized as a highly effective device when one was obtained by the U.S. Army Air Forces in 1944. To properly test the ejection seat, the Army Air Forces required a dummy with the same center of gravity and weight distribution as a human, characteristics that parachute drop dummies did not possess. In 1944, the USAAF Air Materiel Command contracted with the Ted Smith Company to design and manufacture the first dummy intended to accurately represent a human, but only with abstract human features and "skin" made of canvas.

In the late 1940s, the Air Force Aero Medical Laboratory submitted a proposal for an improved model of the anthropomorphic dummy—this request having originated with Air Force scientist and physician John P. Stapp, who conducted a series of groundbreaking experiments at Muroc (now Edwards) Air Force Base, California, to measure the effects of acceleration and deceleration during high-speed aircraft ejections.

Stapp required a dummy that had the same center of gravity and articulation as a human, but, unlike the Ted Smith dummy, was more human in appearance. A more accurate external appearance was required to provide for the proper fit of helmets, oxygen masks, and other equipment used during the tests. Stapp requested that the Anthropology Branch of the Aero Medical Laboratory at Wright Field review anthropological, orthopedic, and engineering literature to prepare specifications for the new dummy. Plaster casts of the torso, legs, and arms of an Air Force pilot were also taken to assure accuracy. The result was a proposed dummy that stood seventy-two inches tall, weighed two hundred pounds, had provisions for mounting instrumentation, and could withstand up to a hundred times the force of gravity, or 100 g's.

A contract was awarded to Sierra Engineering Company of Sierra Madre, California, and "Sierra Sam," as the dummy was affectionately known, was born. A similar contract for anthropomorphic dummies was awarded to Alderson Research Laboratories, Inc., of New York City. Dummies constructed by both companies possessed the same basic characteristics: a skeleton of aluminum or steel, latex or plastic skin, a cast aluminum skull, and an instrument cavity in the torso and head for the mounting of strain gauges, accelerometers, transducers, and rate gyros.

Declassified documentation made available by the Air Force shows that forty-three high-altitude balloon flights carrying sixty-seven anthropomorphic dummies were launched and recovered throughout New Mexico. And as *The Roswell Report: Case Closed* notes, "Due to prevailing wind conditions, operational factors and ruggedness of the terrain, the majority of dummies impacted outside the confines of military reservations in eastern New Mexico, near Roswell, and in areas surrounding the Tularosa Valley in south central New Mexico."

For the majority of tests, the dummies were flown to altitudes between 30,000 and 98,000 feet attached to a specially designed rack suspended below a high-altitude balloon; and on several flights, the dummies were mounted in the door of an experimental, high-altitude balloon gondola. Upon reaching the desired altitude, the dummies would be released and "free-fell" for several minutes before deployment of the main parachute.

Dummies utilized in these operations were typically outfitted with standard equipment, including a one-piece flight suit, which was olive drab or gray in color, and a parachute pack. In addition, the dummies were fitted with an instrumentation kit that contained accelerometers, pressure transducers, and a camera to record movements of the dummy during free fall.

The Balloon Branch at Holloman Air Force Base handled the recovery of the dummies. Under normal circumstances, eight to twelve civilian and military recovery personnel would secure the landing site of one or more of the dummies, and would be complemented by a variety of aircraft and vehicles, including a wrecker, a six-by-six, a weapons carrier, and L-20 observation and C-47 transport aircraft. On one occasion southwest of Roswell, Lt. Raymond A. Madson even conducted a search for dummies on horseback.

Documentation reviewed by the Air Force as part of its attempt to lay to rest the claims that strange corpses were recovered from the New Mexico desert in the summer of 1947 demonstrated that Holloman Air Force Base, New Mexico, has—to date—launched and recovered no fewer than 2,500 high-altitude balloons, with the majority having been launched by the Holloman Balloon Branch. But under what circumstances did these operations begin?

In 1946, as a result of research conducted for Project Mogul, Charles B. Moore, the New York University graduate student working under contract for the Army Air Forces, made a significant technological discovery concerning the use of polyethylene for high-altitude balloon construction. Polyethylene, a lightweight plastic that can withstand stresses of a high-altitude environment differed drastically from, and greatly exceeded the capabilities of, standard rubber weather balloons used previously. As an example of this, polyethylene balloons flown by the Air Force have reached recorded altitudes of 170,000 feet and lifted payloads of 15,000 pounds.

It is also a fact that in the late 1940s, a characteristic associated with the large—and newly invented—polyethylene balloons was that they were often misidentified as flying saucers due in part to the excellent visibility in the New Mexico region. The balloons, flown at altitudes of approximately 100,000 feet, were illuminated during the periods just after sunset and just before sunrise, and appeared as large bright objects against a dark sky. With the refractive and translucent qualities of polyethylene, the balloons appeared to change color, size, and shape. According to Bernard D. Gildenberg, Balloon Branch meteorologist and engineer, so many flying saucer reports were generated as a result of the balloons launched from Holloman AFB that accounts from police and news services were regularly used by Holloman's technicians to supplement early balloon-tracking techniques.

The Air Force concluded that the strange debris recovered by rancher Brazel on the Foster Ranch likely originated with these polyethylene balloons:

As early as May 1948, polythene [polyethylene] balloons coated or laminated with aluminum were flown from Holloman AFB and the surrounding area. Beginning in August 1955, large numbers of these balloons were flown as targets in the development of radar guided air-to-air missiles. Various accounts of the "Roswell Incident" often described thin, metal-like materials that when wadded into a ball, returned to their original shape. These accounts are consistent with the properties of polythene balloons laminated with aluminum. These balloons were typically launched from points west of the White Sands Proving Ground, floated over the range as targets, and descended in the areas northeast of White Sands Proving Ground where the "strange" materials were allegedly found.

Having relegated the reports of strange bodies recovered near Roswell to the world of the crash test dummy, the Air Force then focused its attention upon the claims (many of which surfaced from Roswell mortician W. Glenn Dennis) that alien bodies were taken to the base hospital at Roswell Army Air Field following the events of the summer of 1947. In a section of *The Roswell Report: Case Closed* that runs to no fewer than fifty pages, the Air Force argued that the "Claims of bodies at the Roswell Army Air Field hospital were most likely a combination of two separate incidents."

The first incident occurred on June 26, 1956 (that's correct, 1956), when an Air Force refueling plane caught fire while in flight and crashed, killing all eleven crew members. The corpses of the crewmen were soaked through with fuel and burned beyond recognition, and some even were missing numerous body parts. Some autopsies of the victims were conducted at civilian facilities, and McAndrew's report suggests that this incident was the source of the claim that the military had retrieved gruesome alien bodies that were described as "black" and "very mangled" by witnesses.

The second incident that the Air Force believed led to the claims that alien bodies were transported to the base hospital occurred on May 21, 1959, when Air Force captain Dan Fulgham suffered a serious head injury when the balloon he was piloting crash-landed in New Mexico. His head, severely swollen with blood, was described by one associate as "just a big blob," and McAndrew suggested that Fulgham's condition may have caused a civilian observer at Walker Air Force Base hospital to later report seeing an "alien creature" enter the facility.[9]

Not surprisingly, these conclusions provoked a furor of controversy. The Air Force's report largely and very carefully glossed over the fact that these particular anthropomorphic dummy tests did not begin until the early 1950s, *more than three years after* the Roswell Incident. Likewise, the two events that the Air Force asserted led to the legends of alien bodies taken to the Roswell Army Air Field hospital occurred in the *late* 1950s, long after the purported incident of 1947.

This "time-lag" issue was not lost on the media during the Air Force's press conference at the Pentagon, which accompanied the release of the report in July 1997. When asked by a reporter, "How do you square the UFO enthusiasts saying that they're talking about 1947, and you're talking about dummies used in the 50's, almost a decade later?" Air Force spokesman Col. John Haynes replied, "Well, I'm afraid that's a problem that we have with time compression. I don't know what they saw in '47, but I'm quite sure it probably was Project Mogul. But I think if you find that people talk about things over a period of time, they begin to lose exactly when the date was." [10]

This explanation did not even sit well with some of the Air Force's own people. The Associated Press revealed that no less a source than the project officer at Holloman Air Force Base, Lt. Col. (ret.) Raymond A. Madson wasn't "buying" the latest Air Force explanation of what occurred in Roswell in July 1947 — despite the fact that Madson was cited in the report prepared by the Air Force.[11] UFO researcher Stanton Friedman, who spoke to Colonel Madson, said, "He is adamant that the explanation doesn't fit. Remember that the dummies had to be the same height and weight as air force pilots. None were dropped anywhere near the two crash sites and none were dropped earlier than 6 years AFTER the 1947 events." [12]

Even Walter Haut, the man who issued the original press release from Roswell Army Air Field in July 1947, was not buying the Air Force explanation: "It's just to me another cover-up. If you're dropping a dummy, any dummy would know what a dummy looks like." [13]

FOUR

BALLOONS AND BOMBS

The Air Force dummies clearly exist in the wrong time frame to explain the Roswell event, but it is undeniable that balloons were considered a sensitive issue both during World War II and in the postwar era. In fact, the ancestry of the Air Force balloons that would play a role in Roswell, as well as other features of that event, can be traced back to the Japanese, who were working on some highly advanced and very novel balloon-based projects during the 1940s.

Arguably, one of the best-kept secrets of the latter stages of World War II, the "balloon bomb"—or Fugo, as it was known—was a classified weapon developed by the Japanese military. No fewer than 9,000 such devices were constructed and employed against the United States, largely in retaliation for the "Doolittle Raid" on Tokyo of April 18, 1942.

Thirty-two feet in diameter when fully inflated and holding 19,000 cubic feet of hydrogen, the balloons were made of paper or rubberized silk and carried below them antipersonnel and incendiary bombs. They were launched from the east coast of the main Japanese island of Honshu during a five-month period beginning in the latter part of 1944, and were carried by high-altitude winds more than six thousand miles eastward across the Pacific to North America. Inevitably, most of the balloons failed to reach their intended targets; but around one thousand were estimated to have made it to the States, of which there were approximately three hundred reported incidents, the majority having occurred in British Columbia, Washington, Oregon, California, and Montana.

The idea for a balloon bomb began in 1933, when Lt. Gen. Reikichi Tada of the Japanese military's Scientific Laboratory was made head of the Proposed Airborne Carrier Research and Development Program, the purpose of which was to develop new and novel weapons of warfare. Of those weapons, one that the laboratory envisaged was a constant-altitude balloon that could carry explosives. The plan was that the balloon would be carried to an enemy location by the wind, whereupon a timer device would activate a well-placed bomb. As ingenious as this idea undoubtedly was, it was shelved in 1935; however, as World War II began, the reorganization of the Army resulted in the resurrection of the balloon project under the control of the 9th Military Technical Research Institute. In addition to the research of the Army, a similar project was initiated by the Japanese Navy—using balloons constructed from rubberized silk—and in early 1944, the two projects became one and answered to the Army's 9th Military Technical Research Institute.

The first operational launches against the United States took place on November 3, 1944. Two days later, American authorities realized that something strange was afoot when a U.S. Navy patrol boat spotted a mystery balloon floating on the water sixty-six miles southwest of San Pedro, California. Shortly afterward, shredded balloon debris of unknown origin was found in the Pacific waters near Hawaii; and on December 11 a Fugo balloon was recovered near Kalispell, Montana.

As more and more sightings of the strange balloons were reported and the U.S. government began to grasp the potential enormity of the unfolding situation, a stringent policy of strict silence was put into place—largely to try and eliminate the possibility of panic among the American population and also to deny the Japanese government access to any information on the success of the launches. As evidence of this, on January 4, 1945, the Office of Censorship asked newspaper editors across the United States to avoid reporting on the Fugo attacks. The request was met with large-scale compliance.

To counter the potential threat that the Fugos posed, Army Air Forces (AAF) and Navy fighters, under the control of what became known as "Project Sunset," flew intercept missions to shoot down the balloons. Meanwhile, AAF aircraft and Army personnel working with another operation, Project Firefly, were stationed at critical points to combat any forest fires that might occur in the event that a balloon successfully made it to the mainland and exploded.

Behind the scenes, American authorities had every reason to be concerned: on February 23, 1945, near Calistoga, California, a Fugo balloon was blown out of the skies by the military. Four days later, a Japanese balloon bomb exploded in the air near Goldendale, Washington, and twenty-four hours later, another detonated in the air ten miles northwest of Tacoma. Similarly, and shortly afterward, no fewer than five of the balloons were found in the Mount Rainier park area—but no damage was done—and one Fugo was recovered after crashing into telephone wires at Keyport, near Bremerton. An FBI "demolition squad" was called in after telephone linemen cut down the missile.

During this same time period, the U.S. military succeeded in capturing a number of Fugo devices and was quick to try to understand and utilize this technology for its own purposes. A test-and-evaluation program, largely designed to determine the extent to which the balloons were radar reflective, was undertaken from the Naval Airship Training and Experiment Command at the Chesapeake Bay Annex in Maryland and the Army's Camp Evans Signal Laboratory in New Jersey.

On February 20, 1945, an attempt to launch a Fugo balloon at

Camp Evans failed. Eight days later, however, a second launch took place, with the balloon reaching a height of approximately 1,000 feet before being lost over the ocean. Meanwhile, the attacks continued.

In early March 1945, a Fugo balloon collided with an array of high-tension power lines at the site of the Bonneville Dam, Washington. Power was lost over a considerable area, including at the Manhattan Project's Hanford Works, which was involved in the generation of plutonium for the project's headquarters at Los Alamos. For three days, Hanford was forced to suspend work.[1]

Days later, the Office of Censorship issued another request to the attention of newspaper editors: "Cooperation from the press and radio under this request has been excellent despite the fact that Japanese free balloons are reaching the United States, Canada, and Mexico in increasing numbers. There is no question that your refusal to publish or broadcast information about these balloons has baffled the Japanese, annoyed and hindered them, and has been an important contribution to security."

On June 4, 1945, a Japanese military spokesman boldly and ominously asserted that the Fugo launches were, in reality, little more than test flights for something far more dangerous, including "large-scale attacks with death-defying Japanese manning the balloons." The new balloons, American experts estimated, would be at least sixty feet in diameter and, conceivably, would be able to carry a "pressurized gondola" containing four relatively small men — equipped with oxygen tanks, a considerable amount of food and water, and specialized suits to afford protection for high-altitude flying — to a height of around 30,000 feet as the balloon traveled on its stratospheric, four-day flight across the Pacific to the United States.[2]

The warning of June 4 was reiterated by the Japanese several days later, with a statement that "something big" was about to occur. Forty-eight hours afterward, the *Tacoma News-Times* had much to say about the threat of manned balloon attacks undertaken by "death-defying" Japanese personnel: "Military observers here today refused to become exercised over the Japanese threat of piloted balloons attacking the west coast of the United States in the near future. They classified as absurd the idea that the balloons would be able to do any serious damage, even if they are sent against us."[3]

The idea was not absurd to the Reverend Archic Mitchell of Lakeview, Oregon. The minister had taken his wife and five children out for a picnic in June 1945. They had picked out a shady spot for lunch about sixteen miles in the mountains of southern Oregon. While Mitchell drove the car around by a road, the others hiked through the woods.

"As I got out of my car to bring the lunch, the others were not far away and called to me they had found something that looked like a balloon," Mitchell related. "I had heard of Japanese balloons so I shouted a warning not to touch it. But just then there was a big explosion. I ran up there—and they were all dead."

The clergyman, said the newspaper, was "so dazed from the blast and the shock of seeing everyone killed that he hardly realized two forest service employees had heard the explosion and joined him." They duly covered the bodies, verified that it was indeed a "big balloon" that had carried the bomb to the isolated spot, and quickly took Mitchell to Bly, the nearest town. The forest workers said it appeared that the victims had "clustered around the balloon" and someone had "curiously tugged it enough to detonate one of the bombs carried underneath."[4]

As the *Tacoma News Tribune* of August 15, 1945, revealed, other Fugo balloons had been found by other individuals, all blissfully unaware of the devastation that they could have potentially wreaked: "Near Moxee City, Wash., a sheepherder found a fallen balloon with live bombs, dragged it behind his automobile and kept it in a building two weeks before authorities learned of the incident. A small boy in Washington State found an anti-personnel bomb, which looked to him like a toy airplane. He wound the 'propeller'— the arming device in the nose—until it was within one-sixteenth of an inch of exploding the bomb. The lad was pretty disappointed when his plaything was removed, but not more so than the Indian children near Wapato, Wash., who found part of a paper balloon and used it to make a beautiful tepee in their back yard. They were crushed when the officers snatched it away."[5]

As a result of the escalating publicity and alarm that surfaced when the true extent of the attacks became apparent, Undersecretary of War Robert P. Patterson made the first official, public mention of a balloon bomb, and the Office of Censorship commented on the tragic event at Oregon that resulted in the deaths of the Reverend Mitchell's family, a story that had largely been kept secret for a month. In addition, Patterson stated that this particular Fugo balloon had probably lain undiscovered for some months in the woods and warned there "would be others found" as the snow melted and vacationers traveled into the mountains and the backcountry.

Lyle F. Watts, chief of the Department of Agriculture's Forest Service, told the media: "They take a couple of balloons to a war factory, make a lot of speeches, stir up the workers to a frenzy, then launch the balloons for their trip to the United States." He said the Forest Service was "less worried about this Japanese balloon attack than we are with matches and smokes in the hands of good Americans hiking and camping in the woods."

Revealing hitherto undisclosed details of how the balloon bombs were rigged to fly the Pacific and drop their bombs on the United States, Watts continued: "[T]hey made the trip in the stratosphere by means of an ingenious arrangement of weights and barometric pressure switches."

Having been briefed by knowledgeable government sources, Watts stated that the Fugo balloons were able to cross the Pacific in three to five days, traveling at speeds of up to 125 miles per hour in a layer of air constantly moving from west to east and at an altitude of between 25,000 and 35,000 feet.

Describing the balloons as "hydrogen-filled bags made of five layers of silk paper 35 feet in diameter carrying sandbags and incendiary bombs," Watts explained that "When it drops to 25,000 feet, a barometric pressure switch automatically drops a sandbag. Still traveling east, the balloon goes up again to 35,000 feet. This process of up and down is repeated until the balloon reaches the American coast. And if the Japs have figured right, the last sandbag has been dropped. A second automatic switch then takes over. In place of the sandbags, this one controls incendiary bombs. When the balloon drops to 27,000 feet an incendiary bomb is released. The balloon goes back up, then down again and another incendiary is released and so on as it travels across the United States." [6]

As the war drew to a close, the frequency of attacks on the United States dwindled dramatically, and the media's decision not to report on the incidents had the desired effect. As the Associated Press noted, "The Japanese listened to radio reports, hoping to hear of the bombs' effectiveness. But American editors voluntarily kept the information to themselves and so discouraged the Japanese that they abandoned the project. The Japanese learned of only one bomb landing in the United States. It was one which came down in Wyoming and failed to explode." [7]

On the day the war ended, a Special Research Conduct Outline was issued by the Military Affairs Section of Japan's War Ministry that ordered the destruction of all documentation on the Fugo balloons and other "secret weapons" created by the 9th Army Technical Research Institute.

In early December of that year, Col. Murray Sanders, a Camp Detrick bacteriologist, flew to Washington State under cover of high security to examine debris that had been collected from several recently discovered Fugo balloons. "The balloons were brought in, and we all stood around them, in a circle," recalled Sanders. "All [of] the scientific and military experts, all of us with our own thoughts. We examined them, and then we went away to make our own individual reports. Mine scared them stiff. I told them that if we found Japanese B-encephalitis on any of the balloons we were in real trouble." [8]

On February 9, 1946, the departments of the Army and Navy revealed that a classified study had been undertaken into all aspects of the Japanese balloon bomb situation during the latter stages of the war. The "greatest danger posed" by the balloons, stated the military in its report, was indeed that they would be used by Japanese biological and bacteriological experts for the dissemination of "deadly germs" and viruses such as cholera and typhus. As a consequence, supplies of decontamination chemicals and sprays to counter any possible use of such germ warfare had been quietly and carefully distributed throughout the Western states.

Moreover, a captured Japanese officer had informed American officials that the original goal of the Japanese had been to construct an astonishing 120,000 balloons for use in bombing the United States. The Army further revealed that approximately 10 percent of the balloons sent to America were equipped with radio-sending apparatus, thus allowing Japanese forces on the island of Honshu to track the movements of the balloons. The last balloons were released around April 20, 1945, concluded the military in its 1946 report; nevertheless, said the Army and Navy, intercepted radio signals were heard as late as August 11, 1945, indicating that the Japanese were still studying meteorological conditions over the Pacific with a view to launching even bigger and far more advanced balloons with much larger and far more destructive payloads.[9]

While Japan's Fugo balloon raids did not ultimately live up to their deadly promise, the specter of the balloons continued to haunt American officials for years to come. On March 5, 1949, a bomb from a Fugo balloon was found near Montesano, Washington, and handed over to local sheriff Mike Kilgore. Similarly, the remains of a Japanese balloon bomb, having been carried by high-altitude winds to the wilds of Alaska, were found in 1954, the balloon's payload still lethal after lying unnoticed for ten years. Retrieved by an H-5 helicopter crew of the 74th Air Rescue Squadron from Ladd Air Force Base near Fairbanks, Alaska, its final destination was Wright-Patterson Air Force Base, Ohio, where it was sent for closer inspection.[10]

After the fall of Japan, American forces salvaged files that detailed highly novel plans for much more advanced Fugo-style balloons that were to be manned and utilized in conjunction with
other, equally advanced aircraft. These plans inspired the object
that would eventually crash in the desert of New Mexico and set off
the story now known as the Roswell Incident.

FIVE

MEDICAL MADNESS

The roots of another aspect of the Roswell story—the recovered "alien" bodies—can also be traced back to Japan.

On June 25, 1892, Shiro Ishii, the fourth son of a rich family of Japanese landowners, was born in the village of Kamo, which lies east of Tokyo. With his degree in medicine from Kyoto Imperial University, Ishii enlisted in the Japanese Imperial Guards and in 1922 received a posting to the Tokyo-based 1st Army Hospital. Two years later, Ishii returned to the university to continue his postgraduate studies in the fields of bacteriology, serology, preventive medicine, and pathology; and in 1927, under the supervision of a bacteriology expert, Professor Ren Kimura, he obtained his doctorate for "Research on Gram Positive Twin Bacteria."

Twelve months later, Ishii embarked on a round-the-world trip that took him to many countries, including the United States, France, Germany, and Russia, where he visited establishments engaged in virus research and then fledgling biological warfare studies—this despite the fact that germ warfare research had been summarily banned by the Geneva Convention in 1925. On his return to his homeland, Ishii informed the Japanese War Ministry that bacteriological warfare was likely to become a major weapon of war in the near future and the Japanese military should pursue every available opportunity to capitalize on this new technology.

As a result of his recommendations, and having reenlisted in the military, Ishii attained the rank of major in August 1930 and began working in the Department of Epidemic Prevention at the Army Medical College in Tokyo. Ishii found a number of powerful supporters in the Army: Col. Tetsuzan Nagata, chief of military affairs; Col. Yoriniichi Suzuki, chief of the 1st Tactical Section of Army General Staff Headquarters; Col. Ryuiji Kajitsuka of the Medical Bureau of the Army; and Col. Chikahiko Koizumi, the Army's surgeon general.

In 1936, two bacteriological warfare units were created by order of Emperor Hirohito. One had its base of operations at Mengchiatun and was called the Wakamatsu Unit (later, Unit 100). The other was located near Harbin, Manchuria, which had been occupied by the Japanese Army since 1931. Operating under the control of Ishii, the Harbin unit was known at the time as the Epidemic Prevention and Water Purification Department of the Kuantung Army and was renamed Unit 731 in 1941.

By 1938, Ishii had been promoted to the rank of colonel and his unit had been moved to a new location at Pingfang, where he was now in charge of 3,000 personnel. It was from this period onward that truly dark and disturbing research on human subjects began on a shocking and deadly scale in Unit 731. No fewer than three thousand people (and possibly as many as five thousand), including Chinese prisoners, Russian expatriates living in China, captured allied troops, physically handicapped Chinese and Japanese individuals, and even children were exploited in a wide range of controversial experiments until the close of hostilities in 1945. The experiments involved bacteriological warfare operations, tests to determine the effects of high and low pressures on the human body, the amputation of limbs and dissection of organs from still-living subjects, and studies designed to understand the effects of freezing temperatures on unwitting subjects.

On a number of occasions, Japanese pilots are also known to have dropped plague-infected fleas in eastern and central China, where major outbreaks would later be reported. Similarly, people deliberately infected with virulent diseases were placed in cells with healthy individuals in an effort to establish the ways in which viruses and diseases could most effectively be spread; others were subjected to the horrors of chemical warfare. Equally horrific are the acts described by Takeo Wane, a former medical worker in Unit 731, who has stated that he once had occasion to view a six-foot-high glass jar containing what he believed was a Russian man who had been pickled in formaldehyde; the man had been sliced into two pieces vertically.

As the war progressed, the work of Unit 731 became more advanced and ambitious. For example, Unit 731 personnel were planning an assault on San Diego in 1945. Code-named Cherry Blossoms at Night, the operation was designed to use Kamikaze pilots to attack the city with a deadly plague. Toshimi Mizobuchi, an instructor with Unit 731, stated that the plan was to transport a small aircraft by submarine to the Pacific coastline of the United States, from where it would be launched at night with its deadly cargo of plague-infected fleas. With the atomic bombing of Japan, this potentially disastrous operation did not come to fruition and both it and Unit 731 were brought to a crashing halt.

Only one week after the fall of Japan, Col. Murray Sanders, the Camp Detrick bacteriologist involved in the Fugo balloon affair, undertook a secret mission to Japan to locate Shiro Ishii and determine the full extent to which Unit 731 had engaged in experimentation on human beings. Over the course of ten weeks, Sanders interrogated numerous Japanese military personnel implicated in the activities of Unit 731, including the chief of the army's general staff, Yoshijiro Umezu, and Ishii's personal deputy, Col. Tomosa Masuda. Ishii himself, however, remained in hiding.

Upon arriving in Japan, Sanders came into immediate contact with Lt. Col. Ryoichi Naito, Ishii's right-hand man. However, having been deliberately misled by Naito and his colleagues regarding the full extent to which human experimentation was undertaken, Sanders approached Gen. Douglas MacArthur with the recommendation that Naito and his colleagues should be promised immunity from prosecution for war crimes in return for their cooperation. MacArthur was quick to concur with Sanders.

As he began to dig deeper into the controversy, however, Sanders learned of the sheer scale of the human experimentation in Unit 731 and expressed major concerns to MacArthur about working with Naito and his associates. MacArthur responded by ordering Sanders to remain silent. Notably, and shortly afterward, Sanders was then ordered to return to the United States, and the Unit 731 investigation was continued by a colleague of Sanders, Lt. Col. Arvo T. Thompson.

Although Ishii had been declared dead by Japanese newspapers, he finally surrendered to American personnel from the Counter Intelligence Corps and was vigorously interrogated by Colonel Thompson from January 17 to February 25, 1946. Like Naito, Ishii was a master of obfuscation. He deliberately—and with great success—downplayed to Thompson the actions of Unit 731, carefully maneuvered the interrogations away from human experimentation, and asserted that the bulk of his work had been in the areas of germ research and germ bombs. Nevertheless, as American authorities began to uncover more data, the truth of Unit 731's activities became graphically clear.

However questionable and controversial the unit's work had been, MacArthur considered it to be of overriding importance to the security of the United States. He argued in particular that the results of Unit 731's work should not fall into Soviet hands. As a result, Maj. Gen. Charles Willoughby, head of the Intelligence Department of the Allied Forces Headquarters under MacArthur, coordinated an operation designed to ensure that the United States alone benefited from the interrogation of Unit 731 personnel, the analyses of retrieved documentation and technical and scientific materials, and the recovered bodies and victims found in Unit 731 laboratories.

In April 1947, Gen. Allen Waitt, the commander of the United States Chemical Corps, ordered yet another Camp Detrick bacteriologist, Norbert Fell, to Japan in an effort to try and put together a complete picture of the activities of Unit 731 and its associates. The response from practically everyone Fell spoke with was unanimous: grant us immunity from prosecution for war crimes and we will provide you with complete information on the work of Unit 731.

Despite vigorous protestations—particularly by the State Department—that to accept what was essentially blackmail from war criminals went against established international laws, on May 5, 1947, MacArthur issued a recommendation that resulted in widespread immunity for many of the guilty and the transfer to the United States of a massive body of personnel, literature, data, and medical information on the work of Unit 731.[1]

While the Japanese were undertaking all manner of medical atrocities on human subjects in Unit 731 during the war, Nazi Germany was following a similar and equally chilling path. As evidence of the extreme nature of some of the experimentation undertaken by Nazi doctors during World War II, consider the "work" of one Dr. Sigmund Rascher, who had conducted experiments on prisoners at Dachau. Eager to find out how best to save German pilots forced to eject at high altitude, Rascher and his colleagues placed inmates into low-pressure chambers that simulated altitudes as high as 68,000 feet and monitored their physiological responses as they succumbed and died. Rascher was said to dissect victims' brains while they were still alive to show that high-altitude sickness resulted from the formation of tiny air bubbles in the blood vessels of a certain part of the brain. Of the two hundred or so people subjected to these experiments, eighty died outright and the remainder were executed to ensure that evidence of these atrocities did not leak outside of official channels.[2]

On May 15, 1941, Rascher wrote to SS Fuehrer Heinrich Himmler, informing him that investigations to accurately determine the effects of high-altitude flying on Luftwaffe pilots were practically at a standstill due to the fact that "no tests with human material had yet been possible as such experiments are very dangerous and nobody volunteers for them. . . . Can you make available two or three criminals for these experiments. . . . The experiments, by which the subjects can of course die, would take place with my cooperation."

Within days the fuehrer replied that "prisoners will, of course, be made available gladly for the high-flight research."[3] The results of this research make for grim reading:

The . . . test was without oxygen at the equivalent of 29,400 feet altitude conducted on a 37-year-old Jew in good general condition. Respiration continued for 30 minutes. After four minutes the TP [test person] began to perspire and roll his head.

After five minutes spasms appeared; between the sixth and tenth minute respiration increased in frequency, the TP losing consciousness. From the eleventh to the thirtieth minute respiration slowed down to three inhalations per minute, only to cease entirely at the end of that period. . . . About half an hour after breathing had ceased, an autopsy was begun.[4]

Anton Pacholegg, who worked in Rascher's office, would watch through the observation window of the decompression chamber as prisoners' lungs ruptured in a vacuum: "They would go mad and pull out their hair in an effort to relieve the pressure. They would tear their heads and faces with their fingers and nails in an attempt to maim themselves in their madness. They would beat the walls with their hands and head and scream in an effort to relieve pressure on their eardrums. These cases usually ended in the death of the subject."[5]

In the fall of 1943, the governments of the United States, Great Britain, and the Soviet Union agreed that, once victorious, they would prosecute individuals in Nazi Germany who might have violated international law during the war, specifically with regard to the way in which medically unethical experimentation on human beings had been carried out.

On August 8, 1945, exactly three months after V.E. Day and two days after the bombing of Hiroshima, representatives of the American, British, French, and Soviet governments officially established the International Military Tribunal in Nuremberg, Germany. Allied prosecutors presented cases against twenty-four high-ranking German government and military officials, including Hermann Göring and Rudolf Hess (Rascher had been executed by Himmler in 1944), before an international panel of judges. The trials ran from October 1945 to October 1946 and ended in late August 1947, when the judges handed down seven death sentences and the following ruling regarding all future experimentation with human subjects:

> In order to conform to the ethics of the American Medical Association [AMA], three requirements must be satisfied: (1) the voluntary consent of the person on whom the experiment is to be performed [must be obtained]; (2) the danger of each experiment must be previously investigated by animal experimentation; and (3) the experiment must be performed under proper medical protection and management.

The AMA's official governing body added: "This House of Delegates condemns any other manner of experimentation on human beings than that mentioned herein." Despite the Nuremberg episode, however, the darkest aspect of this controversial story had barely begun.[6]

SIX

PAPERCLIP

As the Nuremberg "war crime" prosecutions progressed, elements of the American military and government were secretly working behind the scenes to bring some of the finest minds within the German medical and scientific communities into the United States to continue their at times highly controversial research, which they had undertaken at the height of World War II. This included studies of human anatomy and physiology in relation to aerospace medicine, high-altitude exposure, and "space biology." The startling fact that some of these scientists were ardent Nazis and even members of the notorious and feared SS seemed not to be a problem to the government of the time; though some people, such as Gen. Leslie Groves, director of the Manhattan Project, expressed serious reservations about the plan. But much pressure was exerted to make sure the plan, called Project Paperclip—so named because the recruit's papers were paper-clipped to regular American immigration forms—was carried out.[1]

"On May 19, 1945, a military transport plane with windows blackened to hide its notorious cargo dropped out of the steely gray skies over Washington, D.C., and lurched down the landing field," according to Linda Hunt, a noted authority on Paperclip. "As the propellers slowed and finally stopped, three figures stepped out of the aircraft. The first was a middle-aged man with a scarred face whose slight build belied his importance."

This man was none other than one Herbert Wagner, who had been the chief missile design engineer for the Henschel Aircraft Company and the creator of the HS-293, the first German guided missile used in combat during World War II.

"Wagner's surreptitious arrival marked the beginning of a massive immigration of Nazi scientists to the United States and a long, sordid chapter in postwar history," said Hunt perceptively. It was on September 3, 1946, that President Harry Truman gave Paperclip his official approval to proceed in earnest.[2] Its aim was twofold: to exploit German scientists for American research and to deny these intellectual resources to the Soviet Union.

Paperclip personnel would end up playing a considerable role in postwar human experimentation on American soil, according to the Advisory Committee on Human Radiation Experiments (ACHRE), which was tasked by President Bill Clinton in January 1994 to investigate unethical medical experimentation undertaken in the United States from the mid-1940s onward. Some sixteen hundred scientists and their dependents were recruited and brought to the United States by Paperclip and its successor projects from the mid-1940s through the early 1970s.

According to an April 5, 1995, memorandum from the Advisory Committee Staff (ACS) to the members of ACHRE:

The Air Force's School of Aviation Medicine (SAM) at Brooks Air Force Base in Texas conducted dozens of human radiation experiments during the Cold War, among them flash-blindness studies in connection with atomic weapons tests, and data gathering for total-body irradiation studies conducted in Houston. Because of the extensive postwar recruiting of German scientists for the SAM and other U.S. defense installations, and in light of the central importance of the Nuremberg prosecutions to the Advisory Committee's work, members of the staff have collected documentary evidence about Project Paperclip from the National Archives and Department of Defense records.

The experiments for which Nazi investigators were tried included many related to aviation research. These were mainly high-altitude exposure studies, oxygen deprivation experiments, and cold studies related to air–sea rescue operations. This information about aircrew hazards was important to both sides, and, of course, continued to be important to military organizations in the Cold War.[3]

In one section of the memorandum titled "Biomedical Scientists at American Facilities," the Advisory Committee Staff revealed:

A number of military research sites recruited Paperclip scientists with backgrounds in aero-medicine, radiobiology and ophthalmology. These institutions included the SAM, where radiation experiments were conducted, and other military sites, particularly the Edgewood Arsenal of the Army's Chemical Corps.

The portfolio of experiments at the SAM was one that would particularly benefit from the Paperclip recruits. Experiments there included total-body irradiation, space medicine and biology studies, and flash-blindness studies. Herbert Gerstner, a principal investigator in total-body irradiation experiments at the SAM, was acting director of the Institute of Physiology at the University of Leipzig: he became a radiobiologist at the SAM.

The Air Force Surgeon General and SAM officials welcomed the Paperclip scientists. In March 1951, the school's Commandant, O.O. Benson Jr., wrote to the Surgeon General to seek more

" . . . first class scientists and highly qualified technologists from Germany. The first group of Paperclip personnel contained a number of scientists that have proved to be of real value to the Air Force. . . ."

General Benson's adjutant solicited resumes from a Paperclip list, including a number of radiation biology and physics specialists. The qualifications of a few scientists were said to be known, so curricula vitae were waived. The adjutant wrote, also in March 1951: "In order to systematically benefit from this program this headquarters believes that the employment of competent personnel who fit into our research program is a most important consideration."

The ACS memorandum also addressed the issue of the extent to which some of the Paperclip scientists had been supporters of the Nazi regime. They located an April 27, 1948, memorandum from the director of the Joint Intelligence Objectives Agency, Navy captain Bosquet N. Wev, to the Pentagon's director of intelligence, that stated: "Security investigations conducted by the military have disclosed the fact that the majority of German scientists were members of either the Nazi Party or one or more of its affiliates. These investigations disclose further that with a very few exceptions, such membership was due to exigencies which influenced the lives of every citizen of Germany at that time."

Wev was critical of overscrupulous investigations by the Department of Justice and other agencies as reflecting security concerns no longer relevant with the defeat of Germany and "biased considerations" about the nature of his recruits' fascist allegiances. The possibility of scientists being won to the Soviet side in the Cold War was, according to Captain Wev, the highest consideration. "Such an eventuality," Wev wrote in an April 27, 1948, report to his superiors, "could have a most serious and adverse affect on the national security of the United States."

One of the most controversial figures in this particularly notorious saga was Hubertus Strughold. Born in Germany on June 15, 1898,

Strughold obtained a Ph.D. in biochemistry in 1922, an M.D. in sensory physiology in 1923, and between 1929 and 1935 served as director of the Aeromedical Research Institute, Berlin. In 1947, as a result of Project Paperclip's actions, Strughold joined the staff of the Air Force's School of Aviation Medicine at Randolph Field, Texas; and in 1949 he was named head of the then newly formed Department of Space Medicine at the school, where, according to documentation uncovered by the ACHRE, he conducted research into "effects of high speed," "lack of oxygen," "decompression," "effects of ultra-violet rays," "space cabin simulator for testing humans," "weightlessness," and "visual disturbances."

The ACHRE memorandum states that "In a 1952 civil service form, Strughold was asked if he had ever been a member of a fascist organization. His answer: 'Not in my opinion.' His references therein included the Surgeon General of the Air Force, the director of research at the Lovelace Foundation in New Mexico, and a colleague from the Mayo Clinic. In September 1948, Strughold was granted a security clearance from the Joint Intelligence Objectives Agency director, Captain Wev, who in the previous March had written to the Department of State protesting the difficulty of completing immigration procedures for Paperclip recruits."[4]

Strughold was naturalized as an American citizen in 1956 and four years later became chair of the Advanced Studies Group, Aerospace Medical Center at Brooks Air Force Base. Strughold, whose awards and honors included the USAF Exceptional Civilian Service Award and the Theodore C. Lyster Award of the Aerospace Medical Association, retired in 1968.[5] And in 1977 the Aeromedical Library at the USAF School of Aerospace Medicine was named after him. In short, Strughold became known as "the father of space medicine." During the war, he was director of the Luftwaffe's aeromedical institute; a Strughold staff member was acquitted at Nuremberg on the grounds that the physician's Dachau laboratory was not the site of nefarious experiments.

"His background," said the ACHRE memorandum, "was the

subject of public controversy in the United States. He denied involvements with Nazi experiments and told reporters in this country that his life had been in danger from the Nazis. A citizen for 30 years before his death in 1986, his many honors included an American Award from the Daughters of the American Revolution."

The final paragraph of the memorandum revealed that "The staff believes that this trail should be followed with more research before conclusions can be drawn about the Paperclip scientists and human radiation experiments. That the standard for immigration was 'not an ardent Nazi' is troubling; in Strughold's case, investigators had specifically questioned his credentials for 'denazification.' It is possible that still-classified intelligence documents could shed further light on these connections."[6]

In time, an absolute wealth of documentation surfaced and reinforced the sheer extent to which Paperclip scientific personnel—including former supporters of the Nazi regime—were integrated into a whole range of government, military, and intelligence operations and projects in the United States. Of specific relevance to the subject matter of this book, however, are the links between Paperclip and the activities of the Army Air Forces in 1947, the year of the Roswell affair.

A February 22, 1947, document prepared by the AAF Aero Medical Center to the attention of the air surgeon of the AAF demonstrates the pressing need in the early part of that year for a full understanding of German research in the fields of aviation and aerospace medicine:

In accordance with directives from higher authority, the Aero Medical Center has given top priority to the completion of the rough translation of manuscripts for the survey of German Aviation Medicine. Additional translators and typists have been employed, and all qualified personnel within the organization have been assigned full time to this project to meet the deadline of 15 April 1947. It is planned that the German and

English manuscripts will be couriered by Major William F. Boseley to the School of Aviation-Medicine, Randolph Field, Texas. The vast amount of original scientific material contained in this survey will constitute, it is believed, a valuable contribution to aviation medical literature as well as a unique reference book for medical research laboratories presently concerned with current Army Air Forces projects.

And thus was set in motion the wheels of a project of truly Frankenstein-esque proportions.

SEVEN

WHiTE SANDS AND THE NUCLEAR AGE

Against this backdrop of human experimentation in Japan and Germany, and research into advanced balloon technology, a third element would be needed to create what would ultimately become known as the Roswell Incident—and that was a ravenous, novel interest in all things nuclear.

In August 1945, as the war drew to a close with the atomic bombing of the Japanese cities of Hiroshima and Nagasaki, Dr. Theodore von Kármán, acting on the orders of the General of the Army, H. H. Arnold, prepared a document titled "Where We Stand: A Report for the AAF Scientific Advisory Group" that examined the feasibility of constructing and flying a nuclear-powered aircraft.

Von Kármán was born in Budapest, Hungary, in 1881. Having moved to the United States in 1930 and obtained his American citizenship in 1936, von Kármán went on to head the prestigious Guggenheim Aeronautical Laboratory. Two years later, he served on a National Academy of Sciences committee advising the Army Air Forces on the use of rocket power to assist airplanes in taking off, and in 1944, he chaired the AAF's newly created Scientific Advisory

Group, which studied the then cutting-edge technologies in rocketry, guided missiles, and jet propulsion.

Ultimately published in the summer of 1946 by Headquarters Air Materiel Command at Wright Field, Ohio, von Kármán's report addressed a variety of areas of advanced aviation research that the military was exploring at the time, including nuclear-powered aircraft. In a section of the document titled "Atomic Energy for Jet Propulsion," von Kármán stated that " . . . no hope for spectacular improvements in range and speed performance of aircraft can be derived from further development of conventional fuels. Use of atomic energy as fuel, however, will radically change this situation."

In his concluding section on atomic-powered aircraft, von Kármán stated firmly:

It seems to me that there are possibilities in the development of nuclear energy for jet propulsion which deserve immediate attention of the Air Forces. To be sure there are problems still to be solved requiring inventive activity of specialists in nuclear physics. However, the main problems are engineering problems requiring inventive genius of the same but different kind. We have to convert the energy liberated by the nuclear reaction into heat of such temperatures as needed for our propulsive devices. Important problems to be solved are in the nature of heat transfer, resistance of materials to heat, corrosion, etc. It appears necessary to find a way, within the limits of necessary security, for engineering talent which could be used to accelerate the progress in the field of propulsion. It would secure us the conquest of the air over the entire globe without range limitations.

Von Kármán then signed off firmly: "It is my feeling that the Air Forces should, as soon as possible, take the lead in investigating the possibilities of using nuclear energy for jet propulsion."[1]

Encouraged by von Kármán's words, Gen. Curtis LeMay and

Col. Donald Keirn, both of the Army Air Forces, strongly urged the development of nuclear-powered bombers. Indeed, as far back as the spring of 1946, they had persuaded Gen. Leslie Groves of the Armed Forces Special Weapons Project to approve Air Forces use of the then vacated S-50 plant at the Oak Ridge National Laboratory to determine whether or not nuclear energy could successfully and safely propel an aircraft.

The initial concept that both LeMay and Keirn envisaged called for a nuclear-powered bomber that was capable of remaining airborne for a distance of no less than 12,000 miles, for a radically extended period of time, and at a speed of at least 450 miles per hour—all without refueling. Needless to say, such range and speed would have ensured the military a nuclear delivery platform that could have struck anywhere in the world and at a moment's notice. The aircraft would require a compact reactor that was small enough to fit inside a bomber; however, it would also need to be powerful enough to lift the airplane into the air, complete with lightweight shielding to protect the crew from potentially hazardous and deadly radiation.[2]

According to a six-page document titled "Brief History of the Aircraft Nuclear Propulsion Project at ORNL" and prepared by personnel at the Oak Ridge National Laboratory: "On May 26, 1946, the U.S. Air Force awarded to the Fairchild Engine and Airplane Corporation a contract which established Fairchild as the responsible agency of the Nuclear Energy for Propulsion of Aircraft (NEPA) project. The purpose of the project was twofold: (1) to perform feasibility investigations and research leading toward the adaptation of nuclear energy to the propulsion of aircraft, and (2) to educate the aircraft engine industry in the field of nuclear science and its adaptation to aeronautical propulsion."

Shortly afterward, the work of Fairchild was transferred to General Electric and the research project was relocated from Oak Ridge to General Electric's Ohio plant. As a result, a number of Fairchild personnel employees transferred to Ohio; however, around two hundred remained in Oak Ridge to join the laboratory's own project: the Aircraft Nuclear Program.

From the mid-1950s onward, however, the whole project would be beset with problems and setbacks, and in 1957 Congress objected to continuing the costly nuclear aircraft project in the face of supersonic aircraft and ballistic missile development—both of which made the mid to late 1940s plans for nuclear aircraft largely obsolete. In response to this congressional decision, research into aircraft shielding and reactor prototype investigations were both shelved, and in 1961, President John Kennedy canceled the remainder of the nuclear aircraft project.

Though the nuclear aircraft program did not ultimately fulfill its initial promise as envisaged in the mid to late 1940s, during the very early years when fledgling research into this particular subject was in its infancy, some decidedly controversial experimentation appears to have been conducted at a secure location deep in the heart of the New Mexico desert.[3]

White Sands Missile Range is a multiservice test facility the prime purpose of which is the support of missile development and test programs for the Army, Navy, Air Force, National Aeronautics and Space Administration (NASA), other government agencies, and private industry. It falls under the operational control of the U.S. Army Test and Evaluation Command, Aberdeen Proving Ground, Maryland. Trinity Site, another national historic landmark at White Sands, is situated near the north boundary of the range, and on July 16, 1945, it was the location of the world's first atomic bomb test.

The Army Research Laboratory's Battlefield Environment Directorate is one of the integral parts of the range—its activities dating back to 1946, when as a then agent of the Army Signal Corps it provided radar and communications support for the German V-2 rocket program. Today, the mission of the laboratory is to maximize worldwide combat and strategic effectiveness by continually improving Army-required, atmospheric-related products.

The U.S. Navy also has a heavy presence at the range, which dates back to June 14, 1946, when an agreement was made to combine its expertise with that of the Army in research studies and test-firing of captured German V-2 rockets. During the late 1940s, the Navy was primarily involved in launching sounding rockets for atmospheric research; and moving on from the V-2, the Navy expanded rapidly with testing of its own Viking rocket.

Situated in the Tularosa Basin of south-central New Mexico, the missile range boundaries extend almost one hundred miles north to south by forty miles east to west; and at almost 3,200 square miles the range is the largest military installation in the country. In addition, White Sands has agreements with the ranchers living in the areas that allow the range to evacuate the residents several times each year. These evacuations, which almost double the size of the range when all areas are used, permit the testing of some of today's long-range missiles.

This range was born during the latter stages of World War II. In late 1944, Maj. Gen. G. M. Barnes, chief of the Research and Development Service, Office Chief of Ordnance, recognized the necessity for the establishment of a program of research and development in the field of guided missiles. More significantly, Barnes astutely realized that if such a project were to proceed in earnest and actually succeed, it was vital that within the continental United States there should be established a secure "range" where test firings of such missiles could take place.

As a result of Barnes's initiative, carefully selected groups of officers and civilian engineers from the Ordnance Department and the Corps of Engineers conducted a detailed study of a whole host of locations throughout the States that might conceivably serve such a purpose. The criteria included a) clear weather for the vast majority of the year; b) very large amounts of open and largely uninhabited terrain over which experimental test firings could be conducted without jeopardy to the surrounding population; and c) easy accessibility to both local rail and power facilities.

The work of the Ordnance Department and the Corps of Engineers led to the conclusion that the area that became known as the White Sands Proving Ground (and that was renamed the White Sands Missile Range in 1958) came closest to fulfilling these specifications.

The site that was designated for the firing facilities was deemed perfect. The huge range over which guided missiles could be flown had a width of approximately forty miles and a length north of the firing point of around ninety miles. South of the firing point, and made available largely to ensure protection against erratic flights straying south, existed approximately forty miles of open terrain that fell under the jurisdiction of the Anti-Aircraft Artillery Battalion activities at Fort Bliss.

Engineering was started in June 1945 and the first actual work began on the site on the 25th of that month. Because of the vital importance of water in such a dry environment, the first work deemed vital was to begin drilling wells. July 1945 saw work begin on the construction of access roads and roadways within the cantonment area, and on July 10, work commenced on the building of the firing facilities. Three days later, an official order activating the White Sands Proving Ground as a "Class II activity" under the command of the chief of Ordnance, was published by the chief of the Army Service Forces at Washington.

Work had progressed sufficiently to permit the movement of troops on to the station during the early part of August 1945. And it was during this period that "C" Battery of the 69th Anti-Aircraft Artillery Battalion—which had been assigned to assist in guided missile work being conducted by the chief of Ordnance—moved on to the White Sands Proving Ground, with its chief goal being to test-fly a missile no later than September 15.

A significant and massively important change was introduced to the program, however, when American troops in Germany succeeded in capturing components for approximately one hundred German V-2 missiles that had been developed, largely as a result of the work of one Wernher von Braun.[4]

*   *   *

Wernher von Braun was born in Wirsitz, Germany, on March 23, 1912, and earned his bachelor's degree at the age of twenty from the Berlin Technological Institute, where he also received his doctorate in physics in 1934. Between 1932 and 1937, von Braun was employed by the German Ordnance Department and became technical director of the Peenemünde Rocket Center in 1937, where the V-2 rocket was developed.

As it became clear that Germany was not going to win the war, von Braun became highly concerned that the SS would follow Hitler's "scorched earth" initiative and would destroy the tons of documents and blueprints that von Braun's team had put together on the V-2, largely to ensure they did not fall into the hands of the Allies. To ensure that this did not occur, von Braun ordered his personal aide, Dieter Huzel, and Bernhard Tessmann, the chief designer of the Peenemünde test facilities, to secure the material in a safe location. As a result of von Braun's actions, no less than fourteen tons of documentation was secretly transferred from the Peenemünde site—and several other locations—into the heart of an abandoned iron mine near the Harz Mountains.

On April 11, 1945, when the U.S. 3rd Armored Division approached the area, they had been advised by Intelligence personnel that they should "expect something a little unusual in the Nordhausen area." This was not an understatement: contained within a large tunnel were freight cars and trucks loaded with component after component used in the construction of the feared V-2. When Col. Holgar Toftoy, the chief of Ordnance Technical Intelligence in Paris, learned of this astonishing discovery, he began organizing "Special Mission V-2," the purpose of which was to transfer the material to the White Sands Proving Ground.

Arrangements were made for the transportation of this huge amount of material by water and rail to Las Cruces, and then by truck over twenty-eight miles of highway and the St. Augustine Pass to the Proving Ground. This shipment consisted of no fewer than three hundred carloads of material and was transported over the mountains to the camp in less than a month.

Von Braun himself came to the United States in September 1945, under contract with the Army Ordnance Corps as part of Paperclip, and worked on high-altitude firings of captured V-2 rockets at the White Sands Proving Ground until he became project director of the Ordnance Research and Development Division Sub-Office at Fort Bliss, Texas.[5]

On October 11, 1945, the 1st Guided Missile Battalion, Army Ground Forces, was constituted and, after months of study, a decision was made to design and construct motor-testing facilities that would have the ability to make static test firings on motors with a thrust up to 500,000 pounds and that could be sustained for two minutes.

In the fall of 1945, the chief of Ordnance addressed an invitation to the chief of the Bureau of Ordnance of the Navy through the Office of the Secretary of the Navy to participate in the activities at the White Sands Proving Ground, his feeling being that great benefit would accrue to both services if such action took place. As a result, the Bureau of Ordnance and Bureau of Aeronautics jointly accepted the invitation and made available funds from both bureaus to augment the facilities at the White Sands Proving Ground.

One particular American scientist who traveled to Europe to interrogate German missile scientists was Ernst H. Krause of the Naval Research Laboratory. Krause returned highly impressed with the status of German missile technology and research, but was at the time unaware of the fact that a significant capture of V-2 technology had been made. When Milton Rosen, one of Krause's NRL staff, proposed building an American research rocket, Krause was highly enthusiastic. As a result, on December 17, 1945, the NRL Rocket-Sonde Research Branch was formalized. Research groups to study cosmic rays, the atmosphere, the ionosphere, and spectroscopy were duly created, and plans were started to develop a new sounding rocket to carry the scientific instruments.

Scientists and engineers in the NRL Rocket-Sonde Research Branch had scarcely begun their work when, on January 7, 1946, they learned from Lt. Col. J. G. Bain, Army Ordnance Department, of the capture of enough parts to build around one hundred V-2 rockets. Plans for a new Navy sounding rocket were quickly set aside in favor of exploiting this treasure trove of technology. Indeed, the Army had already implemented plans for firing the V-2s from White Sands to gain military experience, but had not specifically implemented a scientific research program. Colonel Bain was more than happy to learn that the NRL had already organized a group to meet these ends. Similarly, the NRL, which had the scientific know-how but possessed no actual rockets, was equally pleased and quickly accepted Colonel Bain's invitation to join the V-2 project.

A little more than a week after Colonel Bain's visit to the NRL, approximately fifty interested scientists and engineers from more than a dozen organizations met at the NRL to plan the exploitation of the V-2s. And it was on January 16, 1946, that a "V-2 Upper Atmosphere Research Panel" was created and would ultimately dominate rocket-based research for the next ten years. The first American V-2 static firing took place on March 15, 1946, and the first actual flight came a month later at 2:47 P.M. on April 16.[6]

With research into nuclear-powered aircraft now under way and the White Sands Missile Range firmly established, the stage was set for the Roswell events to explode in spectacular and horrific fashion in the skies over New Mexico.

EiGHT

THE BRiTiSH CONNECTiON

Though the Black Widow's account was certainly controversial, it was not the first time that I had heard a story like hers from a first-hand source. Indeed, a similar account had been related to me five years previously on the other side of the world. Until I met with the Black Widow in the late summer of 2001, however, I had put this strange tale aside as too fantastic to believe without confirmation.

In August 1996, I was contacted quite out of the blue by a man who said that he had some important information that he would like to impart regarding the true extent of the British government's involvement in the area of UFOs. I had heard such claims on numerous occasions before, but agreed, at least, to listen to what he had to say. Less than happy to speak on the telephone or relate his information in the form of a letter, however, he insisted on a meeting over lunch at the sprawling Euston Railway Station, London. "I know what you look like," he told me, "I saw you on *Out of This World*," a reference to a BBC television documentary that I had been involved in and that had been broadcast on British television the previous month.[1]

And so it was that on the morning of August 9, 1996, I set off for my appointment at Euston Station. Ten minutes after I had arrived in the waiting room, a man I estimated to be in his late fifties or early sixties made his way toward me.

"You're Nicholas."

"Yes. You're the man who phoned?"

"We don't have too long," he said in what I perceived to be a deliberately exaggerated, conspiratorial tone while simultaneously scanning the station with obviously faked nervousness.

We retired to the restaurant area of the station, and for the next two hours or so he gave a fascinating account of high-level involvement of the British government in the UFO controversy. Perhaps anticipating that I would ask for some form of proof that he was speaking to me truthfully, the man first opened his black leather briefcase and placed on the table a wealth of documentation pertaining to his employment at the British government's Home Office—employment that centered on immigration issues. As my writing hand struggled to keep up and take notes, he revealed to me a truly bizarre and mind-blowing story. I will refer to this man as "Mr. Levine."

During the early part of 1989, Mr. Levine and several friends within the Home Office who had a purely personal interest in the subject of unidentified flying objects established their own little investigative group, which met informally, usually over drinks in a London bar near Piccadilly Circus, to discuss the latest "UFO news and sightings that were taking place."

Since two of those Home Office individuals held positions of some authority, they would on occasion liaise with influential colleagues and friends in other departments and agencies, including the Ministry of Defense. And although this involvement was wholly personal and unofficial, when it became apparent to senior sources within the Home Office that the group was operating and that one of them was contemplating writing an article for a well-known British UFO journal, those involved were quietly asked to "tone down" their investigations, because it was felt that this behavior was not in keeping with the image that the Home Office wished to cultivate.

Less than happy that their private lives were being intruded upon (all those involved in the group had been careful to restrict their activities to nonworking hours), several of those same individuals protested that their personal UFO investigations had no bearing whatsoever on their work with the Home Office. Not so, they were advised. At the time, they received no further explanation beyond this cryptic comment, but in early October 1989, shortly after they had all attended a UFO conference, everything became crystal clear—terrifyingly so, in fact.

At approximately ten o'clock on a workday morning in the first week of the month, all four members of the group were quietly asked to assemble in the foyer of the Home Office building at Queen Anne's Gate, London, and were driven to a location near Northumberland Avenue, London. On arrival, they were ushered into a building that they immediately recognized fell under the jurisdiction of the Ministry of Defense. Entering a small, dark room with heavy burgundy curtains, they were greeted by a Mr. T., who was reportedly attached to the MoD's elite Defense Intelligence Staff, and a Mr. D., a CIA operative who, they were advised, was on assignment to Britain as part of a joint Anglo-American intelligence operation.

"What does any of this have to do with us?" one of them asked impatiently.

"We want to show you something," D. replied. "Take a seat," he added in a voice that suggested an order rather than a request, and gestured toward a row of chairs. As the four bemused Home Office staff took their seats, they could not fail to see that a film projector and screen had been set up. D. hit the Play button.

As the images on the screen flickered to life, it became clear that the film was aged and of exceptionally poor quality. There was no sound accompanying the film and there were no credits. Indeed, the first image was that of an individual dressed head to toe in some form of bulky "radiation suit" not unlike those worn by persons in the nuclear industry. Then the camera panned to a shocking scene: sprawled out atop a somewhat makeshift table was a strange-looking, and obviously deceased, humanoid body.

As Mr. Levine informed me, the body appeared to be female, was slightly shorter than a fully mature human woman, with an oversize bald head, large black eyes, thick, muscular legs, and a bulging stomach. The entire group watched enthralled and appalled as a team of what were presumed to be medical experts moved in and began to systematically dissect the body with unusual speed. Most distressing were graphic dissections of the creature's genitals and skull.

For almost two hours the group watched this gruesome footage without any word of explanation as to what it was they were viewing. Most unsettling of all was a final scene that reportedly showed an almost identical living creature cowering in a small cell-like room, possibly aware of its comrade's fate.

At the close of the film, D. proceeded to turn on the lights of the room. All of the group were affected by the film to varying degrees and demanded to know what was going on and what it was that they had just viewed.

D. looked toward T. and nodded. What the group had just watched, T. explained, was nothing less than the autopsy of one of five alien creatures recovered from the crash site of an extraterrestrial spacecraft that had plunged to earth in the New Mexico area of the United States in late 1947. The aliens, advised T., were not friendly. They were deceptive creatures with a disconcerting interest in our defense and military capabilities. In more than half a century of visiting our world, they had proved themselves to be unreliable and wholly untrustworthy, and had steadfastly refused to reveal their true intent with respect to the earth and its people.

T. continued that there had been a number of such crash incidents throughout the planet dating back to the late 1930s, and that access to such information was strictly limited to a small body of individuals from a number of countries, including the United States, Britain, Russia, Australia, France, and Japan. Moreover, those same individuals were "in the job for life," and largely operated outside of normal governmental and military guidelines. In other words, they answered to no one.

Why, one of the group wanted to know, were they being exposed to this information if it was deemed so secret? T. explained that there were those within the Home Office who were directly involved with the program, and those same people had expressed deep concern that the establishment of an informal group, however innocent, could possibly compromise the work of those tasked with preserving the safety of both the country and the very planet itself. More important, the identities of those attached to the covert operation would potentially be put under threat if the media and the public UFO research community learned that people working for the Home Office were making their interest in UFOs publicly known.

It was decided that the best course of action was to make it clear to those present why it was so important that they disband their little group: the Home Office simply could not afford to be associated, officially or unofficially, with the UFO subject. Later that day, the group agreed to fold. But the story was far from over.

Three weeks later, all four were once again summoned to the same address near Northumberland Avenue for another meeting. This time, however, the only other person present was the mysterious Mr. T., who then proceeded to relate a far stranger tale.

T. first apologized for the cloak-and-dagger and somewhat heavy-handed treatment dished out by his American counterpart on the previous occasion and then began to elaborate. T. explained that the film they had seen came into the hands of British authorities in early 1981. At that time, he explained, counterintelligence operatives attached to the Royal Air Force's Provost and Security Services (P&SS) at RAF Rudloe Manor, Wiltshire, had been working for some months with their opposite numbers in the U.S. Air Force Office of Special Investigations (AFOSI) and sources from the National Security Agency (NSA) on a top-secret program of disinformation that involved disseminating fabricated crashed UFO accounts and documentation into the public UFO research community.

According to T., the 1980 release of the book *The Roswell Incident* had convinced those "in the know" at AFOSI and the NSA that the secret truth surrounding the Roswell event, which they strongly desired to keep under wraps, would shortly thereafter become impossible to contain. The assistance of the P&SS was required, according to an NSA source, because several British UFO researchers had been briefed by their American friends on certain sensitive aspects of the Roswell affair—and the act of the Americans conducting disinformation operations against British citizens was seen as a distinctly no-go area. So a remarkable operation would be put into place. If the facts could not be kept under wraps, they would be released.

In an ingenious move, the joint NSA-AFOSI-P&SS team decided that via a series of official-looking but fabricated papers they would reveal to certain "meddlesome" players, researchers, and authors in the UFO field the "truth" behind the Roswell affair and the apparent establishment in the wake of the crash of a supersecret group to take control of the situation. But in reality nothing of the sort ever happened.

Instead, these were outright lies that originated in the fertile imaginations of AFOSI counterintelligence personnel and that, as AFOSI well knew, easily would be spotted by keen-eyed UFO investigators. T. stated that these tales centered on three key issues: 1) accounts of crashed UFOs and the recovery of alien bodies; 2) stories concerning underground bases in New Mexico that had been taken over by hostile alien forces; and 3) tales of "alien-induced animal mutilations."

Of course, when the faked material was shown for what it really was, this would also cast doubt on the genuine material pertaining to Roswell that had been uncovered by UFO researchers—albeit, due to the passage of time, at a fragmented and distorted level. In other words, if the truth could not be contained, it would be both confused and, to a limited extent, disseminated. T. explained further that it was during this time period that the film footage showing the apparent alien autopsy had come into the hands of the Provost and Security Services—along with a massive file of documents (amounting to around five hundred pages of material) on UFO crashes, alien autopsies, and secret UFO studies undertaken by the intelligence community of the United States—all of them fabricated and containing a careful blend of fact and fiction and, along with the film, all designed to be surreptitiously "leaked" to certain civilian UFO investigators in 1983. It was then, however, that matters began to deteriorate.

Having worked hand in glove with their American counterparts for several months on this particularly bizarre program, a number of P&SS operatives (and, later, personnel from MI5 and Government Communications Headquarters—the UK equivalent of the U.S.A.'s NSA—who were drafted into the operation) began to have grave doubts about what their American colleagues were telling them.

First, the P&SS team was informed by AFOSI that while the documentation was fabricated, the alien autopsy film was genuine. Subtle checks made by the British, however, had determined that it was nothing of the sort. The film was a fake—albeit a strikingly good one. When faced with this evidence, the Americans stood their ground: "Your information is wrong; the film *is* real."

Second, the P&SS suspected that the Americans had also lied to them about the true nature of what had occurred at Roswell. Mr. Levine stated that T. refused to elaborate on this beyond saying that "while bodies *were* found at Roswell—make no mistake about that—not all of our people were convinced they were alien. Some thought that the Americans had been buggering around and doing something bloody stupid with biological weapons and Japanese prisoners brought over after the war."

If T. could not—or would not—elaborate on this, was Levine in a position to do so? He was. Indeed, he told a story—acquired, he said, "from other friends"—that was gruesome in the extreme. According to Levine, sources within the P&SS had in their possession copies of—literally—thousands of pages of documentation on Project Paperclip, the American government operation that saw numerous German scientific and technical experts transferred to the States at the close of World War II.

Contained within those files, Levine elaborated, were references to the notorious Unit 731 of the Japanese military that conducted all manner of horrific human experimentation, "in the name of science," during the war. Not only that, but the files referenced several cases where grossly deformed and handicapped Japanese people had been "acquired" from mental asylums and institutions throughout Japan for "the benefit of" Unit 731 personnel.

Intriguing and eye-opening was the fact that a number of experiments carried out at the time involved exposing some of these unfortunate people to plagues and lethal viruses, and their corpses were kept "on ice" during the latter stages of the war by Japanese scientific personnel. When the Japanese surrendered in the wake of the atomic destruction of Hiroshima and Nagasaki in 1945, a number of these bodies and "a quantity" of still-living people were found in the remains of Unit 731 facilities (and also German laboratories) by Allied soldiers. These remains were subsequently—and secretly—transferred to the Los Alamos Laboratories, New Mexico, where this dark and disturbing research was continued. Or so Levine's story went.

Of key relevance is the fact that a number of these people, said Levine, were dwarves, handicapped, with enlarged heads, and were used in a variety of experiments in the New Mexico desert that involved everything from biological warfare to high-altitude tests linked with prototype aircraft developed in the immediate postwar era. This, said Levine, was where the stories of alien bodies recovered from crashed UFOs had their origins.

Most alarming of all, the British reportedly learned through official channels of more than a dozen highly suspicious deaths of military and intelligence personnel connected with the events at Roswell "who knew the real truth" [*sic*]. Expressing grave concerns about what they were getting into, the P&SS demanded access to the full and unexpurgated truth.

The Americans stood by their original stance that their British cousins *had* been given the truth: a UFO *did* crash at Roswell, New Mexico, in 1947, and alien bodies *were* recovered by American authorities. In addition, the entire matter was considered to be one of overriding concern from a national security perspective.

Nevertheless, at some point in either late 1981 or early 1982 there occurred an irreconcilable split between the Americans and the British, and the joint project was duly terminated. The Americans demanded that the alien autopsy film footage and the documentation be returned to them—which it was. However, copies of all the evidence had been made by the P&SS, as the Americans suspected it inevitably would be, and remained in a secure location at RAF Rudloe Manor.

In early 1986, stated T., the uneasy alliance that existed between the Americans and the British on this entire affair was reestablished. Mr. Levine informed me that, according to T. and for reasons that he was not aware of, British authorities were by then seemingly satisfied that something strange definitely *had* occurred at Roswell—although concerns were still expressed by British personnel allied to the affair that the Roswell event had more to do with biological and nuclear experimentation than it did with anything that originated on the far side of the galaxy.

Given the group's sincere interest in the UFO subject, T. regretted that he was not in a position to offer any more answers with regard to this particular Anglo-American operation, and shortly afterward, all four men were driven back to the Home Office to resume their normal duties.

As Mr. Levine brought his remarkable narrative to a close, he explained to me that T. had guardedly informed them that the Defense Intelligence Staff and the P&SS strongly suspected that there was *another*—and even more covert—group operating on the fringes of British intelligence that had been involved in the Roswell controversy as far back as 1948. Exactly who these shadowy people were, T. claimed not to know. He did add, however, that "they were not to be fucked around with."

Needless to say, I had a thousand and one questions for the mysterious Mr. Levine. He, however, was not in the mood to answer them.

"I really think I've told you all I can. I always intended this to be a one-way conversation," he said nervously and somewhat apologetically, his eyes once again scanning the station. "You'll have to excuse me now." Then he quickly packed his briefcase; we stood up and shook hands.

"Hang on," I said, anxious to continue the conversation. "Can I publish what you've told me?"

For a moment Mr. Levine's eyes lit up and a slight smile came to his lips. "Yes, you may, but nothing before the end of 2000. Okay?"

"Okay," I replied. "No problem. Is that it?"

"Afraid so." And with that he vanished into the mass of commuters, families, and tourists that were swarming throughout the station. I never saw or heard from Mr. Levine again.[2]

Despite the seemingly incredible nature of Mr. Levine's account, it is one that cannot be dismissed lightly—for a variety of reasons. First, I *was* able to determine his real identity and confirm his employment at the Home Office. That much of the story checked out. But what of the far more controversial aspects—particularly those relating to faked "evidence" and questionable disinformation operations directed at private citizens?

It appears that the American intelligence community *did* begin a covert program of disinformation in the wake of the release of the book *The Roswell Incident*. Similarly, Emmy award-winning television documentary producer Linda Howe was approached in 1983 by U.S. intelligence sources and made privy to material concerning crashed UFO incidents in New Mexico and alien autopsies — even alleged face-to-face contact between elements of the American military and extraterrestrial creatures.[3]

There is also the bizarre story of one Paul Bennewitz of New Mexico, a scientist who was targeted by Air Force Intelligence and the NSA during the same time period, and who was fed such extreme and disconcerting accounts pertaining to hostile aliens holed up in underground bases in New Mexico, crashed UFOs, and alien-induced animal mutilations that he had a complete nervous collapse.[4]

Mr. Levine's assertion that American authorities made available to their British counterparts a large file of material (albeit one that carefully combined fact and fiction) on UFOs, alien autopsies, and crashed spacecraft is provocative, too. In 1986, the highly respected British author Jenny Randles was approached by a former British Army source ("Robert") who claimed to have in his possession hundreds of pages of top-secret material on just those very topics.

As Randles admitted to me in a 1997 interview, the apparent ease with which her source obtained the documents from a secure computer system at Wright-Patterson Air Force Base, Ohio, seemed to beggar belief. However, if in precisely the same year that she was approached the joint AFOSI-NSA-P&SS project of disinformation was relaunched, as T. had advised Mr. Levine was indeed the case, this made matters somewhat clearer. Notably, Randles had been approached with the "crashed UFO files" at the very time that she was digging deeply into a famous UFO "landing" case at Rendlesham Forest, England, which she suspected might have had more to do with a nuclear accident than with anything extraterrestrial.[5]

Researchers William Moore and Linda Howe suggest that all of these "Deep Throat"–style revelations were part of a plan to subtly and slowly acclimatize the public at large to the reality of the ongoing alien situation on Earth. Conversely, as a still-serving employee of Britain's Government Communications Headquarters commented to me, if, as at least *some* of the Provost and Security Services personnel originally suspected, the bodies recovered at Roswell were *not* alien, but were in some way connected with a secret American project dealing with "biological weapons" and "Japanese prisoners brought over after the war," then the act of flooding the UFO community with a mass of confusing, contradictory and outright bogus stories about aliens and crashed UFOs takes on a whole new light.

There is one final matter that cannot be denied—one that made me somewhat guarded and suspicious of not just the combined Anglo-American operation, but also of the less-than-tight-lipped Mr. Levine himself. He was very vocal and precise about his involvement in the UFO subject and the bizarre set of circumstances that came to pass in 1989—circumstances that seem to have had a major bearing on the national security of the United Kingdom. Yet he had no qualms about his story appearing in print post-2000. Of course, the idea that British authorities would not have been able to discern his identity from reading these words is absurd. True whistle-blowers certainly do not spill the beans in such a cavalier fashion, as did the highly talkative Mr. Levine. I know that from experience. They subtly and discreetly point you in certain directions and let you join the dots.

Mr. Levine was neither subtle nor discreet. Plus, his distinctly conspiratorial tone and manner was pure theater and something straight out of a third-rate pulp thriller. I therefore suspect that whatever the truth of this strange affair, Mr. Levine was not the innocent that he claimed to be. Rather, I am of the opinion that he was simply the latest (but surely not the last) player to emerge from the top-secret Anglo-American operation that had its origins in whatever it was that did or did not occur at Roswell, New Mexico, more than half a century ago. For that reason, if for nothing else, I didn't take Mr. Levine's story seriously until I heard the Black Widow's story five years later.

Now here were two people—worlds apart—telling uncannily similar stories. And they would not be the last.

NINE

INSIDER INFORMATION

In the summer of 1952 Bill Salter, a former employee of the Psychological Strategy Board, was brought into an operation to try to identify a Soviet sympathizer at Oak Ridge who was suspected of feeding certain technological information to the Soviets on America's plans to build a nuclear-powered aircraft.

Salter told me that he spent three weeks at Oak Ridge and was involved in forwarding to the suspected Soviet source faked documents that contained a number of deliberate technical errors that would confuse the Soviets if they received them, and that would also assist American intelligence in "chasing the trail after the Russians had them—the handlers, the sources."

Salter said that when he arrived at Oak Ridge there was a man employed in a covert intelligence position there that he knew vaguely. The man—who had previously worked for the Central Intelligence Group (CIG)—had told Salter confidentially about an operation he had been involved in the previous year: 1951.

Salter said that the man had guardedly informed him that he had been ordered to shred a whole file box of documents on the autopsy of five unusual bodies that had been recovered "from a pie-pan object" in the desert somewhere at White Sands in the early summer of 1947. Three of the bodies were relatively normal "but looked like Asians—Japanese," two were handicapped and displayed oversized bald heads and had unusually protruding eyes, and all were about five to five and a half feet in height and dressed in yellow clothlike clothes. Additionally, he stated that the destruction order had come from the CIA and the Armed Forces Special Weapons Project.

According to the file, the bodies had been recovered following the crash landing of a balloon and gondola that was specifically designed to determine the effects of very high altitude flight exposure experiments on human subjects. Salter was advised that, in a clearly delineated period that extended from May to August 1947, several vehicles had been involved in high-altitude, radiation, and biological warfare experiments at White Sands and elsewhere in the New Mexico desert and that there had been a number of fatal accidents.

Salter claimed to me that he was "told of the truth by an old friend from the Department of Energy," who was "very aware" of the scandal that broke at that time concerning the radiation experimentation carried out on American citizens in the 1940s. The bodies were indeed deformed and handicapped humans used in experiments that went wrong, Salter informed me firmly. However, the horrific nature of some of the experimentation—and, most crucially, the fact that it tied the American government to some of the most notorious and diabolical figures in Unit 731—meant that elements of the military and intelligence community wanted the story systematically buried at all costs, even more than half a century later.

"A crashed flying saucer and spacemen story is a big one," said Salter in quiet but deliberate tones. "Fifty-year [old] experiments using [people] in high-altitude experiments is an even bigger one. If you're concerned that the thing is getting out and you want to hide the second story, there's no better way to do it than by telling the first." [1]

Al Barker worked with the Army's Psychological Warfare Center

(PWC) in the early-to-mid-1950s, and stated unequivocally that elements of the government, military, and intelligence communities feared in the late 1940s and throughout the 1950s that if the Soviets uncovered the truth about the Nazi and Japanese links to the "high-altitude idiocy" at White Sands and elsewhere, this would have caused major repercussions between the United States and its allies in the postwar world. Hence the cover story put out by the Psychological Strategy Board and, later, by the Army's Psychological Warfare Center that the bodies were from a crashed UFO in case the Soviets, the press, UFO researchers, and America's allies came snooping.

Notably, Barker was very knowledgeable about Japan's Fugo balloon raids on the United States and the work of Unit 731. He claimed to have read classified documents showing that the Japanese carried out experiments on people with several specific syndromes in 1944–45 and he asserted that it was bodies with some of these defects that were recovered at White Sands and nearby in the New Mexico desert and led directly to the "alien body" legends.[2]

The specific syndromes that he referred me to were Hutchinson-Gilford progeria syndrome, Werner's syndrome, and Ellis-van Creveld syndrome. An examination of available data reveals astonishing similarities between descriptions of people exhibiting these conditions and the descriptions of the bodies recovered in the aftermath of the events at Roswell and elsewhere in the New Mexico desert in 1947.

Ellis-van Creveld (EVC) syndrome is a form of short-limbed dwarfism. Children with EVC are diagnosed at birth because of noticeably short limbs and other characteristic features. The middle parts of the limbs are primarily affected, with the shortening more apparent in the lower limbs. As the child gets older, knock-knee, or genu valgum, occurs, which can require surgery, and the hands are short and wide and have an additional digit next to the fifth finger. In scientific terms this is referred to as postaxial polydactylysm and occurs in virtually 100 percent of individuals with EVC. In addition, 10 to 20 percent of people with EVC have an additional digit on the feet. Adult height ranges from forty-two to sixty inches and skin manifestations include problems with nails and teeth. Changes in the EVC gene are also responsible for a related syndrome, Weyers acrofacial dysostosis, in which individuals may display mild short stature, extra fingers and toes, and dental abnormalities.[3]

The first formal description of what would come to be known as the Hutchinson-Gilford progeria syndrome was presented at a meeting of the Royal Medical and Chirurgical Society in 1886 by the renowned English physician-surgeon Jonathan Hutchinson. In his presentation to his medical colleagues in 1886, Hutchinson described "the case of a boy three and a half years old, who presented a very withered old-mannish appearance. His skin was remarkably thin, in some places not being thicker than brown paper. The genitals presented a marked contrast to the rest of the body, being in a state of a normally plump child. He had no nipples, their sites being occupied by little patches of scar."

Those afflicted with progeria only rarely exceed four feet in height during their brief lives. All body hair, including the eyebrows and eyelashes, either fails to develop or is lost; there are also skeletal and structural abnormalities, such as a receding chin, an oversized, bald head, beaklike nose, and protruding eyes. Voices are usually thin and high-pitched. Children with progeria usually have an average life span of twelve to thirteen years, and survival beyond twenty years is rare.

Like the Hutchinson-Gilford syndrome, Werner's syndrome is a progeria disorder. It is also known as *"progeria adultorum"*—progeria of the adult—and is the most common of the premature aging disorders. In the United States, Werner's syndrome is rare. Indeed, the estimated incidence is one case in a million individuals. Highly illuminating, however, is the fact that Werner's syndrome is more common in Japan and Sardinia than in any other regions in the world. In fact, of the approximately 1,000 cases currently reported, *more than 800 can be found in Japan*—the direct result of the fact that in Japan first- and second-cousin marriages are more common than in the

West. Unlike progeria, the onset of definitive symptoms in Werner's syndrome rarely begins before age twenty. Affected individuals seem perfectly normal as children, but they generally stop growing altogether early in the adolescent years. Men are rarely more than five feet tall, with women several inches under that.[4]

"Can you supply any documents or leads on this that I can follow up on?" I asked, hoping to gather yet more information before the Grim Reaper came calling on what was undoubtedly a rapidly diminishing body of aged individuals.

Barker immediately referred me to the life and work of one Robert Alexis McClure, who Barker stated was deeply involved in the "crashed saucer cover," and added that McClure's plans were based on similar tales spread in late 1940s New Mexico by a source whose identity Barker was extremely careful not to reveal, but "who was Pentagon brass in the fifties."[5]

In late 1942, McClure was selected by General Eisenhower to be chief of psychological warfare for the European and Mediterranean theaters. When the war ended, this group evolved into the Information Control Division, becoming the focal point for the de-Nazification of Germany. In 1948, McClure was assigned as the chief of the New York Field Office of the Army's Civil Affairs Division. Here he implemented education programs in the occupied countries of Germany, Austria, Japan, and Korea. Throughout his post-world-war II tours McClure was an unfailing proponent of the full integration of psychological warfare into the Army's arsenal of weapons.

From the various positions he held in World War II, McClure was very familiar with the Office of Strategic Services (OSS) and greatly appreciated its capability and established the Office of the Chief of Psychological Warfare. From this platform, he also was determined to reestablish a special operations force on the lines of the OSS. He recruited two other officers: Aaron Bank of the OSS and B.G. Russell Volckmann, who led Philippine guerillas during World War II. With Volckmann writing the doctrine and Bank as the first commander of the newly created 10th SFG(A), McClure was successful in selling the concept to the U.S. Army; as a result, in May 1952, the U.S. Army Psychological Warfare Center was established at Fort Bragg, North Carolina.[6]

From the National Archives at Maryland, I uncovered a significant body of data on McClure and his work with the military. And although the files that might have linked him with the events at White Sands remained elusive, the available material presented a clear and remarkable picture of a man who was a true genius in the field of psychological warfare.

Barker asserted that another individual with a deep awareness of the creation and dissemination of both fabricated documents and bogus tales on crashed UFOs was a Maj. Gen. Edward G. Lansdale. I was already keenly aware of who Lansdale was. In *Strange Secrets: Real Government Files on the Unknown*, I had detailed how in the 1950s Lansdale — who, like Bill Salter, had served in the war with the Office of Strategic Services and later became deputy assistant to the secretary of defense for Special Operations — was personally involved in a highly bizarre psychological warfare operation during the uprising in the Philippines that involved spreading faked stories to the superstitious Huk rebels to the effect that there were bloodthirsty vampires known as Asuangs on the loose in the area.

Regrettably, Lansdale was already dead; he had passed away in 1987. However, the startling fact that he was implicated in an event that involved spreading spurious tales (concocted by official sources, no less) about vampires suggested to me that his involvement in carefully disseminating bogus crashed UFO accounts seemed quite plausible.[7]

"I guarantee you won't find any files on this," Barker warned me. "Those people aren't going to leave tracks. McClure, Lansdale, Oak Ridge, White Sands, the balloons, nothing's left now. It will have been destroyed years ago — the documents, photographs, the bodies are all gone. But I will tell you this much: the goal behind much of this was based on studies to try and create both conventional and unconventional delivery systems for nuclear, biological, and chemical weaponry.

"I mean that plans were looked at to one day build a platform, an airplane, as a delivery system for biological warfare. This was a giant Fugo setup with an airplane. There were also far-ahead plans for a nuclear-powered airplane. But one of the crucial issues of this plan was how would the crew of an airplane designed as the delivery system be affected by prolonged high-altitude flying and nuclear exposure from the aircraft's power source? These were the purposes of using the guinea pig crews in balloons and at least two airplane flight tests."

Interestingly, and as an aside, Barker stated that at least two rumors pertaining to UFO crashes that emanated from Kingman, Arizona in 1953 in reality involved somewhat similar tests to those already referred to, but they employed primates loaded into "drone" aircraft.[8]

While the image of an unmanned drone aircraft packed with a "crew" of monkeys flying across—and ultimately crashing in—the deserts of the southwest might sound laughable and bizarre in the extreme, official papers establishing that such tests were indeed undertaken have surfaced. A document titled "Early Cloud Penetration," dated January 27, 1956, prepared by the Air Research and Development Command at Kirtland Air Force Base, New Mexico, states in part:

In the event of nuclear warfare the AF is confronted with two special problems. First is the hazard to flight crews who may be forced to fly through an atomic cloud. Second is the hazard to ground crews who maintain the aircraft after it has flown through the cloud. . . .

In the 1953 Upshot-Knothole tests, monkeys were used so that experiments could be conducted on larger animals nearer the size of man. QF-80 drone aircraft were used, their speed more nearly approximating that of current operational aircraft.[9]

As Barker explained, "This isn't directly linked with the [White Sands] situations, but it is prima facie evidence of unusual aircraft flights using a nonconventional guinea pig crew for aviation tests." [10]

Of course, what's most shocking is that the conventional guinea pigs in the earlier test were human.

TEN

DESERT SECRETS

Certainly the most enigmatic character that surfaced during the course of the research for this book was the "Colonel." I first met the Colonel when he introduced himself to me after I had delivered a lecture at a UFO conference held in Henderson, Nevada, in November 2003. At the time, he presented himself simply as someone with an interest in UFOs who had read some of my books. We spoke for a few minutes about allegations of UFO crashes in Britain, and then went our separate ways. Shortly afterward, the Colonel contacted me and apologized for having initially misled me about his true intentions for getting to know me. He had something he wanted to tell me.

Having spent fifteen years operating deep within the heart of American intelligence, the Colonel claims that in 1969, while working with the Defense Intelligence Agency, he read a top-secret document that, as far as he is concerned, laid to rest the tales about flying saucers and alien bodies recovered from the desert of New Mexico in the summer of 1947 and told the true story about the Roswell events.

The Colonel states unequivocally that there has *never* been the crash and recovery of an alien spacecraft. Like Al Barker, Bill Salter, and the Black Widow, however, the Colonel maintains that the Roswell and other 1947 events were given a "crashed UFO cover" to hide research that was linked with classified high-altitude balloon experiments and the Nuclear Energy for Propulsion of Aircraft project.

"Back in 1969," he began, "I was shown—let me say that to you—a large file on several experimental aircraft that were flown at White Sands in [the] summer [of] 1947. I *will* tell you that my exposure to the file came about from certain things I was involved in from 1959 to 1968. In that time I was with several operations, although not many—maybe four or five—where [the DIA] sent false UFO stories to the Russians, to the Communists: sightings, flying saucer landings at military facilities, stories that we had crashed UFOs and bodies of space aliens. I was fascinated by all of this because I couldn't understand why we were doing it.

"But there was a team of nine or ten psyops people that worked out of the Pentagon at the time and whose whole day's work was to create and push these tales. They have these wonderful scenarios and they are so complex: space aliens coming from Venus that want us to disarm—nuclear; UFOs seen by astronauts; bodies of frozen spacemen under the CIA at Langley; aircraft destroyed by UFOs; briefings on UFOs for [President] Nixon; so many things and all of it absolutely false and just to be fed to Russia and occasionally to UFO writers. They would create these beautifully crafted documents, just like the real thing, ten or twenty pages long. You couldn't tell them from the real thing. There would be bogus CIA, DIA, Air Force documents, whatever was needed.

"Well, over at DIA some of our people were involved in getting these files to certain people in Russia—military, intel guys—a controlled release, if you will. Then we sit back and listen to the chatter in the Kremlin. And our people at DIA would prepare a report on whether the Soviets had bought into the stories. Where those reports went, I don't know. But this fascinated me—not so much because it worked and got the Russians bent out of shape, but why are we doing it? What's the reason? What's the incentive? What's the gain for us?

"In 1969, I'm due to get out: retirement. And I've had an offer from a D.C. outfit working in the private sector and this appeals to me. But before I leave—about six weeks before—I have this meeting with one of our people, an old friend from the Ike years. Let's go to a bar for drinks for a retirement celebration, he says. We're sitting there with boilermakers and martinis and he . . . says, 'You ever wonder why we have all that going on with the Russians and the faked UFO things?' I play it casual and say, 'Sometimes, I guess.' I can see he's trying to gauge my reaction and I stay cool. He then comes out and says, 'You want to know?' I shoot back, ' . . . , what the hell are you doing and why are you asking these questions?' He just kind of smiles and says we'll discuss it at work the next day. So we just get back to our drinks and it's forgotten.

"Next day comes around and he comes up to me and invites me to take a walk down to his office. We get there and there is this large file on his desk just sitting there and full of manila folders inside. He smiles, says to take a seat, and he asks me, 'Do you want the truth about UFOs?' Well, I'm wondering if this is some sort of setup as with the Russians. I'm thinking, Are they thinking I'm part of some Russian setup and with me retiring they want to know am I going to be compromised back in the real world?

"I tell [my source] this and he just laughs that I think he thinks I've been turned. But he's real casual and says it's no big deal. He passes me the box and says, 'Read it; there's no problem.' And that's what I did. It was a bizarre and a surreal situation, but I trusted—and still to this day trust—[him]. We talk about it sometimes today even, and what we know, and after I told him about you speaking with Salter and Barker, [he] says, 'Go ahead. Tell him.'"[1]

According to what the source told the Colonel, the one aspect of the entire UFO controversy that concerned the Pentagon during the early years of its involvement in the subject more than any other was the 1950 publication of the book *Behind the Flying Saucers* by Frank Scully. Although the book was widely panned by critics on publication, it went on to become a huge bestseller and told the story of how the government had retrieved several alien spacecraft, along with their dead extraterrestrial crews, that had crashed to earth in New Mexico and elsewhere in the late 1940s and had initiated a supersecret project to deal with the situation.[2]

In reality, the Colonel's source said there were no such crashes of alien spacecraft in the United States in the late 1940s—or at any other point in time—and as a consequence no alien corpses have ever been recovered, either. However, the Scully book caused consternation within official circles for one specific reason: the stories of crashed and retrieved UFOs as related to Frank Scully by his sources were in fact highly distorted accounts of the recovery of the vehicles and bodies at White Sands, as the Black Widow, Bill Salter, and Al Barker had described to me, and that had to be kept under wraps at all costs. In other words, stressed the Colonel, it was not the UFO controversy per se that alarmed the military and the intelligence community, but a series of classified events that had been perceived—wrongly—to be of relevance to that same controversy.

The Colonel elaborated: "It was known at the time—early fifties—through intelligence channels that the Russians were deeply interested in these crash stories and there was a fear that if they dug into Scully's saucer tales, and similar ones that were in circulation at the time, then they would uncover the real truth about the balloon projects, the biological warfare, and the human experiments. So someone in the Pentagon comes up with a plan. We know from experience with the atomic bomb and the Rosenbergs that if the Russians want to know what was going on, eventually they will find out. That we can't afford back then; so instead of trying to stop the Russians, we give them exactly what they want.

"In April 1951 there is a brainstorming session in D.C. with agency people, psychological warfare people, [and] some of Truman's people. They work on this plan to create faked documents and stories, coach some chosen witnesses with faked saucer tales, and really flood Russian intelligence channels with so much saucer disinformation that the real secret that we want hidden—the White Sands crashes that the Russians and some of the saucer people like Scully mistakenly believe to be UFOs—stays hidden and gets swamped by the lies. Our secret is safe and the Russian teams and the UFO writers like the [Donald] Keyhoes, the [Frank] Scullys, and the [Leonard] Stringfields, that are looking into all this, are spending so much time on the faked material, bogus pilot sightings, bogus radar reports, and our faked rumor mill that the White Sands stories get buried deeper and deeper and deeper and get more and more confused and discredited. And so after [he] tells me this, I read the file."

According to the Colonel, the file he read referred to the crashes, in May and July 1947, of two prototype aircraft that were based upon the highly advanced and novel "flying wing" designs of the German aviation geniuses Reimar and Walter Horten.

"This was kind of a weird-looking aircraft—maybe eighty feet wide with severely arced-back wings, with a cabin where the pilot would be in a prone position to pilot the bird. [It was] based on the Hortens' flying wings and gliders, but powered. And it had a rear compartment that could hold, maybe, four people in rows of two. This is like an elongated half-moon. Or two thirds of a flying saucer with the ass cut out.

"There had been the high-altitude balloon experiments going back to May 1947 or maybe before that I understand you have already been told about and that led to some of these Roswell legends—the bodies in the desert, if you will. Well, those accidents had occurred when the parachutes [on the capsules] didn't open and we have the crashes and the body recoveries at White Sands. But at the same time as that is going on, our guys are working right then with a contingent from the Fugo people—the Japanese balloons—and the [Unit] 731 people.

"[The Japanese] have this plan if the war had continued to make a new Fugo, if you will: a huge balloon setup—huge—that would have had a piloted, powered glider attached to it, below, that would have been kind of like our lifting bodies that came in the fifties. The plan is for these to fly very high over enemy territory, and for enemy territory—I mean the States—and the aircraft would be detached from the balloons by the crew and be used for biological warfare agent dispersal to a specific target as a kamikaze. That way, they don't rely on the old-style Fugos where they launched them and have to just hope they hit a decent target.

"So when we take Japan after the [atomic] bomb, we find huge files on all this: the balloon plans [and] the biological warfare suicide plans with aircraft fixed to these giant balloon setups. We even find some of the scientists and even the damned pilots that were going to be on the first experimental attack. Well, the Fugo people are brought over after the war, our guys take this further, and the Japanese go along with it because, for them, the alternative is [a] life [sentence] or execution for war crimes. They *have* to go along with it, despite Japanese pride about not wanting to work with what they see as their enemy. But they're softened a bit when we do a deal with them and the prosecution and death threats get thrown out.

"We see from their blueprints that this could be the perfect weapon delivery system: fly a balloon setup real, real high over Russia, release the bird, do the drop—whether a bomb or a bioweapon—and have the pilot get his bird back to the nearest friendly land. Remember, even though this is a new and strange idea, it was only one of a whole lot of things under discussion, including ICBMs, new bombers, and such like, if you will. This was just one of many strange projects. Some got canceled—as this one was in late 1947—and some didn't. And believe me, if people who are skeptical of all this tell you that the entire history of White Sands and Holloman has been documented from the 1940s and they can't find anything on these tests and accidents, they're wrong.

"Coincidentally, the design and shape of the vehicle—kind of a broad, flying heel—was one that some of the NEPA people wanted to follow with their nuclear aircraft research; so they want to see this thing fly, see how it moves and how it responds in a flight situation. So, you have some of the cleared NEPA people there, the Paperclip people, some of the Fugo and [Unit] 731 guys we brought over, a bunch of Strughold's high-altitude people, and a few others.

"They begin trials of the aircraft in early February 1947 and make the first few tests at a relatively low level—a couple of thousand feet. Seven or eight of these aircraft had been constructed by that time. In the beginning the first tests with the aircraft were towed—by glider—into the air and the first flight went okay. The flight test was [conducted by] the Army Air Forces using guys who had been with the 82nd Airborne in the war; they were experts towing gliders, and before the balloon tests, they get this towed into the air by a Douglas DC-3 [known as a C-47 during World War II]."[3]

The Colonel also stated that copies of at least *some* of the Japanese blueprints of the "really advanced aircraft and gliders" that played a role in the construction of the aircraft flown at White Sands were found along with the V-2 document cache hidden in the Harz Mountains, Germany, by Wernher von Braun's team and were brought to White Sands for translation into English as far back as October 1946.

The Colonel continued his account: "*Everyone* was pinning his hopes on this. But then they have to do follow-up trials. LeMay and von Kármán had been talking about getting a nuclear aircraft in the air since 1945 and the brass wants quick results. The Paperclip people are involved because some of this is based on the Nazis' [plans] to build something like what you might call a flying saucer or rounded wing and the Air Force wants to know if a saucer style is going to be a feasible design project for them. The NEPA people arrive because they think this is a good design for their nuclear aircraft—if they can ever get it off the ground—and some of their people also need high-altitude data. So *everyone's* there, watching and waiting, if you will.

"Things actually go okay. The 82nd guys do a good job and there's a guy in the aircraft doing what he's told to do: get it airborne, see how it flies, how it responds and handles itself, and get it back on the ground at White Sands in one piece. Everyone's happy. They repeat the tests several times and all is still going good. Then comes the real test. The Air Force and NEPA still need to know what the deal is in the upper atmosphere: are our guys going to be seriously affected by long-term exposure to whatever's up there—altitudes, cosmic radiation—and what about an atomic engine? How will that affect our boys? So then we have the first test—of what I think were only two tests, although there could have been more with NEPA— that you could say led to the Roswell stories, one connected with NEPA and one with biological weapons.

"The first was late May, and between February and May one of these aircraft is fitted with prototype shielding materials that NEPA have just had shipped in from the University of Chicago, and a supply of radioactive materials to try and simulate a nuclear-powered flight and how a crew might be affected or protected. And so we have an aircraft launched again on a tow by the 82nd. This is for the benefit of NEPA. We have this aircraft with a crew this time. They bring in the other people for the test. You know what I mean: the crew, God help the poor sons of bitches. This is because they also plan this crude experiment—*very* crude—for the next flight and that some people that want the NEPA project to succeed are pushing for.

"This time, like I just told you, the aircraft is fitted—internally and throughout—with experimental shielding material that was based on work [undertaken] at the Metallurgy Committee at the University of Chicago in the war, and a quantity of radioactive materials is loaded into the aircraft. The whole point of this is to see how this shielding stands up to the material, if there are any adverse effects, contamination in flight in an aircraft of this design, and to what extent it's going to shield a crew from contamination—using new materials, plastics, metals—and also the pilot, who is very, very securely shielded."

When I asked the Colonel to clarify what he meant by the term "radioactive materials" as it related to the experimental flight, he informed me that it's "a term I use for technological research that is still partly classified today and I'm not sure how speaking on this affects me. Not classified because of the technology, but because of certain nonethical things done with the technology in the 1940s as it relates to the nuclear aircraft programs."

This naturally raised even more questions; and in response to further probing, the Colonel told me that in the early part of 1947, two German scientists, August Reis, a physician, and Fritz Morhard, a mechanical and electrical engineer, undertook unique research designed to convert heat energy from an atomic pile into electrical energy. The research, added the Colonel, was of great interest to the "nuclear aircraft people and the White Sands guys" and "a device built by us out of the research of these guys" was loaded aboard the aircraft because "an application for using this technology in a nuclear aircraft situation had been realized even if it wasn't perfected yet."

The Colonel became distinctly uneasy when I asked for further clarification. He repeated that he had no wish to elaborate on certain data pertaining to this aspect of the story beyond stating that "We knew there was potentially shielding problems [*sic*] with this device; so you have the crew put on board to see how hot—radioactive—this all gets and how they are affected and how the aircraft is contaminated or not."

Despite the enigmatic and carefully worded nature of this aspect of the Colonel's account, data has since surfaced that appears to provide corroboration for his remarks. Based on the names the Colonel provided, I undertook research at the National Archives, Maryland, that led to the discovery of some now declassified but formerly top-secret documents generated in the summer of 1947 by Headquarters, Army Air Forces, Washington, D.C. The documents make direct reference to the work of Reis and Morhard (and a colleague, Max Ostenrieder, a biochemist) and specifically refers to "a revolutionary method" of "converting heat energy from atmospheric and other sources such as atomic pile directly into electrical energy at high power levels" developed by the trio and that was of interest to the Air Materiel Command at Wright Field, Ohio. The documents even reveal that Morhard, Ostenrieder, and Reis had been hired to work for the military under the jurisdiction of the controversial Paperclip program.

The Colonel continued his account: "Although this is to try and better understand the situation for NEPA and radiation exposure in a nuclear airplane situation, some of the people aren't happy about this—using a guinea pig crew of people with severe disabilities, you know? But four souls are loaded into the airplane—just strap them into the seats. This is planned to go real high. Okay, it's a very crude experiment. But back then, what are they going to do? There is *no* nuclear engine back then—none at all. But there *is* a need for a simulation of a nuclear flight with prototype shielding materials that isn't just done in a lab scenario and they sure as shit aren't going to contaminate our boys, so the need is for the other people to understand human contamination and how the aircraft is going to be contaminated or how the shielding resists the radiation experiment. They worked with what they got back then and what they considered would give them good results in high-altitude and nuclear research, and if it also benefits NEPA, then let's go for it. The Russians are going to be the next big problem, if you will, and everyone's getting pressured for results for something really new and so that's what they are going do. But it doesn't happen. There's a problem.

"I don't think the full details of the accident were ever really understood, but there's a twenty-minute flight and the aircraft comes in to land at White Sands. There's a problem and on its approach it hits hard, flips over, and in a couple of seconds it's all over. Now, the pilot has major protection but the thing hits the ground hard, skids, flips over, splits, and so you have this aircraft and these bodies lying there on the range. This is major—believe it.

"The Armed Forces Special Weapons [Project] people are there; they handle the recovery and they contain the site. The pilot's just about okay and two of the other people are alive, just screaming and screaming, crawling around in a daze in the damned desert heat.

Screaming and hollering, wailing like crazy people while the other two are dead. No one wants to go near them—the radiation, the screams, the way they look with their deformities, this weird aircraft. The Special Weapons people are afraid, ball-shrinking afraid. They actually haven't been told what it is they're recovering or what the crew is, apart from that it's a classified project, and they haven't seen anything like this. Ever. Hell, no one has.

"Well, the area is cordoned and it takes a couple of days to get everything cleaned up, and the dead bodies and the survivors are taken away, to a D.C. hospital, I believe was the place, somewhere. Then comes the analysis. Now, the report I read referred to a technical appendix that went into greater detail about the analysis of the crash, why it happened, what went wrong and such. That I never saw. And I will admit there are parts I don't recall after thirty years.

"But I can tell you for certain these facts: that a highly classified experiment involving a simulated nuclear-powered aircraft flight happened on White Sands in May of 1947. It involved a powered lifting body, a glider aircraft, that was based on the work of the Horten people and the Japanese Fugo people's plans for their aircraft balloon setup, and had on board handicapped people that were taken from American hospitals that had been taken from the Unit 731 labs. Experimental radiation shielding and an amount of radioactive material was used that was meant to simulate as close as possible the output that might be expected from a nuclear power source when we have one. It malfunctioned. It crashed. Those *are* the facts.

"Well, that story is incorporated into the Roswell story today, and if you know where to look you will find aspects of that in the bigger Roswell picture. And I can tell you that some of the body descriptions that people have made in connection with Roswell are really of the bodies from the White Sands crash and not the one that came shortly after at the ranch with Brazel. This is not because the witnesses are lying but because they believe that [the event] they were involved in *was* the Roswell story; but really it was just a part of it, and of course with memories it's so long ago. But that incident was [in] May [1947]. This whole mess in the desert from May to August 1947 with the lifting bodies and the high-altitude balloon pro-grams—all of this has all been rolled into one unholy mess that the UFO people call the Roswell Incident. And the reason why there was so much going on in one place with these tests was Nuremberg. They all know that Nuremberg would be the clampdown that will eventually end all this and so the brass is screaming in early 1947 to get as much work done in the desert and away from spying eyes as possible before the shutdown comes. But the bigger incident—the one that *really* can be called the Roswell Incident—is the July thing, if you will."

In addition to the work designed to understand the problems as-sociated with nuclear-powered aircraft that led to the White Sands crash of May 1947, the Colonel states, during the same time frame, elements of the military were keen to understand and expand even further upon the plans that the Japanese had to build a revolution-ary Fugo balloon that was to be coupled with an experimental air-craft for the dispersal of biological warfare agents over a hostile country.

"When the Fugo and the Unit 731 files are examined after the transfer of all of this material and some of their people to here, our guys that are looking into the biological warfare angles are shocked—*very* shocked—to see the extent that the Japanese have things planned: highly advanced, very strong, and very large balloon systems with very maneuverable and combat-ready, sleek aircraft—one like a dart, one more like a half-moon—fixed below that would be lifted extremely high, that would be taken across the Pacific, and that when it was released over here would cut through the sky to a target kamikaze-style and release biological agents, toxins, what-ever. This is all highly advanced and far more advanced than the original [Fugo] balloons. There's no doubt that if it hadn't been for Hiroshima, these aircraft would have been used in some ways against us.

"There were pictures and drawings in the file of prototype models—small-scale models—that had been built by the Japanese. And in May 1945 there had apparently been a test flight of one of these aircraft, but without the balloons. This is pretty similar to the Horten vehicles, pretty sleek and kind of like a combination of a stealth fighter and a flying wing. But they are *this close* to building a full-scale, armed version that would travel by balloon over the Pacific with a crew in the aircraft below the balloon. This is to be a totally remodeled and reworked aircraft and will have a pressurized cabin area and food, all the provisions needed for a high-altitude flight to the States.

"Well, it's made very clear to [the Japanese], as I told you, that working for us is the proverbial offer they can't refuse—the only option, if you will. There *is* no alternative. So, under very strict security, in late 1946, a team—the Japanese scientific team—is brought to an area of White Sands where the documents are translated, where we get to see their mock-ups and files [and] pictures, and a plan is set to duplicate what the Japanese had planned. Plus, we have the real coup: the crew of the prototype that flew in Japan.

"You must remember that this is all happening at the same time as Nuremberg is going down and we are pushing to get all this moving before Nuremberg comes down hard on everything and closes it down. But Paperclip—with the Nazis—is moving ahead and so working with Japanese war crime people is seen as okay too by some.

"But when their order is given to destroy everything when the war is all but over—the Fugo notes and files, the Unit 731 files—some of the Japanese refuse. It's seen as failure by them that they're being ordered to destroy their hard work and just accept defeat to us. They're fierce, proud little bastards, you know?

"So, the team goes to ground: the scientific team, the crew that would have piloted the first aircraft, and some of the people from 731. They are on the mainland in Japan and we have people in 731 that we threaten with execution—or we offer them freedom from prosecution if they help—unless we get to see everything they have and where it is. We *know* there is more—more files and Lord knows what else. So some of the 731 guys give their buddies up and some of them don't. But we find them—in a deep underground setup with a railway system used by the Japanese Army for weapons storage and transport. There are files and files, boxes and boxes of documents, guys from the Fugo project, and even the crew for the first prototype flight. We get all this back to [the United States]. We do deals—I guess not too different from Paperclip—and they get a guarantee to continue their work and, if they do, there's no trial for war crimes.

"So this is the picture: we have a device based on the Horten work that is *extremely* similar to the Japanese aircraft. In fact, some of the White Sands people thought that it was so close that there had been some German collusion on all this with the Japs, but that was never proven, even though there *were* Japanese documents found in the von Braun files in the [Harz] mountains. But this device, and our devices based on this and the Horten boys' work, is good to go for the job; and so deep on the [White Sands] Proving Ground and away from anyone who isn't cleared, there is the test with the balloons.

"Everyone's anxious because much of this is being done by the Japanese, and we are kind of letting them do their thing, and people are freaked by the fact that we have Japanese people here that are absolutely not our friends—not at all. The Japs are angry that we have them, angry that Japan is defeated, angry that they are working for us, and pissed that they have no choice. So no one is happy and everyone is tense about security. And the crew, by the account I read, were fierce little fuckers. In their minds, they had their mission to launch a very destructive kamikaze attack on us by high-altitude balloon—which probably would have worked so well—and we screw it up for them. Then on top of that they have to come work for us. Right or wrong, I guess you *can* see their point.

"And space and weight are key issues when you're trying to fly a high-altitude, fully pressurized aircraft across the Pacific below a huge balloon, at forty or fifty thousand feet, with food and water, and you need to keep weight low and optimize everything. So the crew was chosen because they were small guys—five foot max. Just like the Roswell legend says: smaller bodies, Asian faces, and quite human-looking, because that's exactly what they were. Well, the test is ready—this is just intended as an up and down . . . not a full-scale test yet—and there is the balloon array and the lifting body, and this is planned to be a relatively low-level situation: just get the balloon and the aircraft in the air, have the pilot release the vehicle, get it on the ground, and then we can recover the balloon later as we track where it goes and do more detailed flights. . . ."

The problem, the Colonel elaborated, was that not long after the balloon array and the aircraft became airborne, the pilot radioed hearing a loud noise from the rear of the aircraft. Later analyses would determine that the huge array had been struck by lightning. Notably, according to *New York Times* weather maps for July 1947, there were numerous thunderstorms recorded in the state of New Mexico on July 2, 6, 7, and 8.

The result was apparent chaos on board the aircraft, and the careful attention paid to ensuring that the balloon and the lifting body were separated at a very low level was placed in dire peril. Indeed, stated the Colonel, at a height estimated to be 12,000 feet, there was a lurch, and the aircraft became partly detached from the huge balloon array; and to the horror of those monitoring the situation on the ground and based on an analysis of air-to-ground radio communication with the pilot, it began to spin wildly out of control beneath the balloons, with its nose pointing toward the ground.

"By now, the whole thing is way outside of the Range and everything's gone bad; this is where the Roswell thing comes into it. The brass is freaking. No one knows the exact location at this time, though—where it's going to come down. But the problem is that this was only meant to be an on-range thing, or at least relatively close by. By the time everyone comes to the realization that this thing has failed—and failed big-time—it's miles away and on its way to Lord knows where.

"The lifting vehicle and part of the balloon array comes away and the weight of the vehicle brings it down maybe twenty miles from the ranch. The Roswell ranch, I mean. There is just enough of the balloon array to slow the descent, but the bird had still hit the ground hard. Everyone's killed: the pilot and the rest of the crew.

"Well, I say that everyone's killed, but there were references in the file to survivors, or [people] who were critically injured and died later. The weird thing is that no one—by 1969 when I read the file—seemed to know if the story about the survivors [was] true or a rumor or maybe something to confuse the story, and it's left open, I guess because this is a file that was a look-back based on personal memory with most of the original files having been destroyed way back when to hide all this.

"And something else. There is a reference in the file that was never really confirmed from an interview with a White Sands guy about a similar accident on the Range in May 1947 in which another of these aircraft flown by balloon crash-lands but with a surviving crew. That I can't confirm to you happened, though. But with Roswell, you have the remains of this weird aircraft laying [sic] in the desert, and these small Japanese bodies in flight suits, some inside and a couple thrown out, and a small bunch of balloon debris. Now, there's no potential radiation contamination as with the May [1947] crash, but this is still potentially a major incident, if you will.

"The brass freak. Now what? They have this team ready for recovery in the event of an accident—again, from the Armed Forces Special Weapons Project. But they're at White Sands as before, which is where this was supposed to come down—just up and down and nice and simple. So they have to then send a team into the air to locate the crash site. And then they have to get the recovery team out there and move in to secure everything—contain the aircraft and the balloons, remove the bodies, clean the site up like it never happened. Now, although the crash site was located, this was the following morning, and the cleanup and containment of everything took about three days.

"You have got to realize this is early days—nearly sixty years ago—and a lot of this was people not really knowing what the hell they were doing and just coming up with dipshit ideas and hoping for the best. But then they hit another problem—and it's a *real* problem. There's a section of material missing from the whole upper side of the aircraft that looks to be about nine feet long, and it's clear as soon as they get to the site that most of the balloon system and all the associated technical materials from the balloons is missing.

"Seems that as the aircraft detached after the lightning strike, there was a problem, and a part of its outer coat is literally ripped away and remained fixed to the remaining balloons, probably where the lightning hits. Worse still, they're missing one body of the crew that looks to have been sucked out the vehicle when the upper section came away, or perhaps more likely when it's spinning vertically and hanging from the balloons and after the [upper] section is gone.

"Now, the recovery of the aircraft, the crew, the pilot, and that part of the balloon array was done secretly and successfully. Not a damned soul outside of the military saw anything. If they tell you they did, they're damned liars. But the missing material cannot be found. Neither can the body. But remember, we are only talking about a nine-foot-long piece—shattered—of the lifting body, one five-foot-long human body, and the rest of the very large balloon array that was the Brazel debris field. They searched the first night, sent aircraft up again, but it's missed. At least, until the rancher guy finds it. Make no mistake, he saw it all—the remains of the rest of the balloons, the lightweight covering materials from the aircraft's frame that was missing, and the last body, which he finds about a half mile from the debris field. They tried, but you know you can't hide something like this. It's going to come out.

"The rancher takes the debris to town, everyone agrees on that, wondering what is it? Then you know the rest. The Roswell base gets to hear it and [Jesse] Marcel comes out with [Sheridan] Cavitt. Right now those two don't know the truth of it all because White Sands doesn't even know that Brazel has found the debris and taken it to town. So Marcel and Cavitt take the materials back to base and there's the big thing about is it a flying saucer or is it a weather balloon? Now, whether or not that was a genuine screwup or whether this was a real attempt to hide the truth, I don't know. That was never a part of the file. But either way it worked. It hid the real picture.

"Cavitt's dead now and not here to answer for himself, but after the press hear of it and then the White Sands people realize that the flying disk wreckage is really a part of their experiment, Cavitt receives orders from Washington to get back out to the site; there's more to this and he is officially briefed on it. They only tell him a part of the story, though. They *do* tell him that this is a classified White Sands balloon experiment and it came down and we need to secure the debris that's left. But they leave out the part about the bodies and the lifting body—of course—and maybe hope that animals got to the missing body before anyone sees it. After all, they still have the rest of the bodies to work with and do crash analysis. No need to tell [Cavitt] and complicate things even more.

"Cavitt's people are to lend any and all assistance to a team from the Armed Forces Special Weapons Project that is going to clean up the remainder of the ranch site, and Cavitt is to be the coordinating point for intelligence between Special Weapons and Roswell. This is because they decide now to route the rest of the material through Roswell—where the stuff Brazel brought in can be got hold of and so have it all together in one place and not floating around everywhere—and then send everything on to Wright Field, where the Foreign Technology guys were at and who were the right people to look at the crash and examine what went wrong.

"So, Cavitt speaks with the rancher who is in town being briefed by the military on what to say to the press guys, and the rancher's real quiet and disturbed. Cavitt tries to be the good cop and asks what's up, and Brazel blurts out he saw something else that he hasn't told: a body. A little guy in a flight suit, smashed to a complete pulp, but still recognizable as a smaller-than-normal human shape. He won't go near it.

"Cavitt wonders what has he got himself into and is on the phone to his contacts at White Sands: 'The rancher says he found a body.' And you know that the White Sands people are just groaning and thinking, Now a fucking civilian is in on the story. Cavitt says, 'Brazel says he found a body; a little guy all busted up at the scene.' 'Where is the body now?' asks White Sands, knowing that Brazel has found the last bit of evidence. Brazel has left the body out in the sun; he's scared shitless by it, not knowing what the hell it is: Japanese-looking, small, smashed, decomposing. And by the time the Special Weapons people are out there, the poor little fucker has decomposed real, real bad; so he looks real strange to Brazel after a couple days in the sun.

"And so, as you know, this issue of the bodies being scattered everywhere after an incident like this was something that kicked them in the ass to speed up research into ejection capsules from high-altitude craft to keep all the crew contained in one place, pretty much, in the event of an accident, and avoid shit like this. I heard that at least one or two UFO crashes in the 1940s were probably based on people really seeing some of these ejection capsule experiments with handicapped people used. Several of these failed badly and killed the crews near White Sands—by 'crews' you know what I mean again, and where you have a small emergency vehicle eject from the main vehicle and drop by parachute."

Interestingly, the Colonel believes, "based on a few things I heard and still hear," that the bodies examined by Dr. La June Foster in broadly the same time frame were not from the Roswell event directly, but were in reality the victims of one of these failed ejection capsule experiments, which was itself part of a larger project to better understand how the human body reacts to rapid decompression at high altitude. To illustrate this, the Colonel provided me with a series of documents that originated with the surgeon general, USAF, covering the period 1947 to 1952 and all titled "Physiological Aspects of Hypoxia in Rapid Decompression to High Altitudes."

As the documents make abundantly clear, the physical effects of exposure to high altitudes, rapid decompression, and plans for new and novel escape systems from aircraft were all considered of paramount concern and interest to the military in the late 1940s.

The Colonel then continued his account: "But most of the Special Weapons people who were at the two recovery sites—the ranch site and the first one—were not briefed on what the hell they were guarding. Need to know. And at White Sands they see these deformed, dead bodies, some with big, bald heads, some small and severely handicapped, smashed outside of this weird aircraft that they aren't allowed to approach because of the security surrounding the whole project. Then at the Roswell site you have a similar aircraft but with the Fugo guys on board, and these two stories are going to fuse—at least to an extent with the same people involved in certain aspects of the story. And what are they going to think when they see the really strange bodies? You *know* what they are going to think—the fucking Martians are coming. Washington brought photographic people in to both sites—told them not a damned thing: 'Just take the pictures, get the film processed, and give it to us.'

"You think you can stop these people talking? Hell, no! So you have people at White Sands without the clearance hearing rumors about these weird bodies found on the Range and the high-altitude balloon tests. You got others talking about this weird-looking aircraft loaded aboard a flatbed by Special Weapons; and then the Roswell thing with real 'little men' found, and then the press release about first it's a flying saucer, then it's a balloon. It's all going to fuse into one, you know?

"So, the remaining body goes to Roswell for a classified flight to Wright Field, with this body in cold storage, or what's left of him, for autopsy and crash analysis. Imaginations are going to go everywhere and people are going to link all these things into one holy mess. And the people at Roswell are flipping out because they really aren't involved in *any* of this directly but are getting all the flak and becoming the fall guys to hide what's really up to the White Sands people.

"Then the Washington brass flip: 'What are those SOBs at Roswell doing saying they found a saucer?' Roswell get[s] chewed out because even though it was no saucer they found, there was no authorization to tell the press they found *anything;* and the fear for Washington was that the press would go for the saucer story big-time and really dig deep and eventually find the truth about the nuclear test at White Sands and this Fugo thing. So you have to keep it mundane, and so the Roswell people like Marcel become the fall guys to calm it down. Like: 'Yeah, sorry. All of these things you might hear: just a weather balloon. Our guys fucked up and can't tell a balloon from whatever. No flying saucers, no green men, just a weather balloon. Just our guys getting it wrong.'"

As the Colonel admits, more than a quarter of a century has passed since he read the documentation in question; and there are—he also concedes—some parts of the report that he no longer recalls. He is adamant, however, that the story he told me is essentially correct and explains what really occurred all those years ago in New Mexico.[4]

ELEVEN

CORROBORATiON

It is important to note that despite the controversial nature of the Colonel's account, corroboration for it can be found in both documents and accounts by others. While it has long been acknowledged that rancher Mack Brazel was responsible for bringing the recovered debris from the Foster Ranch to the attention of the sheriff's office and personnel at Roswell Army Air Field, much less is known about Brazel's alleged personal knowledge of the solitary body that the Colonel asserts was also found on the ranch. Of course, if the Colonel's testimony stood alone, then one could rightly question its veracity. However, it does *not* stand alone.

For example, the research team of Tom Carey and Donald Schmitt found a witness with important data pertinent to this aspect of the story. Before he died, Meyers Wahnee, who was a pilot and aircrew commander of the 714th Bomb Squadron, 448th Bomb Group, told his family of the 1947 Roswell events during the last year of his life.

"Of special interest to us," wrote Carey and Schmitt, "is his testimony to his wife and two children about 'decomposing body parts' found among the debris at the Foster ranch. 'It really happened,' he told them." [1]

Similarly, and again according to Carey and Schmitt, in 1994 Dee Proctor inexplicably drove his ill mother, Loretta Proctor, to a remote location on the former Foster Ranch, where he told her that Mack Brazel had found "something else." Carey and Schmitt stated: "This site is located about 2.5 miles east-southeast of the debris field. Loretta Proctor eventually recovered, but what was it that would cause a son to risk the health of his mother to embark on such a dangerous and uncomfortable trek? The question now seems to us to have been answered. Loretta will not volunteer anything beyond the 'something else' statement for now, and Dee, who is now 59, will not talk to anyone." [2]

Important data that may corroborate other aspects of the Colonel's account comes from Timothy Cooper, a California-based writer and private investigator. In a telephone conversation with Colonel Paul Helmick, former commanding officer with the Alamogordo Army Air Force, Cooper was told "the Air Materiel Command was preparing for a series of high altitude experiments that were to augment a program at the White Sands Proving Ground, in late June of 1947." Cooper stated that "[Helmick] did not say what was going to happen, only that the Atomic Energy Commission, the Armed Forces Special Weapons Project and the Department of Ordnance had secured portions of the Tularosa Range and the White Sands Proving Ground for a highly classified project." [3]

Cooper also questioned Helmick specifically on the issue of experimentation involving nuclear-powered aircraft: "Do you remember when the Army was testing an experimental aircraft at the White Sands Proving Ground and it crashed? The Armed Forces Special Weapons team from Sandia Base went to recover it."

Helmick replied: "That was tested at Trinity some thirty miles northwest of Alamogordo. They test flew an atomic-powered craft near Trinity in July [1947 and] that is when they found *something else* in the desert." [4]

Despite the enigmatic nature of this final comment from Helmick, the Colonel considers the statement—which was made when Helmick was in his early nineties—to be a reference to the recovery of the White Sands aircraft in May 1947, which *was* of critical interest to the NEPA team because of the simulated nuclear experimentation; although the vehicle was *not*, itself, nuclear powered. The Colonel also considers the reference to the recovery of "something else" to be related to the July 1947 recovery of balloon materials, aircraft debris, and the single body found on the Foster Ranch by Brazel.[5]

Timothy Cooper also spoke with one Albert Collins, who, in the early to mid-1940s worked for Berkeley and at Occidental College on the Manhattan Project, the one project more than any other that proved instrumental in determining the outcome of World War II, when atomic bombs destroyed the Japanese cities of Hiroshima and Nagasaki. Notably, Collins's testimony provides valuable corroboration to the whistle-blower data imparted thus far.

Albert Bruce Collins was born in New York on May 12, 1912, and died on December 31, 1990, from coronary disease. He had graduated from Occidental College in 1942 and worked initially at Berkeley, California, and later at the University of Chicago. In late 1943, Collins was assigned to Los Alamos, where he and other enlisted technicians with college education in certain sciences and technologies were assigned to a project headed by a civilian scientist in charge of machining "special metal" components for a "device" that was being constructed for the Army.

According to his obituary, published in the January 10, 1991, edition of the *Big Bear Grizzly*, Collins was known as Big Bear Valley, California's "watchdog." Detective Tom Bradford of the San Bernardino County Sheriff's Department remembered Collins as a man who "stood his own" in legal matters (often representing himself in court) and was instrumental in officiating several arrests.[6]

Crucially, according to Collins, during the war " . . . New Mexico was abuzz with unusual research into nuclear powered aircraft and bizarre biological experiments. Some people were losing their clearances for no apparent reasons. All I know is the scary feelings everybody had who was asked to do experiments on stuff that nobody ever saw before and how we were later threatened if we talked about anything we saw, felt or heard."

Of paramount relevance is the fact that one of the rumors that Collins was acutely aware of centered on "autopsies of midget people with mongoloid heads that were accidentally exposed to high doses of radiation at Los Alamos."[7] But where were these strange-looking people and bodies coming from? A clue came from a nurse who had served in the Medical Laboratory at Los Alamos during the war and whose story eerily paralleled that of the Black Widow. Cooper recalled:

"She casually mentioned to me over coffee that 'bodies' were being flown to Los Alamos periodically from late 1945 to sometime in 1947. I asked her if she had seen these 'bodies' and she said no, but others had. I asked her where these 'bodies' were coming from. She said she did not know, but it was rumored that they were human experiments for biological and nuclear medicine research. She thought they may have come from Japan after the war. She said they were small bodies with deformed heads and limbs. The eyes were abnormally big, she was told. She said they were being flown in on special transport planes equipped with refrigerator units to keep the bodies from decomposing."[8]

One of those who suspected almost a decade ago that the answer might lie in that direction was Vicki Ecker, the editor of the newsstand publication *UFO Magazine*:

A favorite knee-jerk comment aimed at anyone even lightly prone to conspiratorial thinking is this reliable old saw: "But everyone knows the government can't keep secrets!" Well, the recent horrifying disclosures about America's nuclear tests during the Cold War roundly put the lie to that. Hundreds—perhaps thousands—of innocent people were victimized by scientists and military who hid the truth about the effects of nuclear substances on the human body. Shades of those hideous Nazi experiments! And more such secret tests are undoubtedly tucked away. What if the Roswell crash was a failed nuclear experiment—either ours or somebody else's? The site was not found to be radioactive, the answer comes back. Well then, perhaps it wasn't nuclear, but if it was, that aspect has been kept secret. Maybe it was still a test of some kind, using shaved monkeys—or even worse, captured Japanese prisoners, for instance—as experimental passengers on an ill-fated flight. Ergo, "alien bodies."

It's even possible that some secret technological advances had brought into existence a remarkably thin but unbendable, unbreakable metal substance à la . . . Roswell debris. The concept of casting molten steel into very thin sheets, after all, dates back to the mid-nineteenth century.

"Now I ask," one conspiratorial thinker rightly asks, "Which scenario is more plausible? A visitor from outer space? Or experiments conducted by our government?"[9]

Writer Jacques Vallee makes a noteworthy and relevant comment in this regard also: "The material recovered in the [Roswell] crash itself, while it remains fascinating, was not necessarily beyond human technology in the late Forties. Aluminized Saran, also known as Silvered Saran, came from technology already available for laboratory work in 1948. It was paper-thin, was not dented by a hammer blow, and was restored to a smooth finish after crushing."

Vallee continues:

"Roswell was the site for the very first air base equipped with atomic bombs. If a special type of balloon or drone, designed to monitor atmospheric radioactivity in the area, had been flown over New Mexico, such a device might well have been brought down during a thunderstorm. Given the extremely high sensitivity of anything related to the bomb or radioactivity at the time, it would have been a high priority, top secret task to recover any lost device of that type and to explain it away at all costs: as a weather balloon, as a radar test instrument, as a probe, or even as a crashed flying saucer." [10]

In a fashion very similar to that of the Black Widow and Jacques Vallee, Martin Cannon, an investigative writer, has made a number of relevant statements about the Roswell controversy. Indeed, Cannon's theory that the events in the New Mexico desert were linked with high-altitude experimentation that was also allied with test flights of prototype devices designed to deliver atomic and biological payloads is highly reminiscent of the assertions of the Colonel and the Black Widow.

"The Navy possessed jet-type drone airplanes which took air samples during the 1946 Hydrogen bomb tests on Bikini atoll," stated Cannon. "Some of these drones even carried passengers—test animals, flown through the clouds rising after an atomic explosion. . . . A government report dated July 3, 1948, lists a number of options and rejects most of them. But the final delivery option—'Use of Drone Planes'—elicits the following commentary: 'As a result of discussions with representatives of the Air Corps, it is believed that the use of drone planes to transport the radioactive materials, and dispersed by one or more of the methods described above, may prove to be the most practical. The main advantage lies in the fact that the shielding problems are greatly simplified.' This same report, under the heading 'Method of Delivery,' notes that, 'It is now believed that high altitude missions are the type that merit the most attention.'" [11]

One person who was—initially, at least—very vocal on the issue of whether or not some form of secret terrestrial device came to grief at Roswell was a former employee of the CIA, the Marine Corps, the Air Force, and who later became the Special Assistant for Defense, Space and Science and Technology to Congressman Ken Kramer—Karl Pflock.

Commenting in 1994 on the allegations that alien bodies were recovered in the New Mexico area as part of the so-called Roswell Incident, Pflock was willing, at the time, to conclude that there were indeed "human-like but strangely disfigured bodies" recovered in the New Mexico desert in 1947 and that those same bodies were "associated with some very unusual wreckage." However, Pflock, too, was careful to point out that "Even if there were bodies—and I believe there were—they may not have been of unearthly origin. In which case, Roswell turns out to be a significant chapter in early Cold War history, akin to the currently unfolding disclosures about the U.S. government radiation experiments spawned in the same era."

Pflock later changed his opinion and became a champion of the theory that what was recovered at Roswell was nothing more extraordinary than a Project Mogul balloon; yet it is interesting that his initial thoughts veered toward the possibility of an event connected to "US government radiation experiments."[12]

Equally as important as the corroborative testimony and opinions cited above is the body of documentation that has surfaced that supports the accounts of the Colonel and the other whistle-blowers. For example, with respect to the Colonel's statement that paperwork concerning the early years of research at White Sands was, and still is, absent from the official record, consider the following document that originated with Holloman titled "RANGE SAFETY 1947–1959," and that makes a number of intriguing and relevant statements:

The handling of range safety problems at the Air Force Missile Development Center, Holloman Air Force Base, New Mexico, has passed through three distinct phases. From the establishment of the Air Force's guided missile program at Holloman until the integration of the Holloman and White Sands Proving Ground test range in September 1952, Holloman was responsible for safety aspects of all its tests, including rocket-sonde and balloon flights and research and development drone tests as well as missile tests in the narrow sense. Naturally there were many occasions for close coordination between the Air Forces at Holloman and the Army at White Sands on range safety criteria and procedures, for instance when the flight pattern of a missile took it over both of the adjoining test ranges.

Notably, and crucially, the document also states: "Little information is available on specific events with regard to range safety during this period."[13] Needless to say, if, as this document demonstrates, Holloman's own historians had "little" access to the history of the early years of research at Holloman and its links with activities undertaken at White Sands, then the idea that such a monumental story as this could remain successfully buried for decades seems not so unusual after all.

In addition, a number of documents have surfaced from the files of one Otis Benson that appear to have a bearing on the Colonel's account. Born in Minnesota in 1902, Benson was appointed commander of the Aeromedical Research Unit, Wright Field, Ohio, in September 1940; and in 1949 he was named commandant of the School of Aviation Medicine and initiated a broad aeromedical research program, including studies in acclimatization to altitude, explosive decompression, air evacuation, human factors in aircraft accidents, and high-altitude escape.[14]

Benson's name turns up in a series of documents that appear highly relevant to the issue of experimental lifting body and balloon experimentation occurring in the key period of early to mid-1947. The documents focus on several key issues: a) "special flying operations"; b) "experiments on mutations in extreme altitudes"; and c) "capsule ejection at very high speeds." A May 20, 1947, document titled "Special Procedures," from the deputy chief of the Air Staff to Colonel Benson states: "The Army Air Force's Tactical and Technical Liaison Committee, in conjuction with the Atomic Energy Commission, has initiated action to determine the requirements for procedures to ensure the relative safety of those concerned with special flying operations.

"The Army Air Forces Tactical and Technical Committee has requested the service of a 'Research Flight Surgeon' representing Headquarters, Army Air Forces, for ninety (90) days TDY at Kirtland Field incident to the work of this Project. It is suggested that the officer selected have some background of Radio-Biology." [15]

Another document, dated July 1, 1947, about budgetary requirements to continue research into two unspecified projects and written by Benson, states:

Distinct progress has been made in aero medical research during the past (1947) fiscal year. In these passing twelve months, much has been learned about the ability of the human body to withstand fairly high "G" forces of short duration, such as would occur in ejection vertically from a disabled aircraft or downward ejection in which negative "G" forces are applied. There have been two highly successful human ejections during flight at about 260 miles per hour and these experiments will be greatly extended in the next three months at higher speed utilizing a greater variety of aircraft. Progress has been much slower and less distinct in human studies directed toward "capsule" ejection at very high speeds. Undoubtedly, much of the data being obtained in other ejection experiments will apply.

A partial pressure suit has been developed that will permit life in a vacuum and laboratory personnel have made simulated ascents to 106,000 feet utilizing it. The pilots of the S-aircraft have been fitted with models of the suit to permit full altitude exploitation of the experimental aircraft. Progress has been made on all medical aspects of prone position for pilots. Explosive decompression has been further studied and men subjected to this phenomenon from 40,000 to 65,000 feet. The development of oxygen generating plants has progressed and there have been forward strides in perfecting all of the components of aircraft and personnel oxygen equipment. New aircraft liquid oxygen systems have been flight tested to 45,000 feet with satisfactory results. Work is continuing on studies of cockpit cooling and the cooling of pilots employing airflow suits. Human limits of tolerance for hot cockpits have been defined after adequate studies. Much has been learned on air safety monitoring following atomic bomb explosion and new fields of endeavor defined as a resultant. Finally, many studies of the psychological aspects of aircraft accidents have been made to define accident proneness and some interesting data brought to light.[16]

Though this document is intriguing, a true smoking gun is a September 22, 1947, document titled "Analysis of Factors Contributing to 'Pilot Error' Experiences in Operating Experimental Aircraft Controls," which was prepared for the Office of the Air Surgeon:

Enclosed for your information is a copy of Research Memoranda TSRAA-694-12 from Psychology Branch, Aero Medical Laboratory, subject as above. Incidents of errors in Experimental Aircraft controls were obtained through accident reconstruction and written 621 Project reports.

The recent air accidents at White Sands Proving Ground, as outlined by 28 May Collection Branch, Air Intelligence Requirements Division Report dealing with mutant experiments of extreme altitude flight, capsule ejection, and decompression effects, could be classified under six major categories as follows: (1) substitution errors, (2) forgetting, (3) adjustment errors, (4) reversal errors, (5) unintentional activities, and (6) unable to reach controls.

The reference to "recent air accidents at White Sands Proving Ground" suggests that the Black Widow, Al Barker, Bill Salter, and the Colonel have indeed imparted accurate data. The document continues:

In regards to radio-biological hazards, the Army Air Forces Tactical and Technical Liaison Committee, in conjunction with the Atomic Energy Commission, has initiated action to determine the requirements for procedures to assure the relative safety of those concerned with "special" flight operations. The Army Air Forces Tactical and Technical Liaison Committee requested a "Research Flight Surgeon" representing Headquarters, Army Air Forces to conduct radio-biological hazard studies incident to the work of this project. These studies were performed at Kirtland Field and all data was classified "Restricted Data" under the provisions of AAF Letters 46-22 and 46-22A.

The document then elaborates on the two crashes of experimental vehicles that occured at White Sands and in the near vicinity:

As to the actual causes of the two incidents on 25 March and 4 July 1947, of the loaned S-Aircraft (PF), analysis of the engine design and thrust stress factors, P9 personnel and Atomic Energy Commission consultants in conjunction with advisory people from Army Air Forces Scientific Advisory Group, and Armed Forces Special Weapons Project, could not fully agree as to the exact cause of engine failure in both cases. One plausible problem has been examined which might help in correcting "Pilot Error" operation. Interaction of symbolic instrumentation with tactile manipulation of flight controls and pilot shielding in high performance operation, has been a continuing factor of study by Research and Development.

Notably, the next—and final—section of the document implies that at least a part of the flying saucer mystery was born out by a series of high-level experiments that began in the New Mexico desert in 1947:

Recent inquiries from other commands and government agencies requesting information about experimental projects as being the cause of so-called "Flying Saucers," [have] prompted the control of Restricted Data. A case in point was the request by Eighth Air Force AC/AS-2 to Headquarters, Strategic Air Command, that a central control of Restricted Data be established contrary to AAF Letter 46-24, 10 March 1947, Par. 24(1). To insure tighter security and access to Project Restricted Data, a new policy has been in affect. Under a recent decision by the Military Liaison Committee to the Atomic Energy Commission, "Top Secret—Restricted Data" can now be transmitted by couriers who have [been] cleared for access to "Restricted Data." The present War Department Courier Service did not meet the requirements as mentioned. Presently Headquarters, Research and Development has assumed this responsibility.[17]

Still more data exists that supports the whistle-blower testimony of Al Barker, the Colonel, Bill Salter, and the Black Widow. In 1997, *Popular Mechanics* magazine published an article written by columnist Jim Wilson on the Roswell controversy and the Air Force's assertions that the recovered material found at the Foster Ranch originated with a Mogul balloon. In part, Wilson revealed that *Popular Mechanics* had been "alerted to a forthcoming release of documents" that could possibly shed more light on what happened at Roswell.

Not only that, Wilson very specifically stated that the magazine had been "told" that "the documents scheduled for future release will tell of a Japanese counterpart to Operation Paperclip. One of its purposes was to determine if the Japanese had constructed a suicide-piloted version of the Fugo incendiary bomb. . . . [*Popular*

Mechanics] suspects the craft that crashed at Roswell will eventually be identified as either a U.S. attempt to re-engineer a second-generation Fugo, or a hybrid craft which uses both Fugo lifting technology and a Horten-inspired lifting body. In either case, Japanese engineers and pilots brought to the U.S. after the war to work on the project could have been the dead 'alien' bodies recovered at the crash site." [18]

The documents that Wilson referred to ultimately did not surface into the public domain; however, the magazine was far from finished with Roswell. Following publication of the Air Force's "Crash Test Dummy" report in 1997, Wilson once again turned his attention to Roswell:

"[A] close reading suggests there may be more to 1940s-era balloon testing than the government is willing to reveal, even now. The new report makes specific reference to a robust high-altitude-balloon research effort that included manned projects. In one especially striking passage, McAndrew reveals, 'Polyethylene balloons flown by the U.S. Air Force have reached an altitude of 170,000 ft. and lifted payloads of 15,000 pounds.'"

This seems to be an inordinate amount of weight for a nuclear tracking device, but not at all unusual for something along the lines of an experimental lifting-body-style vehicle.

Jim Wilson then asks exactly the right question: "[W]hat else besides the Mogul balloons were launched in this era? It would help settle the matter if the Air Force would look at projects by other government agencies that would have used these balloons in their intelligence gathering." [19]

There can be no doubt that the article authored by Wilson, even though it is clearly presented as just a theory, is *very* similar to the accounts of Salter, Barker, the Black Widow, and the Colonel. It certainly can't be attributed to "coincidence." All four of the whistle-blowers I spoke to deny speaking with Wilson for his article, however—and that strongly suggests there are still others out there that know the truth of this dark affair.

*   *   *

On the issue raised by *Popular Mechanics* of what else might have been test-flown by balloon in New Mexico during the summer of 1947, the Colonel makes a number of perceptive comments: "A lot of the Roswell people make a big deal about Brazel finding a large field of wreckage at the ranch. Well, that's true. But many of them ignore one important part of the story: the amount of debris Brazel found was way too much to have come from the one aircraft that other witnesses report crashed at the second site. But the aircraft, if you will, or UFO, as the believers have it, is described as a solid vehicle, an aircraft, whereas the ranch debris is flexible, lightweight wreckage. So the debris at the ranch is of something distinctly separate from the vehicle from which the bodies were recovered rather than being a component of it and was constructed from something totally, totally different. The [UFO] writers never explain what that 'something separate' might be or even *why* it should be different. But look at it in the context of two devices, a large balloon system and the lifting body, and the mystery of why there were two distinct and very different sites and with very different materials at each site is gone.

"Don't forget, too, that the descriptions of the debris described by the original witnesses *do* sound very much like balloon materials—with a few odd properties that can be explained from the parts of the lightweight coating materials that Brazel picked up and also from parts of the balloons that were polythene [polyethylene] with an aluminum covering, which wasn't widely seen then—and hardly ever by civilians back then. Even some of those descriptions that the alien supporters use in their books, and those that dispute the Mogul idea talk about, *still* sound like balloon material. Look at what some of the witnesses say in the Weaver report and there's no doubt they are describing balloon debris. No doubt.

"And maybe most important is that as Brazel himself had said, he had found [weather] balloons in pretty much the same location at least twice before. So, this whole area was swarming with balloon tests after the war, absolutely swarming. Just give that a thought:

Brazel recovers at least two balloons before Roswell and then there's Roswell that *does* sound like balloon debris, even if the UFO writers don't buy it. But if it sounds like balloon material, it looks like it, it crashes where the principal witness had already found two previous balloons flown by our guys, and was near where classified balloon launches such as Mogul and others were [occurring], then it sure as shit *is* a balloon."

The original witnesses to the Roswell debris certainly *did* describe what sounds suspiciously like balloon-borne debris. The testimony of three witnesses is recorded in the Air Force's 1994 report on the Roswell affair. According to Major Marcel's son, Jesse A. Marcel, Jr., "There were three categories of debris: a thick, foil-like metallic gray substance; a brittle, brownish-black plastic-like material, like Bakelite; and there were fragments of what appeared to be I-beams." Similarly, Loretta Proctor, Brazel's neighbor at the time of the event, stated: "Brazel came to my ranch and showed my husband and me a piece of material he said came from a large pile of debris on the property he managed. The piece he brought was brown in color, similar to plastic. . . . 'Mac' [*sic*] said the other material on the property looked like aluminum foil. It was very flexible and wouldn't crush or burn." And Bessie Brazel Schreiber, the daughter of rancher Brazel, stated unequivocally that "The debris looked like pieces of a large balloon which had burst. The pieces were small, the largest I remember measuring about the same as the diameter of a basketball. Most of it was a kind of double-sided material, foil-like on one side and rubber-like on the other."

The Colonel had further, highly perceptive data to impart: "The bigger problem too, with the balloon controversy is that a bunch of false locations and dates for the crash had been spread in case the Russians came looking, and so no one to this day really knows if this happened on July 1, or 2 or 3 or 4, or even sometime before, maybe. So when you have the alien believers saying that the Mogul flight dates, or the size of the debris area, or the wind directions for Mogul flights don't tie up with the date or the location of the crash site [where] Brazel found the material—and therefore this means the material wasn't Mogul and *must* therefore have been extraterrestrial—that doesn't really mean much. All of these guys are working with data that's only partly complete and may not even relate to the correct day of either the crash or the recovery.

"And they're working with Mogul data, which has *nothing* to do with the real picture anyway. Mogul is just a convenient cover. Arguing about whether or not wind and weather records or the size of a Mogul balloon indicate or don't indicate that [a Mogul balloon] might have been taken in the direction of the ranch is irrelevant when it wasn't a Mogul balloon. Mogul is the diversion; the conflicting dates, the dummies, the crash sites are a diversion; and it's all such a great cover because Mogul *was* being tested in the same area, and that goes for the dummy flights, too: all in New Mexico and all close—in aerospace terms—to White Sands, the ranch, Holloman, [and] Alamogordo. You couldn't plan a better series of covers for this experiment to confuse people if you tried." [20]

If, as the Colonel has asserted, the key event that led to the legend of the UFO crash at Roswell involved a "next generation of Fugo" balloon that was responsible for launching an experimental aircraft that catastrophically crashed, then who better to enlist into the study of how and why the Roswell experiment failed than an expert on those very same balloons?

Keeping that question in mind, recall the earlier testimony of former Counter Intelligence Corps operative Lewis "Bill" Rickett, who stated that one of those he worked closely with on an investigation of the crash at Roswell was Dr. Lincoln La Paz of the University of New Mexico.

That La Paz was the director of the university's Institute of Meteoritics and was later involved in a study known as Project Twinkle, the purpose of which was to investigate sightings of strange "green fireballs" seen in the New Mexico region and elsewhere in the late 1940s and early 1950s, has led many commentators to assume that this logically infers an otherworldly point of origin for the Roswell wreckage.[21] While it is true that La Paz *did* undertake work for Project Twinkle and *was* a renowned expert on meteorites, *he was also one of the government's leading experts on Fugo balloons during World War II.*

As evidence of La Paz's deep connection to the wartime studies of Fugo balloons undertaken by the government, consider the following press release titled "New Mexican Had Lookout Job for 'Japanese Germs'" and issued by the University of New Mexico shortly after the close of hostilities in 1945:

Dr. Lincoln La Paz of the University of New Mexico was in the thick of the fight against Japanese plans to send disease germs into America by balloon, said President J. P. Wernette of the University today. Commenting on stories from the Navy in Washington revealing that use of germs and viruses in the Jap balloon-barrage was an enemy project as the war came to an end, Dr. Wernette said that Dr. La Paz, head of the department of mathematics and the University's Institute of Meteoritics, was with the government's secret anti-balloon project during the war.

"If the war had not ended when it did, in the opening stages of a full-scale balloon offensive which probably would have taken place between October 1945, and now, when the velocity of the west wind at high altitude is greatest, this country would have had unpleasant experiences," Dr. La Paz said today. "People most concerned were trained scientists, and stockmen, too, he said. Anthrax spores could have been sent over in the paper balloons in great numbers, and Manchurian sheep pox could have easily struck the hooved animals of this country because the disease has not been found here and there would be no natural immunity," Dr. La Paz went on.

"But the Japanese, using radio devices to locate their balloons on the flight to this country, apparently did not realize that we could pick up the signals and find the balloons before they reached the mainland," said Dr. La Paz."[22]

A similar press release issued by the University of New Mexico—also in late 1945—provides more data on La Paz and his research into Fugo balloons and meteorites:

Observers, watching for meteors, thought they had something when they saw some brilliant lights in the sky from February to May, 1945. And they did, said Dr. Lincoln La Paz, mathematics department head at the University of New Mexico and director of its Institute of Meteoritics, today.

The displays were actually made by Japanese balloons, Dr. La Paz said, revealing the history of a scientific study of meteors which went on before and during the time that *Dr. La Paz was busy in secret government work of studying and combating the balloon offensive.* [My italics.]

Nevertheless, a few months later, on Nov. 29, 1945, a great meteorite fell slowly across northern California and Nevada, and observers mistook it for everything from a jet plane to a Hollywood publicity stunt. Members of the Society for Research on Meteorites and the American Meteor Society thought at first that it was a new type [of] Japanese balloon bomb.[23]

As all of the material in this chapter amply demonstrates, there is a wide and varied body of evidence corroborating the testimony of those whistle-blowers who have asserted the events at Roswell resulted from a series of secret trials and experiments. And the story is still far from over.

TWELVE

HiTLER'S DiSKS

Having learned that I had spoken with the Colonel, Al Barker agreed to reveal other pertinent data, which he had previously held back because, he explained, "I don't want all of this on my shoulders."

In mid-1947, according to Barker, White Sands test-flew three unusual-looking aircraft: one of these was of an almost classic flying saucer design that was recovered in a semiconstructed state from a German weapons factory in 1945; and two were prototype vehicles built in the United States that Barker, too, perceptively, describes as "half-moon" in shape or "like a shoe heel bent out of shape," and that were based on the designs of the Horten brothers of Germany.

"Now, if you hear that we were flying fantastic machines at speeds of thousands of miles an hour that the Nazis had designed, you're wrong. That's not true at all. These *were* saucerlike, but more like an ellipse, and they certainly did not fly around the States at thousands of miles an hour. Hell, you think we would be building bombers and missiles if we had that technology? But, sure, we had a few tests of these aircraft and several crashes, aborted takeoffs, failed landings. We just could *not* get these things stable. I know—

absolutely know—that there were aborted takeoff and landing crashes at White Sands of these aircraft: two Horten and one somewhat of a disk. Do I think that this is where the crashed UFO stories came from? I *know* that's where some of the crashed UFO stories came from, with others from the balloon capsules and the lifting bodies."

Expounding further, Barker asserts that post-1949, and as a direct result of the 1947 crashes, the flying saucer project was "not closed but modified and we began looking into delta aircraft, bat wings, and aircraft that were more like today's stealth aircraft. And of course, there was a realization that missile technology was going to replace much of the work that our bombers had been involved in during the war, and that would make a lot of this obsolete by the fifties, anyway."

Barker also expounds on the link between the Nuclear Energy for Propulsion of Aircraft operation and the Aircraft Nuclear Project and the work being undertaken at White Sands in 1947: "NEPA were doing their work; White Sands were doing theirs. Both groundbreaking—potentially, at least—but both separate, too. But we heard that there were people at NEPA that were very interested in the 1947 UFO sighting reports and there was a kind of informal group at NEPA that thought—wrongly—these were Russian or maybe even interplanetary. And some of these sightings, even though they weren't known as saucers then, took place in March and April 1947, when we began the flights, and so NEPA got involved way back when, when we began testing these things. Now, because NEPA's area was nuclear propulsion, they figured that maybe that's what powered these things. Well, this was wrong—totally wrong. What was tested at White Sands was certainly revolutionary but mostly jet propelled, and we even test-flew one with props.

"But the problem is that the NEPA people were looking at this and wondering what's happening. They weren't stupid, they were going to figure it out eventually, and if that happened in an environment where we weren't pulling the strings, then you would get problems with information spilling into the open. No one wanted that with the Russians around, so we briefed some of the senior people [at NEPA]. 'Yes, we've been testing these things out in New Mexico on the Range and at other locations. But no, these things aren't nuclear powered and they aren't Russian or interplanetary. We've had some successes and we've had some failures, and this is a classified project that might give us the upper hand with the Russians.'

"Well, NEPA understood this, but then they surprised us by saying that they had their people take a look at some of the flying saucer reports because they were worried that it was the Russians, and they got thinking about combining their work on nuclear propulsion into our flying saucer designs and the Horten designs. Before this, they were thinking of a relatively normal aircraft design but with a modified nuclear reactor as a power source.

"This sounded good to everyone: White Sands was doing its thing; NEPA was doing its, too; and maybe this was something that everyone could get involved in. And that's how NEPA was invited to see the aircraft at White Sands and how they got involved—peripherally—in the 1947 crashes with the bodies and the incident on the Sands with the nuclear simulation."

An FBI document offers valuable corroboration for Barker's assertions that there *were* people at the NEPA project that believed some flying saucer reports were the result of secret test flights of man-made, nuclear-powered vehicles. The document, titled "Flying Discs" and dated September 21, 1949, was prepared by FBI operative D. M. Ladd and marked for the attention of FBI director J. Edgar Hoover. It states:

I thought you might be interested in the following information concerning "Flying Discs" which has been furnished to the Bureau on a confidential basis by Colonel Clyde D. Gasser, Air Materiel Command, U.S. Army, who is the principal army technician at the Nuclear Energy for the Propulsion of Aircraft Research Center at Oak Ridge, Tennessee.

Colonel Gasser stated that he knew nothing of an official nature concerning "Flying Discs" other than the fact that they are believed by Air Force Intelligence officials to be man-made missiles, rather than some natural phenomena. It was his belief that a great deal of information has been compiled concerning these missiles by Air Force Intelligence, and that research on the matter was being extensively done at Wright Field, Dayton, Ohio.

Colonel Gasser then continued with his own ideas as to what might be the nature of these discs which ideas he had formulated through review of those known facts and theoretical conjectures of himself and other scientists concerning the nature of flying discs and methods of propulsion for such type of aerial mechanism. According to him, flying discs have long been a theoretical possibility, and, in fact, a possibility which would indicate one of the best means by which to break through the barriers of the supersonic area. He stated that scientists have, for many years, been attempting to develop this type of aircraft. Some experimentation has been done even in the United States, but insofar as is known in the United States, at the present time, there have never been any practical developments. As a second factor of consideration, Colonel Gasser stated that insofar as is known to U.S. scientists at this time, there is no known chemical fuel which would make possible tremendous range of flight such as is ascribed to the reported "flying discs." According to Colonel Gasser there is only one possible fuel which could be utilized which is in accord with present theory, and that is the utilization of atomic energy.

This report is particularly noteworthy for two reasons. To begin with, it officially confirms—as both Barker and the Colonel asserted—that there *were* people attached at a very high level to the NEPA project in the late 1940s who were interested in utilizing flying saucer technology and suspected (mistakenly, it transpired) that at least *some* UFOs seen in American airspace employed then fledgling nuclear-energy-based propulsion systems. The document also provides testimony from a credible source—the "principal army technician" at NEPA, no less—that research into flying-saucer-like aircraft *had* indeed been undertaken in the States, but that, largely, the results were lacking in terms of making truly radical aviation-based advances—as Al Barker stated was the case.

Barker continues: "The biggest problem that was always there for NEPA—it never went away—was how do you test-fly a nuclear aircraft without killing or burning up the crew in the process? And how do you assess what the radiation damage might be? You can't ask the crew to sit there and just take it. And there's the biggest problem of all: not having a working prototype of a nuclear reactor in 1947 that can be installed in an aircraft to get completely accurate results. That was just too advanced—Buck Rogers—and years away. So there we have the radiation experiment at White Sands and other experiments at Los Alamos and Oak Ridge on handicapped people, trying to determine how the human body absorbs and reacts to radiation: total body irradiation, without having a working nuclear engine for the aircraft. This was all crucial to the NEPA people.

"But you must be made aware that it wasn't strictly NEPA that was doing this research. It was people, people high up in our military, that knew what NEPA needed, and they pushed for these things to be done, even if the experiments aren't going to give completely accurate results—as with the radiation, for example.

"I'm not proud that I kept this a secret; I'm not proud that I know. But the Japanese had done unspeakable things to these people. Well, it was probably inevitable that someone is going to realize that there is a huge research value to looking at the way in which people and bodies have been used by [Unit] 731 in high-altitude [experimentation], pressurization tests, injecting of plagues and viruses, chemicals, and—later, here—exposure to radiation. Like it or not, we needed those results and we wanted to run other tests. And I have to say to you, many of these people had already been experimented on before we received them. Absolutely, we needed to know what had been done and the effects. We did.

"So, after [Gen. Charles] Willoughby and [Gen.] MacArthur began moves to grab the [Unit] 731 discoveries, this was seen as a 'go' signal, and the bodies and the people were all brought here, secretly brought to Los Alamos first and then to a location in Chicago. No one wanted to say it or be the first, but there was a tremendous potential to using these people. The gains in aviation medicine, nuclear medicine, [and] biological warfare—potentially—were huge. But everyone was sitting on these experiments, doing nothing, with these people in a secure hospital in Chicago, and everyone was waiting for 'go.'

"Word came down that this was to be a highly classified project: 'If it helps us get an edge on the Russians, do what you have to do with these people, but you keep it classified and you commit nothing to paper.' They knew—we all knew—that this was going to be damned and dirty. No one wanted to be responsible for using the handicapped [people]. It was: 'Do what you have to do; if we can use these and learn what the [Unit] 731 people did, then maybe . . . ' Well, maybe that was true, but maybe that was some of these people trying to justify the experiments and easing their consciences."

According to Barker, when "in late 1946" permission was granted to begin operations using these people, "it was like a snowball down a hill. Things got bigger and bigger and went faster and faster, mainly because Nuremberg was on their tails. Everyone had their own pet projects with these people. There was so much going on in New Mexico that having a Horten aircraft crash in the same year and place as some of these high [altitude] balloon experiments was not a bit surprising. People were out of control with these projects. And the desert was big enough for everyone to have their slice.

"There were also the glider tests with NEPA that you know about," and, he states, there were very controversial experiments in which already-dead, deformed bodies held at Los Alamos were exposed to massive amounts of radiation or dissected and used in similar nuclear, chemical, and biological experimentation. "This was the main link with NEPA on all this: trying to determine the effects of radiation on the human body and how that would translate to a crew being protected or—worse—contaminated by radiation from a nuclear engine."

But things got much darker than that, according to Barker. "The bigger problem," he reveals, "was that there was a finite number of people. Overall, we are talking about perhaps forty people and twenty bodies that were split between the agencies and that had been brought over mostly from Japan and some from Germany— mostly of normal-looking people such as the scientists and the crew on the Roswell lifting body, but maybe twenty, too, with a range of [conditions including those of] dwarfs, what I call the 'big head' people and terrible deformities—mental and physical. But what do you do when the supply runs out? You need to carry on—right or wrong."

Barker maintains that a solution to the problem was soon forthcoming. "They made deals here with mortuaries, with funeral homes, with asylums, hospitals—even prisons—where they would make an under-the-table payment in return for dead bodies and living handicapped people. Now, this is where, again, these stories about alien bodies appeared. You go along to a funeral home, an asylum, and you can't take away the body of somebody's husband or wife. That just won't work. So you only take those that won't be missed.

"Back then, there was a hell of a lot of stigma with mental and physical handicaps, and a lot of people were handed over at birth to hospitals. The families didn't want to deal with it—maybe *couldn't* deal with it. The hospital or the asylum agrees to look after them for what might be a short life. So, again, we do the deals with these places: 'If you have someone that won't be missed—and *only* someone that won't be missed—we'll deal with it for you. Let us know; you get the payment.'

"So again, all through this period of about very late 1946 to about August 1947 and *maybe* earlier, based on some things I heard of, we had these bodies and strange-looking people used in medical tests across the country—in the desert, at Los Alamos, at Oak Ridge, everywhere.

"Well, after Nuremberg in August [1947], a lot of this—not all, but a lot—was shut down. People were getting tense about using bodies and handicapped people in ways that went against Nuremberg and other things. But they aren't going to prosecute anyone or everything comes out and everyone's implicated. So files are burned, bodies are gotten rid of, you won't talk about this, it never happened and if anyone comes calling—the press or whoever—we begin spreading these tales about crashed UFOs and alien bodies. And it worked.

"But there are going to be things we can't foresee—accidental viewings of these things—and there were. You get a high-altitude balloon come down somewhere off the Range with a dwarf body on board, you get two bodies used in an early ejector capsule test at White Sands, it goes off course. A recovery team is sent out and maybe a civilian sees the cleanup and talks. You even get corpses of handicapped people laid out near atomic test sites to measure the radiation afterward. A prototype glider crashes. Then, years later, you have all these rumors spring up everywhere: bodies in the desert, the military, people being warned, strange flying contraptions.

"Now, if you look at the NEPA files from 1948 on, you'll see all these debates about using humans in test flights and nuclear medicine tests—Can we do it? Is it legal? Is it ethical? That might sound odd when you consider everything that happened in New Mexico in 1947. But remember that this is all in the context of Nuremberg; and NEPA—or the people that were pushing for NEPA to succeed, is more accurate—started over again, trying to get official sanction to use people. The earlier days of having people in the military secretly going ahead with the bodies and people in 1947 were all gone by two years later.

"So, right or wrong, we tried to make these advances in the early years, but then it all gets blown away when everyone starts backing away with Nuremberg, so it's back to the beginning and trying to get permission—official permission—to do these things, and not as they had before, kind of under the table, nothing in writing and un-officially. You know, getting the job done without too many people asking questions or even knowing. But after Nuremberg, everyone's getting jittery and it all comes to a halt. But check into what NEPA was doing in 1948 and 1949 and you'll see what they wanted to do with people—which was based on what White Sands and Los Alamos had done two years earlier—and you'll get an angle on the frustration about not getting permission to continue these experiments after [1947]. But you'll also get an idea from their thinking of what came before. If you dig you'll find a lot of material after 1948 about the things NEPA wanted to do—with people, maybe even the prisoner things, as some of that had a lower level of classification. But the pre-'49 material—that's where you are going to find problems in getting the files."

Finally, Barker concludes, "I'm not proud of all this, but it *is* the truth."

"And how do you feel about it all now—the things that happened, your role and knowledge?" I asked.

After a stony silence, Barker uttered quietly, "What was done, was done. It's gone. History. Forgotten. Old men with old memories."[1]

It is a matter of record that in the latter years of World War II, the Nazis *had* been working to perfect both circular- and elliptical-shaped aircraft, as Al Barker has claimed. It must be stressed, however, that controversy abounds with regard to the extent that this work was or was not successful. That research, at least, was under-taken in this field by Nazi Germany is not in doubt, and this can be demonstrated by examining a series of papers released officially under the terms of the Freedom of Information Act by a variety of agencies. Take, for example, the Air Force report of January 3, 1952 (on the subject of flying saucer sightings investigated by the Air Force in the late 1940s and early 1950s), from Brig. Gen. W. M. Garland to Gen. John A. Samford, Air Force director of intelligence:

It is logical to relate the reported sightings to the known development of aircraft, jet propulsion, rockets and range extension capabilities in Germany and the USSR. In this connection, it is to be noted that certain developments by the Germans, particularly the Horten wing, jet propulsion, and refueling, combined with their extensive employment of V-1 and V-2 weapons during World War II, lend credence to the possibility that the flying objects may be of German and Russian origin. The developments mentioned above were completed and operational between 1941 and 1944 and subsequently fell into the hands of the Soviets at the end of the war. There is evidence that the Germans were working on these projects as far back as 1931 to 1938. Therefore it may be assumed that the Germans had at least a 7 to 10 year lead over the United States.[2]

A CIA document of 1954 showed similar concerns: "A German newspaper (not further identified) recently published an interview with George Klein, famous German engineer and aircraft expert, describing the experimental construction of 'flying saucers' carried out by him from 1941 to 1945. Klein stated that he was present when, in 1945, the first piloted 'flying saucer' took off and reached a speed of 1,300 miles per hour within 3 minutes. The experiments resulted in three designs: one designed by Miethe, was a disk-shaped aircraft, 135 feet in diameter, which did not rotate; another designed by Habermohl and Schriever, consisted of a large rotating ring, in the center of which was a round, stationary cabin for the crew. When the Soviets occupied Prague, the Germans destroyed every trace of the 'flying saucer' project and nothing more was heard of Habermohl and his assistants. Schriever recently died in Bremen, where he had been living. In Breslau, the Soviets managed to capture one of the saucers built by Miethe, who escaped to France. He is reportedly in the U.S. at present."[3]

Two of the most persuasive accounts that posited a direct link between the Nazi war machine and circular-shaped aircraft came via two individuals interviewed by FBI agents in 1957 and 1967, respectively. In the 1957 case, agents at Detroit recorded that they had spoken with a Polish man who had been a prisoner of war in Germany during the hostilities of 1939 to 1945 and who surreptitiously came upon "a circular enclosure approximately 100 to 150 yards in diameter protected from viewers by a tarpaulin-type wall approximately 50 feet high, from which a vehicle was observed to slowly rise vertically to a height sufficient to clear the wall and then to move slowly horizontally a short distance out of his view, which was obstructed by trees."

This vehicle, observed from approximately five hundred feet and in the vicinity of the prisoner-of-war camp, the FBI was informed, was "circular in shape, 75 to 100 yards in diameter, and about 14 feet high, consisting of dark gray stationary top and bottom sections, five to six feet high." The documentation continued that an "approximate three foot middle section appeared to be a rapidly moving component producing a continuous blur similar to an airplane propeller, but extending the circumference of the vehicle so far as could be observed." The man mentioned that the incident had been witnessed by a work crew of sixteen or eighteen men, consisting of Russian, French and Polish POWs, who had discussed this incident among themselves many times.[4]

The second document concerns a man who appeared at the Miami Office of the FBI on April 26, 1967, and furnished the following information relating to a circular-shaped aircraft that he allegedly photographed during November 1944.

Sometime during 1943, he graduated from the German Air Academy and was assigned as a member of the *Luftwaffe* on the Russian Front. Near the end of 1944, he was released from this duty and was assigned as a test pilot to a top secret project in the Black Forest of Austria. During this period he observed the aircraft. . . . It was saucer-shaped, about twenty-one feet in diameter, radio-controlled, and mounted several jet engines around the exterior portion of the craft. He further described the exterior portion as revolving around the dome in the center which remained stationary. It was his responsibility to photograph the object while in flight. He asserted he was able to retain a negative of a photograph he made at 7,000 meters (20,000 feet).

According to him, the above aircraft was designed and engineered by a German engineer whose present whereabouts is unknown to him. He also assumed the secrets pertaining to this aircraft were captured by Allied Forces. He said this type of aircraft was responsible for the downing of at least one American B-26 airplane.

He has become increasingly concerned because of the unconfirmed reports concerning a similar object and denials the United States has such an aircraft. He feels such a weapon would be beneficial in Vietnam and would prevent the further loss of American lives which was his paramount purpose in contacting the Federal Bureau of Investigation.[5]

Meanwhile, across the Atlantic and during the same time frame, British authorities had uncovered a similar body of data. A Secret Air Ministry report dated 1957, for example, states that "A review by the *Daily Worker* newspaper of a book recently published on German wartime weapons contained references to a German flying saucer which was flown at a speed of 1,250 mph to a height of 40,000 feet."[6] Similarly, in 1998, the British government declassified a two-volume document—titled "Unorthodox Aircraft," previously withheld at top-secret level and dating from the period 1948 to 1951—that dealt with British intelligence interviews with former prisoners of war who had seen unusual and radical aircraft in the vicinity of German and Russian airfields and military installations.

Interspersed throughout the reports are a variety of foreign newspaper clippings about circular-shaped aircraft and the Nazi attempts to build and utilize such vehicles. Moreover, copies of the file were distributed to a whole host of British agencies and departments, including the Joint Intelligence Bureau, the Air Ministry's Scientific and Technical Intelligence office, MI10 at the War Office, Air Intelligence, and an elite Air Ministry division known as A13.[7]

As these examples demonstrate, the intelligence communities of both the American and the British government were extremely interested in knowing the extent to which the Nazis had made advances with respect to circular and elliptical aircraft—and possibly capitalizing on this new and emerging technology—just as Al Barker maintains.

Both Barker and the Colonel have stated that at least two of the aircraft that were test-flown at White Sands in 1947 and led to the legend of the Roswell Incident were based on the revolutionary aircraft designs of the Horten brothers, Reimer and Walter. A document dated December 16, 1947, classified secret, and prepared by Lt. Col. Harry H. Pretty of the U.S. Army for Headquarters Berlin Command, delves deeply into the life, history, and work of these aviation geniuses:

> The Horten brothers . . . are residing in Goettingen at present. . . . Reimer is presently studying advanced mathematics at the University of Bonn, and is about to obtain his doctor's degree. It is believed that when his studies are completed he intends to accept a teaching position at the Institute for Technology . . . sometime in February or March 1948.
>
> . . . [Reimer] . . . is the one who developed the theory of the flying wing and subsequently of all the models and aircrafts built by the brothers. Walter, on the other hand, is the engineer

who tried to put into practice the several somewhat fantastic ideas of his brother. The clash of personalities resulted in a continuous quarrel and friction between the two brothers. Reimer was always developing new ideas which would increase the speed of the aircraft or improve its maneuverability; Walter on the other hand was tearing down the fantastic ideas of his brother by practical calculations and considerations.

[The two brothers] worked together up to and including the "Horten VIII" a flying wing intended to be a fighter plane. . . . After the "Horten VIII" was finished, one of the usual and frequent quarrels separated the two brothers temporarily. Walter went to work alone on the "Horten IX," which is a fighter plane of the flying wing design, with practically no changes from the model VIII except for the engines. . . .

The model of this aircraft . . . was tested extensively in the supersonic wind tunnel . . . of the aero-dynamic testing institute . . . located in Goettingen. The tests were conducted in the late summer of 1944 under the personal supervision of Professor Betz, chief of the institute. Betz at that time was approximately sixty years old and next to Prandtel (then seventy-eight years old), was considered to be the best man on aerodynamics in Germany. Betz's attitude toward the flying wing is very conservative to say the least. Basically he is against the design of any flying wing. According to the official reports about the tests, air disturbances were created on the wing tips, resulting in air vacuums, which in turn would prevent the steering mechanism from functioning properly. This seems logical as, of course, neither the ailerons nor the rudders could properly accomplish their function in a partial vacuum created by air disturbances and whirls.

In spite of this, the report reveals, two Horten IX's *were* built and test-flown at Rechlin in the fall of 1944. One of the two planes developed engine trouble while the pilot was trying to ascertain the maximum rate of climb. The right jet stopped suddenly, causing the aircraft to go into an immediate spin and then to crash; the pilot was killed.

After extensive tests, the German Luftwaffe commissioned the Horten IX and ordered immediate mass production, with the first order going to Gothaer Waggon Fabrik, located in Gotha, in January 1945. The Luftwaffe requested that ten planes be built immediately and that the entire factory concentrate its efforts on the production of the Horten IX. However, upon receipt of the plans, the technical manager of the firm submitted a number of suggestions to improve the aircraft—largely with the intention of eliminating the Horten brothers as the inventors and modifying the vehicle to such an extent that it would be seen as his brainchild rather than that of the Hortens. Production of the Horten IX would never begin in earnest, however.

When, in the final stages of the war, American troops occupied the town of Gotha and the Nazi war machine began to deteriorate, the original designs in possession of the Horten brothers were quickly and quietly hidden in a salt mine in Salzdettfurt, only to be discovered by British authorities in the summer of 1945, along with a host of additional documentation relating to their work.

As a result, the Horten brothers were invited to go to England in the late summer of 1945, where they remained for approximately ninety days. Reimer proved unwilling to cooperate unless an immediate contract was offered to him and his brother. Walter, on the other hand, not being a theoretician, was unable to comply by himself and Reimer was sufficiently stubborn not to move a finger. The brothers returned to Germany.

Upon their return, Walter remained in contact with British authorities and was actually paid a salary by the British between October 1945 and April 1946, as the British contemplated offering him employment. Walter subsequently had an argument with his brother and the two decided to part ways. In due time, Reimer headed off to the University of Bonn to obtain his degree, and Walter married Fraulein von der Groeben, former chief secretary to Luftwaffe general Ernst Udet.

"But, it was with the German saucer files, the Horten files, and the data from the Brits in 1945," states Barker "that we began working on prototypes of what became the White Sands aircraft and that then led to the saucer tales and sightings of 1947. Hell, there was so much secrecy back then that we were even hiding things from each other: keep the FBI out of the loop, or keep this away from these people or those people."[8]

Barker's reference to the FBI being kept in the dark is notable. In early July 1947, Brig. Gen. George F. Schulgen, chief of the Requirements Intelligence Branch of Army Air Corps Intelligence, met with Special Agent S. W. Reynolds of the FBI with a view to determining if the Army Air Forces could solicit the assistance of the Bureau on a regular basis in its investigation of the flying saucer mystery.

General Schulgen advised Reynolds that "every effort must be undertaken in order to run down and ascertain whether or not the flying discs are a fact and, if so, to learn all about them." The foremost thought on General Schulgen's mind was that the saucers were man-made in origin. He confided in Special Agent Reynolds that "the first reported sightings might have been by individuals of Communist sympathies with the view to causing hysteria and fear of a secret weapon." It was for this reason that the Army Air Forces sought the FBI's assistance.

General Schulgen guaranteed the FBI "all the facilities of [my] office as to results obtained," and outlined a plan that would involve the FBI in both locating and questioning witnesses to UFO sightings to ascertain whether they were sincere in their statements that they had seen flying saucers or whether their statements were prompted by personal desire for publicity or political reasons.

Schulgen was careful to advise Reynolds, too, that "It has been established that the flying discs are not the result of any Army or Navy experiment." Based on the testimony that we have seen thus far, however, this statement appears to have been wildly inaccurate and the Bureau was, seemingly, deliberately misled.

Following the meeting between Schulgen and Reynolds, FBI director J. Edgar Hoover instructed his agents to begin investigations into flying saucer sightings in the manner suggested by General Schulgen. As a result of these investigations, on August 15, 1947, the FBI learned of the distinct possibility that the military's involvement in the flying saucer subject possibly extended beyond that of mere observer.

In a memorandum to Edward A. Tamm, the FBI assistant director, D. M. Ladd of the Bureau's Domestic Intelligence Division wrote the following: "The Director advised on August 14, 1947, that the Los Angeles papers were carrying headlines indicating that Soviet espionage agents had been instructed to determine the facts relative to the flying discs. The article carried a Washington date line and indicated that Red espionage agents had been ordered to solve the question of the flying discs, the Russians being of the opinion that this might be some new form of defense perfected by the American military. The article further recalled that during the recent war pieces of tinfoil had been dropped in the air for the purpose of off-setting the value of radar being used by the enemy forces and that these aluminum discs might be a new development along this line. The Director inquired as to whether the Bureau had any such information." [9]

Suspecting that if the Russians were snooping around, the saucers had to be American in origin, Special Agent Reynolds of the FBI's Liaison Section was directed by J. Edgar Hoover to make further inquiries with the Army Air Forces. On August 19, 1947, Reynolds met with a lieutenant colonel from Air Forces Intelligence, whose name is blacked out of the document. They discussed the entire secret weapon issue, as well as the possible consequences should the Bureau uncover details of a top-secret, domestic research-and-development program. Following their candid discussion, a remarkable memorandum captioned "Flying Discs" was prepared by Reynolds for the attention of Hoover. It is this document perhaps more than any other that indicates that the American military *was* testing flying-saucer-type aircraft in the summer of 1947:

Special Agent S. W. Reynolds of the Liaison Section, while discussing the above captioned phenomena with Lieutenant Colonel [X] of the Air Forces Intelligence, expressed the possibility that flying discs were, in fact, a very highly classified experiment of the Army or Navy. Mr. Reynolds was very much surprised when Colonel [X] not only agreed that this was a possibility, but confidentially stated it was his personal opinion that such was a probability. Colonel [X] indicated that a Mr. [Deleted], who is a scientist attached to the Air Forces Intelligence, was of the same opinion.

Colonel [X] stated that he based his assumption on the following: He pointed out that when flying objects were reported seen over Sweden, the "high brass" of the War Department extended tremendous pressure on the Air Forces Intelligence to conduct research and collect information in an effort to identify these sightings. Colonel [X] stated that, in contrast to this, we have reported sightings of unknown objects over the United States, and the "high brass" appeared to be totally unconcerned. He indicated this led him to believe that they knew enough about these objects to express no concern. Colonel [X] pointed out further that the objects in question have been seen by many individuals who are what he terms "trained observers" such as airline pilots. He indicated also that several of the individuals are reliable members of the community. He stated that these individuals saw something. He stated the above has led him to the conclusion that there were objects seen which somebody in the Government knows all about.

Special Agent Reynolds then pointed out to the colonel that if flying saucers did indeed originate with a highly classified domestic project of the military, it was wholly unreasonable for the FBI to be expected to "spend money and precious time conducting inquiries with respect to this matter." The colonel concurred with Reynolds, and indicated that it would have been extremely embarrassing to Air Forces Intelligence if the saucers proved to be American in origin.[10]

Perhaps sensing that he was getting close to uncovering the truth behind the UFO puzzle, Reynolds then made inquiries with the Intelligence Division of the War Department for an opinion on the theory that some shadow government operation was responsible for the many flying-saucer-type objects seen over North America.

The War Department, however, issued a flat denial that it was in any way implicated in the UFO issue. In a report written up later, Reynolds noted that he was given "the assurance of General Chamberlain and General Todd that the Army is conducting no experiments with anything which could possibly be mistaken for a flying disc." Nevertheless, the FBI continued to view the subject of flying saucers and the military's involvement with deep suspicion, and rumors continued to circulate within the higher echelons of the FBI that it was being denied access to the full and unexpurgated facts— just as Al Barker said they were.[11]

THiRTEEN

BODY SNATCHERS

History has shown that the Nuclear Energy for Propulsion of Aircraft (NEPA) operation and the Aircraft Nuclear Program (ANP) did not prove feasible in the long term. In the immediate postwar era and through the following decade, however, there *was* a real belief that the projects would succeed; and conducting research — such as the simulated nuclear aircraft flight at White Sands in 1947 — to determine the potential effects of both radiation and high-altitude exposure on human beings was seen to be of paramount importance and relevance to those projects. Once the Unit 731 bodies were used up and covered up, concerted efforts were made to find other human subjects for the continuation of radiation exposure experiments.

That NEPA was, as Al Barker had told me, lobbying to try and secure official permission to use human beings, and particularly prisoners, in nuclear aircraft experimentation in the post-1947 period is not in doubt. Documentation generated as a result of a meeting held in Chicago on June 23, 1948, which focused on the work of NEPA's Medical Advisory Committee makes this point perfectly:

The NEPA Medical Advisory Committee is attempting to determine what will happen to humans exposed at infrequent times to amounts of radiation which are higher than those accepted as permissible for peace time operations. The Committee, with the exception of one member, feels that such information cannot be obtained by animal experiments nor by clinical observations and that the information sought is sufficiently important to justify the use of humans as experimental subjects. The Committee therefore recommends, that the Armed Services arrange for and conduct unclassified experiments on man which will make possible the accurate prediction of biological changes resulting from known levels of radiation exposure.

The Committee is not in a position to make recommendations as to where these tests can be conducted other than that they should be carried out at some federal, state, or Armed Services prison, where life prisoners are incarcerated and where arrangements can be made with the prison authorities to cooperate in the experiment. The selection of the prison is a matter for top military consideration. Continued cooperation of the prison staff and prisoners for a matter of many years will be required.

On April 3, 1949, in Washington, D. C., the NEPA Medical Advisory Committee approved data compiled and tabulated by its Subcommittee on Literature dealing with effects of radiations and estimates of radiation damage to humans. It also approved a report of its Subcommittee on Human Experimentation that "the Armed Services arrange for and conduct unclassified experiments making possible accurate prediction of biological damage in man from known levels of radiation exposure."

Two months later, on June 3, 1949, the Joint Panel on Medical Aspects of Atomic Warfare (Research and Development Board) endorsed in principle the conduct of live human experimentation in the nuclear aircraft projects to determine levels of human tolerance to ionizing radiation and the establishment of militarily acceptable dosages.

This was followed by a meeting in Chicago on October 4, 1949, in which the NEPA Medical Advisory Committee approved detailed plans for the conduct of its recommended research, and stated that live human experimentation should be considered the *"Number 1 recommendation."* [My italics.]

On February 1, 1950, however, the Committee on Medical Sciences learned that certain elements of the Atomic Energy Commission Medical Group did not favor human experimentation. In view of this development, NEPA Committee members requested a restudy of the problem in the light of the implications of the policy of the AEC Medical Group. At its following meeting, the Committee on Medical Sciences revoked its previous endorsement of the action of its panel approving the NEPA's recommendation and voted to refer the matter back to the panel for further consideration.

By mid-September 1950, the NEPA Research Guidance Committee (the successor to the NEPA Medical Advisory Committee) proposed that various prominent individuals be solicited to assist in persuading influential agencies to work for approval of human experimentation, the results of which were needed "not only by NEPA but by the Armed Services as a whole and Civilian Defense."

By December 1950, NEPA was—as Al Barker maintained—expressing both concern and frustration that research on live subjects was being thwarted in certain quarters: "At the meeting of the NEPA Research Guidance Committee on this date, it was recognized that unless AEC or some other highly influential agency recommends human experimentation, the NEPA proposal would never be carried out by the Armed Services." [1]

A January 5, 1950, document titled "Radiation Biology Relative to Nuclear Energy Powered Aircraft Recommendations to NEPA" and prepared by the NEPA Medical Advisory Committee offers similar observations: "For many reasons it is desirable that the aircraft carry a crew. This implies that the reactor will be surrounded with shielding adequate to protect the crew against radiations escaping from the reactor. . . . [I]t is necessary to determine the amount of radiation a human can reasonably tolerate in a given number of doses, at given repetition frequencies, and at given intensities, so that shield weights can be minimized. This knowledge is only partially available."

Although this statement was made in January 1950, it suggests that some research had already been undertaken—albeit "partially"—with regard to understanding the effects of radiation on the crew of a nuclear-powered aircraft. In many ways, this dovetails very well with the statements of Barker and the Colonel about early, fledgling research that was, essentially, "people not really knowing what the hell they were doing and just coming up with dipshit ideas and hoping for the best"—such as that involving the radiation experiment over White Sands in the summer of 1947.

A letter from M. C. Leverett, technical director of the nuclear aircraft program, to Dr. Shields Warren, director of medicine and biology at the Atomic Energy Commission dated February 12, 1951, adds further weight to Al Barker's assertions that in the post-Nuremberg era it became increasingly difficult to obtain official sanction to conduct radiation research on human subjects for the NEPA project:

Dear Dr. Warren: In connection with our work on Nuclear Powered Flight, we have as you know called together a group of highly qualified experts in the general field of radiology and the effects of radiation upon human beings, in order to assist us in defining the limiting exposure to which we should plan to subject the crew of a nuclear powered airplane. One of the actions taken by this group of experts was the formulation of a program of recommended research necessary, in their opinion, for adequate coverage of the radiobiological aspects of nuclear flight. Among the recommended research projects was the

Nick Redfern

highly controversial one of human experimentation which this group strongly recommended and gave a position of highest priority. For almost two years the various members of this Committee have been making efforts to gain governmental approval of their recommendation regarding human experiments. These efforts have been largely unsuccessful and we and they have come finally to the conclusion that further efforts in this direction would be a waste of energy. We are therefore discontinuing our efforts to obtain governmental approval for experiments on humans along the lines recommended by our Advisory Committee.[2]

History shows that NEPA failed to get the extensive human trials it wanted in the post-1947 era, amid controversies that surfaced in part, at least, as a result of the Nuremberg trials. However, equally controversial research that has a bearing on the material contained within these pages *was* undertaken by other agencies.

Much of what is known about this highly controversial research comes from the work of the Advisory Committee on Human Radiation Experiments (ACHRE), officially appointed by President Bill Clinton on January 15, 1994. ACHRE's purpose was to investigate reports of what might possibly have been unethical medical experimentation conducted on human beings and funded by the government as far back as the mid-1940s and up until the mid-1970s. The members of the advisory committee were fourteen private citizens from around the country: a representative of the general public and thirteen experts in bioethics, radiation oncology and biology, nuclear medicine, epidemiology and biostatistics, public health, the history of science and medicine, and law.

ACHRE sought answers to a number of crucial questions, including: a) How many experiments were conducted or sponsored by the government, and why? b) How many were secret? c) Was anyone—deliberately or otherwise—harmed? d) What was disclosed to those subjected to risk, and what opportunity did they have for consent? e) By what rules should the past be judged? f) What remedies were due those who were wronged or harmed by the government in the past? g) How well do federal rules that govern human experimentation today work? and h) What lessons could be learned from the experiments?

The President directed the Advisory Committee to uncover the history of human radiation experiments during the period 1944 through 1974 for the following reason: it was in 1944 that the first known human radiation experiment was planned in the United States, and it was in 1974 that the Department of Health, Education and Welfare adopted regulations governing the conduct of human research—a watershed event in the history of federal protection for human subjects.

With the assistance of hundreds of federal officials and agency staff, the committee retrieved and reviewed hundreds of thousands of government documents, some of which were secret and were declassified only at the committee's request. Even after this extraordinary effort, the historical record remained incomplete, however, and the committee conceded that "some potentially important collections could not be located and were evidently lost or destroyed years ago."

Nevertheless, the documents that *were* recovered led to the identification of nearly four thousand human radiation experiments sponsored by the federal government between 1944 and 1974. In the great majority of cases, however, only fragmentary data could be located and the identity of subjects and the specific radiation exposures involved were typically unavailable. These case studies included

Experiments with plutonium and other atomic bomb materials

The Atomic Energy Commission's program of radioisotope distribution

Nontherapeutic research on children

Total body irradiation

    Research on prisoners
    Human experimentation in connection with nuclear
       weapons testing
    Intentional environmental releases of radiation
    Observational research involving uranium miners and
       residents of the Marshall Islands.

The experiments, the committee explained, were conducted to advance biomedical science; some experiments were conducted to advance national interests in defense or space exploration; and some experiments served both biomedical and defense or space exploration purposes. Interestingly, as the committee noted, "in the great majority of these cases only fragmentary data are available."

Although the Atomic Energy Commission, the Defense Department, and the National Institutes of Health recognized at an early date that research should proceed only with the consent of the human subject, the committee found little evidence of rules or practices of consent except in research with completely healthy subjects. For example, it was commonplace during the 1940s and 1950s for physicians to use patients as subjects of research without their awareness or consent.

Government officials and investigators, stated the committee "are blameworthy for not having had policies and practices in place to protect the rights and interests of human subjects who were used in research from which the subjects could not possibly derive direct medical benefit."

And the committee also noted, "Information about human experiments was kept secret out of concern for embarrassment to the government, potential legal liability, and worry that public misunderstanding would jeopardize government programs. . . . [T]here is no evidence that issues of fairness or concerns about exploitation in the selection of subjects figured in . . . policies or rules of the period."

Similarly, with regard to the Nuremberg episode, the committee concluded:

It would be historically irresponsible to rely solely on records related directly to the Nuremberg Medical Trial in evaluating the postwar scene in American medical research. The panorama of American thought and practice in human experimentation was considerably more. . . . In general, it does seem that most American medical scientists probably sought to approximate the practices suggested in the Nuremberg Code and the AMA principles when working with "healthy volunteers." Indeed, a subtle, yet pervasive, indication of the recognition during this period that consent should be obtained from healthy subjects was the widespread use of the term *volunteer* to describe such research participants. Yet, as Advisory Committee member Susan Lederer has recently pointed out, the use of the word *volunteer* cannot always be taken as an indication that researchers intended to use subjects who had knowingly and freely agreed to participate in an experiment; it seems that researchers sometimes used *volunteer* as a synonym for *research subject*, with no special meaning intended regarding the decision of the participants to join in an experiment.

In the late 1940s American medical researchers seldom recognized that research with patient-subjects ought to follow the same principles as those applied to healthy subjects. Yet . . . some of those few who asked themselves hard questions about their research work with patients concluded that people who are ill are entitled to the same consideration as those who are not. That some did in fact reach this conclusion is evidence that it was not beyond the horizon of moral insight at that time. Nevertheless, they were a minority of the community of physician researchers, and the organized medical profession did not exhibit a willingness to reconsider its responsibilities to patients in the burgeoning world of postwar clinical research.[3]

But for perhaps the most shocking example of the way in which we know that human beings *were* indeed utilized for radiation-related experiments at the height of the Cold War, we have to turn our attention to Project Sunshine. Although not directly allied with the events at White Sands, the history and activities of Project Sunshine serve as perfect examples (and, perhaps far more important, as *documented* examples) of the way in which human beings were utilized in Cold War radiation and biological experimentation in a fashion very similar to the top-secret Roswell-related events described in this book.

The Advisory Committee on Human Radiation Experiments looked into a whole range of Department of Energy-related scandals involving the use of human beings in radiation tests from the 1940s to the 1970s. One memorandum, dated June 9, 1995, and prepared by ACHRE's Advisory Committee Staff, is titled "Documentary Update on Project Sunshine 'Body Snatching'":

. . . As part of Project Sunshine, which sought to measure strontium-90, the AEC [Atomic Energy Commission] engaged in an effort to collect baby bones from domestic and foreign sources. As discussed in the prior memorandum, the project involved the use of a cover story (those without clearance being told that the skeleton collection would be used to study naturally occurring radiation, and not that from fallout). Key participants in Project Sunshine at its onset included the AEC's Division of Biology and Medicine (DBM), its Director John Bugher, Columbia University's Dr. J. Laurence Kulp, and the University of Chicago's Dr. Willard Libby (who became an AEC Commissioner).

The memorandum then refers to Dr. Willard Libby and his work in more detail:

A 1955 transcript classified as "secret" (located in the classified materials at the National Archives and recently declassified at the Committee's request), sheds more light on the role of tissue sampling in Project Sunshine. The transcript shows that considerable thought had been devoted to best ways to establish channels to procure "human samples," and the impact of secrecy on the effort. AEC Commissioner Willard Libby, who was a primary proponent of Project Sunshine, explained the great value of "body snatching," and noted that the AEC had even employed an "expensive law firm" to "look up the law of body snatching. . . ."

The meeting was then turned over to Dr. Libby, who was now an AEC Commissioner. Dr. Libby began by stating that there was no effort more important to the AEC than Sunshine. However, "[t]here are great gaps in the data." He explained that: "By far the most important [gap] is human samples. We have been reduced to essentially zero level on the human samples. I don't know how to get them but I do say that it is a matter of prime importance to get them and particularly in the young age group."

The supply of stillborns had evidently been shut off: "We were fortunate, as you know to obtain a large number of stillborns as material. This supply, however, has now been cut off also, and shows no signs, I think, of being rejuvenated."

Therefore, Libby told the audience, expertise in "body snatching" would be highly valued: "So human samples are of prime importance and if anybody knows how to do a good job of body snatching, they will really be serving their country."

Libby recalled that when Project Sunshine was created in 1953, a law firm was hired to study this problem: "I don't know how to snatch bodies. In the original study on the Sunshine at Rand [The Rand Corporation] in the summer of 1953, we hired an expensive law firm to look up the law of body snatching. This compendium is available to you. It is not very encouraging. It shows you how very difficult it is going to be to do legally. . . ."

The conferees discussed the need for a wide enough variety

of samples to cover age ranges and potential variations among body parts. Dr. Kulp, from Columbia, explained that there were "channels": "We have the channels in these places where we are getting everything. We have three or four other leads where we could get complete age range samples from different other geographic localities. These three are Vancouver, Houston, and New York. We could easily get them from Puerto Rico and other places. We can get virtually everyone that dies in this range. . . ."

Finally, there was discussion of the need for resources from other countries. Colonel Maxwell of the Armed Forces Special Weapons Project suggested the Armed Services could provide some help for specimens of the local population. The possibilities included Germany, a native hospital in Formosa and the Navy unit in Cairo.[4]

This passage is particularly revealing for one reason: when I spoke to the Colonel, he firmly asserted that personnel from the Armed Forces Special Weapons Project were deeply involved in the recovery of the handicapped Japanese bodies from the May 1947 incident at White Sands. It is therefore notable that in 1955, when the Project Sunshine discussions were well under way, one Colonel Maxwell, also of the Armed Forces Special Weapons Project, stated firmly that he knew how to acquire certain "specimens" from "a native hospital in Formosa. . . ."

Interestingly, when this testimony became public knowledge, new sources surfaced with their own dark and disturbing tales—all of which centered upon radiation experiments involving the bodies of children and physically handicapped and deformed individuals. For example, on June 6, 2001, Reuters, in a news release titled "Babies and Stillborns Used in Nuclear Experiments," revealed:

British newspapers reported that some 6,000 stillborn babies and dead infants were sent from hospitals in Australia,

Canada, Hong Kong, South America, the UK and the US between the 1950s and 1970s without the permission of parents for use in nuclear experiments. According to the reports, the US Department of Energy used the bodies and some body parts for tests to monitor radioactivity levels of the element Strontium 90 in humans. . . .

. . . The <u>Observer,</u> a British newspaper, also stated that British scientists also conducted tests on babies sent from Hong Kong and the research did not end until the 1970s. A government spokesman for Hong Kong announced that his country will investigate further into the reports.[5]

Then on June 12, 2001, Western Australia Newspapers Ltd. (WAN) revealed that "people with severe disabilities were used as human guinea pigs during British nuclear tests at the Maralinga Test Site in Australia in the 1950s. According to the allegations, a control group was flown to the British test site as part of an experiment to determine the effects of radiation on humans. The group died after being exposed to the radioactive fallout." While such claims were dismissed as unsubstantiated in a final report of a royal commission into British nuclear tests in Australia in December 1985, no less a source than Dr. Robert Jackson, director of the Center for Disability Research and Development at Edith Cowan University in Australia, expressed concern that the royal commission did not hear testimonials from pilots.

Dr. Jackson first discovered details of these gruesome events in the 1980s when he was the regional director for the Western Australia Disability Commission. Of key relevance to the subject matter of this book is an approach made to Dr. Jackson by a man who claimed to be a pilot and who had flown a "planeload" of disabled people from the UK to the Maralinga Test Site. The pilot told Dr. Jackson, "We didn't fly them out again."[6]

This documentation is of profound importance to the whistleblower testimony presented in this book. First, it confirms that in the late 1940s and early to mid-1950s research *was* undertaken to determine how live subjects might react in a nuclear aircraft situation. Second, it confirms that bodies were indeed "snatched" for radiation experiments. And finally, there is the testimony offered to Dr. Robert Jackson, director of the Center for Disability Research and Development at Edith Cowan University in Australia, that at least some of these test subjects displayed evidence of severe physical handicaps.

The truth of this dark affair was kept secret—hidden behind a thick curtain of bizarre crashed UFO rumors.

FOURTEEN

THE CRASHED UFOS THAT NEVER WERE

Crashed UFO stories have played a key role in hiding deep dark government secrets for half a century. The first example may be found not in the archives of America's intelligence community, but within the pages of an obscure novel that hit the bookshelves just eleven months after the Roswell Incident.

Published in Britain in June 1948, Bernard Newman's book *The Flying Saucer* was the first in the world to deal with the emotive topic of crashed flying saucers. A prolific author, Newman (who died in 1968) wrote more than a hundred books on subjects ranging from real-life espionage to global politics and current affairs. It was his foray into the world of crashed UFOs that was perhaps most notable, however. *The Flying Saucer* tells the tale of an elite group of scientists that decide to "stage" a series of faked flying saucer crashes, with the express purpose of attempting to unite the world against a deadly foe that, in reality, does not exist.

It would appear that Newman's novel was prompted by a speech made by former British prime minister Sir Anthony Eden, who in 1947 said: "It seems to be an unfortunate fact that the nations of the world were only really united when they were facing a common menace. What we really needed was an attack from Mars."

The Flying Saucer begins with a series of worldwide "UFO crashes" involving distinctly terrestrial vehicles secretly built for this specific task, the first in England, the second in New Mexico, and the third in Russia. The "crash sites" are carefully chosen and involve the three major powers that emerged from the carnage of World War II. But the work of the scientists has only just begun. Not content with creating its bogus UFO crashes, the team takes things one step further and constructs a faked "alien body," created from the remains of exotic animals, which is pulverized in one of the crashes and is then presented to the world's scientific community as evidence of the alien origin of the creatures that pilot the craft.

As a result of these events and with remarkable speed, the many and varied differences between the governments of the earth dissolve under the "Martian" threat, and the final chapter of Newman's book sees practically every international political problem hastily resolved.

Newman's book could be dismissed as little more than fantasy, if not for evidence that suggests otherwise. His undemanding civil service job in the Ministry of Works may have been a cover for some other activity. "Somehow he seemed able to take extremely long and, for those days, exceedingly adventurous holidays, including lengthy stays in Eastern Europe and Russia," noted researcher Philip Taylor in the November 1997 issue of *Magonia* magazine with reference to Newman's unrevealing autobiography, *Speaking From Memory.* "His destinations invariably seemed to include areas of particular political interest: for example several extended holidays to Germany in the 1930's."

Taylor also notes that Newman claimed to have prepared a report on the German rocket site at Peenemünde in 1938, which he sent to the British Foreign Office. And adding yet more mystery to the story is an article published in the *New York Times* in 1945 that describes Newman as having spent most of the First World War acting as a double agent in the German intelligence service. While New-man was indeed fluent in German, the idea of a then eighteen-year-old "boy spy" operating within the German forces and influencing senior officers stretches credulity to the breaking point, states Taylor, adding that "an addendum to Newman's obituary in the [London] *Times* contains a reference to the alleged episode that relegates it to the realm of fiction."

While that may be the case, what we have here, albeit in a fictional format, is a top-secret project that utilizes the crashed UFO scenario as a cover story for other purposes. It does seem unlikely that Bernard Newman could have been operating on mainland Europe as a "double agent" in German intelligence; and yet, the ever-present rumors that Newman had high-level links with the British government should not be ignored. Did Newman learn of the plans to make use of the crashed UFO subject as a tool of psychological warfare and subsequently pen his own novel around this planned operation? Or, incredibly, did Newman's story galvanize American intelligence to follow a similar path? There seems to be no clear answer. We can be certain of one thing, however: less than a year after the events at Roswell, an author who had numerous high-level, official connections and who had written extensively on espionage issues, wrote a book that specifically linked the worlds of crashed UFOs, bogus flying saucer tales promoted by officials, and psychological warfare.[1]

Moving from the realm of fiction to that of nonfiction, the story stays essentially the same. It's worth noting, for instance, that one of the "Recommendations" of a Technical Report prepared by the Air Force's flying saucer study, Project Grudge, in August 1949, states: "That Psychological Warfare Division and other governmental agencies interested in psychological warfare be informed of the results of this study."[2]

The Department of Defense's official definition of "psychological warfare" is: "The planned use of propaganda and other psychological actions having the primary purpose of influencing the opinions, emotions, attitudes, and behavior of hostile foreign groups in such a way as to support the achievement of national objectives."[3]

Of course, "influencing the opinions" of people (whether Soviet or otherwise) who were snooping into the stories of strange bodies and unusual aircraft found in the New Mexico desert in 1947 would have been of paramount importance to those tasked with hiding the truth. And it *was* indeed during this particular time frame that a host of crashed UFO accounts began to surface—a number of which show clear signs of official creation and dissemination.

Both Bill Salter and Al Barker have stated unequivocally that in the early 1950s the government's Psychological Strategy Board (PSB) and the Army's Psychological Warfare Branch (PWB) spread spurious UFO tales (including crashed UFO accounts) to the Soviets in an effort to mask the true nature of the events in New Mexico. Of course, if the PSB and the PWB *were* involved in the creation and dissemination of bogus, crashed UFO stories in the early 1950s, then one would expect to see some evidence of this—however scant or fragmentary. And if one digs deep enough, one does indeed find it. A 1952 document from then CIA director Walter B. Smith to the director of the Psychological Strategy Board titled "Flying Saucers" states:

"I am today transmitting to the National Security Council a proposal in which it is concluded that the problems connected with unidentified flying objects appear to have implications for psychological warfare as well as for intelligence and operations. I suggest that we discuss at an early board meeting the possible offensive or defensive utilization of these phenomena for psychological warfare purposes."

According to Gerald Haines, historian for the National Security Agency and the CIA, in the early 1950s, "The CIA . . . searched the Soviet press for UFO reports, but found none, causing the group to conclude that the absence of reports had to have been the result of deliberate Soviet government policy. *The group also envisioned the USSR's possible use of UFOs as a psychological warfare tool.* [My italics.] In addition, they worried that, if the US air warning system should be deliberately overloaded by UFO sightings, the Soviets might gain a surprise advantage in any nuclear attack. Because of the tense Cold War situation and increased Soviet capabilities, the CIA Study Group saw serious national security concerns in the flying saucer situation. The group believed that the Soviets could use UFO reports to touch off mass hysteria and panic in the United States. The group also believed that the Soviets might use UFO sightings to overload the US air warning system so that it could not distinguish real targets from phantom UFOs."

Significantly, the CIA Study Group "did find that continued emphasis on UFO reporting might threaten 'the orderly functioning' of the government by clogging the channels of communication with irrelevant reports and by inducing 'hysterical mass behavior' harmful to constituted authority. The panel also worried that potential enemies contemplating an attack on the United States might exploit the UFO phenomena and use them to disrupt US air defenses."

This, in essence, is the CIA's official stance with respect to the UFO puzzle. The CIA was most concerned about the way in which the Soviets might exploit the UFO subject as a tool of psychological warfare and spread bogus UFO accounts to clog intelligence channels.[4]

In other words, it was not UFOs per se that particularly interested or alarmed the CIA, but the way in which the subject itself could be manipulated for other, more novel purposes. And, as we shall now see, it was during these formative years that the American intelligence community began to realize how it, too, might make use of the UFO mystery to further muddy the waters concerning the incidents in New Mexico in 1947. And so it was that in the same time period that CIA director Walter B. Smith recommended the manipulation of the UFO subject for psychological warfare purposes, three bogus crashed UFO tales surfaced—all of which bore the hallmarks of official involvement, both in their creation and dissemination.

Next to the so-called Roswell Incident of July 1947, certainly the most-talked-about "UFO crash" of all is that which is alleged to have occurred in the vicinity of Aztec, New Mexico, in 1948. According to information related to author Frank Scully in the late 1940s, and subsequently published in his bestselling 1950 book *Behind the Flying Saucers*, the wreckage of four alien spacecraft, and no fewer than thirty-four alien bodies, had been recovered by American authorities as a result of a number of separate incidents in 1947 and 1948, and were being studied under cover of the utmost secrecy at defense establishments in the United States.

Scully was willing to admit that the bulk of his information had come from two primary sources: Silas Mason Newton, who was described in a 1941 FBI report as a "wholly unethical businessman," and one "Dr. Gee," allegedly the name given to protect eight scientists, all of whom had supposedly divulged various details of the crashes to Newton and Scully. According to Scully's sources, one such UFO was found in Hart Canyon, near the town of Aztec, in March 1948.

After the Aztec saucer had crashed, said Scully, it was found essentially intact by military personnel that gained access to the object via a fractured porthole. Inside they found the bodies of no fewer than sixteen small, humanlike creatures, all slightly charred and undoubtedly dead. The UFO was then dismantled and the bodies of the crew were transferred to Wright Field, Dayton, Ohio, for study.

At the time of its release, Scully's book caused a major sensation. In both 1952 and 1953, however, J. P. Cahn, a reporter who had previously worked for the *San Francisco Chronicle*, authored two detailed exposés, which cast serious doubt on the claims of Newton and "Dr. Gee"—identified not as "eight scientists" but as one Leo Gebauer, who had a background equally as dubious as that of Newton.

Yet, as the years have shown, the Aztec crashed UFO incident re-
fuses to roll over and die—indeed, it has now spawned a whole industry. In 1974, for example, Professor John Spencer Carr revealed
that he had in his possession credible information on the case, including testimony from a senior Air Force officer who was allegedly
involved in the retrieval of the Aztec UFO. Twelve months later,
however, the story was once again demolished, this time by a UFO
researcher and writer named Mike McClellan in a persuasive paper
titled "The UFO Crash of 1948 Is a Hoax." [5]

In view of this exposé, it was something of a surprise when, in
1987, the researcher William Steinman released his own, massive
book on the case, *UFO Crash at Aztec*, which asserted that the incident *did* occur and that Frank Scully's book was in essence factually
correct. And to complicate things still further, following the release
of Steinman's book, *Fate* magazine reported that "[the book] draws
on speculation, rumor, unnamed informants and unbridled para-
noia to defend and elaborate on the original story."

Here we see the major problems with the Aztec story: both Newton and Gebauer were, at best, dubious con men. Scully published
their testimony without question and Steinman made the fatal mistake of largely looking at the affair from the perspective of a believer.
As a result, the whole story remains unresolved—even after more
than half a century. Did a UFO crash to earth in the harsh deserts of
New Mexico? Were the key players in the story all that they appeared to be? Or was the Aztec UFO story part of an officially or-
chestrated operation—coordinated by the military—to hide the
truth about the disturbing and radical experimentation that had occurred at White Sands, Los Alamos, and Oak Ridge in the mid to
late 1940s, as the Colonel, Al Barker, Bill Salter, and the Black
Widow have suggested?

While official documentation pertaining to the events at Roswell is
practically nonexistent, not so with Aztec, which supposedly occurred
nearly twelve months later. Frank Scully's mysterious "Dr. Gee," Leo
Arnold Julius Gebauer, is the subject of an FBI file that totals no fewer

than 398 pages, of which fewer than 200 pages have been declassified under the provisions of the Freedom of Information Act.

The available papers amply demonstrate that Gebauer was a colorful character. He had numerous aliases, including Harry A. Grebauer, Harry A. Gebauer, Harry A. Greybauer, Harry A. Barbar, Leo A. J. Gebauer, Leo Arnold Julius Gebauer, and Arnold Julius Leopold Gebauer. And as a confidential FBI report of December 19, 1941, states, Gebauer had made some disturbing statements some seven months previously: "What this country needs is a man like Hitler; then everybody would have a good job. . . . It would be a God's blessing if we had two men in the United States to run this country like Hitler. The English people are nothing but a dirty bunch of rats. We should stay to home and tend to our own damn business and let Germany give England what they had coming."

Silas Mason Newton, Frank Scully's main source for the Aztec crashed UFO story, attracted his own share of controversy. An FBI document from 1970 reveals: "Silas Newton, presently under indictment [in] Los Angeles, California, for fraud, returned to [the] Silver City, New Mexico, area January 1970, and began to organize what appears as a mining swindle." And even today, the Aztec story continues to perplex and intrigue. A fascinating piece of documentary evidence relative to the Aztec case surfaced in the late 1990s, thanks to investigative author and former CIA employee Karl Pflock—and it is one that may ultimately shed more light on the psychological warfare angle of the crashed UFO mystery:

In 1998, under curious circumstances, I was made privy to a fascinating document about one of the most controversial cases of the Golden Age of Flying Saucers, the so-called Aztec crash of 1948. I had little more than passing interest in the case until 1998, when a source, who insists on complete anonymity, showed me a handwritten testament, set down by the key player in this amazing, often amusing, truth-is-stranger-than-fiction episode.

[I]t seems that what I was shown was . . . something penned by sly old Silas Newton, but what can we say about the veracity of its content? After the *Denver Post* revealed he was Scientist X, Newton received two visitors at his Newton Oil Company office in Denver. These men claimed to be with a highly secret U.S. Government entity, which they refused to name. Were they Air Force OSI agents, who Newton hyped into something more mysterious? Newton writes, "They grilled me, tried to poke holes in my story. Had no trouble doing it and laughed in my face about the scientific mistakes I made. They never said so, but I could tell they were trying to find out if I *really* knew anything about flying saucers that had landed. Did not take those fellows long to decide I did not. But I sure knew *they* did."

Pflock expands further and the tale becomes decidedly intriguing: "Newton's visitors told him they knew he was pulling a scam and then gave him what may have been the surprise of his life. 'Those fellows said they wanted me to keep it up, keep telling the flying saucer story and that they and the people they worked for would look out for me and for Leo. I could just go on doing what I always did and not worry about it.'"

Pflock asks: "Did the U.S. Government or someone associated with it use Newton to discredit the idea of crashed flying saucers so a real captured saucer or saucers could be more easily kept under wraps? *Was this actually nothing to do with real saucers but instead some sort of psychological warfare operation?*" [My italics.][6]

The key figures in this puzzling and bizarre story (Silas Newton, Frank Scully, and Leo Gebauer) are all long dead, but their legacy ensures that whatever did—or, indeed, did *not*—occur at Hart Canyon in March 1948, the legend of the little, dead aliens of Aztec, New Mexico, continues to live on, much to the satisfaction of the government, one strongly suspects. And the tales of spurious crashed UFO tales concocted out of (or, at least, promoted by) the fertile imagination of the American intelligence community do not end there. Indeed, there is good evidence that other tales of crashed UFOs have a similar origin.

Much of the disinformation that surrounds the Roswell puzzle can be traced back to the early 1950s and one Robert Alexis McClure, according to the Colonel and Al Barker. The Colonel asserts that McClure played a part in the U.S. Army's Operation Klondike — one of the few operations where it's been uncovered and confirmed that a crashed UFO story was used as a cover for other activities. Following the collapse of Nazi Germany, several of Hungary's national treasures, including the fabled Crown of St. Stephen, were handed over to the United States military for safekeeping. They were duly delivered (in the early 1950s) to Fort Knox in an elaborate operation codenamed Klondike. The treasure was eventually returned to Hungary in 1978. This would be just another story of political intrigue were it not for one strange fact: according to a memorandum in the State Department, the soldiers designated to guard the treasure were told that the boxes contained "the wings and engine of a flying saucer."

This type of misinformation may well have been common. "Is it effective?" asks researcher William Moore. "Certainly in the Klondike situation it was, because unsubstantiated stories about parts of a flying saucer being stored at Fort Knox continue to be part of the UFO crash/retrieval rumor mill to this very day. How many other similar rumors have a similar origin is anybody's guess."[7]

Also according to the Colonel, in the early 1960s, a Soviet spy known to be operating in Washington, D.C., was suspected of having received classified data from someone allied with the U.S. Army's Foreign Technology Division (FTD). A plan was hatched to reveal some very specific but bogus information to the traitor that could be easily traced to the Soviet contact when it was passed on — thus identifying the traitor as well.

The concocted story, states the Colonel, was that in 1961, the FTD had got its hands on a quantity of strange, metallic debris from a crashed UFO that was being analyzed under cover of the strictest security. This story was duly and carefully leaked to the suspected Soviet sympathizer, and apparently the ruse worked: the traitor passed on the information to his Russian handler and arrests were quickly and quietly made without any real secrets having been compromised. Interestingly, the Colonel states that as with the Operation Klondike and Fort Knox stories, this led to rumors among officials that the Army's FTD had gotten its hands on crashed UFO materials.[8]

Perhaps of relevance to this incident is the 1997 publication of one of the most controversial UFO books of all time: *The Day After Roswell*, cowritten by William J. Birnes and Lt. Col. Philip J. Corso, who was a prime mover in the Army's Foreign Technology Division in the early 1960s. Corso claimed that while he was with the FTD he had hands-on access to recovered debris from the Roswell crash of 1947—debris that Corso asserted until his dying day was extraterrestrial in origin. The Colonel believes that, wittingly or unwittingly, Corso's story can be traced back to the ruse laid down to smoke out the Soviets' informant.

The Colonel states that, in reality, the odd metal material that the FTD obtained and utilized in its operation was nitinol. In 1961, nitinol, which stands for Nickel Titanium Naval Ordnance Laboratory, was discovered to possess the unique property of having shape memory (returning to its original shape when heated), which a number of individuals claimed the recovered materials on the Brazel ranch possessed.

The Colonel states that shortly afterward a supply of nitinol was presented to the FTD to begin smoking out the Soviet source with a crashed UFO story. How this all relates to the Corso story is not fully clear, but it is an intriguing slant on the whole controversy, and it should be noted that it was during this precise time period in which nitinol came to the fore, 1961 to 1962, that Corso served with the FTD.[9]

There is one other aspect of Corso's story that is worthy of comment. Despite the fact that Corso was a champion of the notion that an alien spacecraft crashed at Roswell, even he conceded that the object was not of a typical flying saucer design, but instead bore an uncanny similarity to some of the designs of the Horten brothers. "At the very last," Corso stated, "[General Nathan] Twining had suggested, the crescent-shaped craft [recovered at Roswell] looked so uncomfortably like the German Horten wings our flyers had seen at the end of the war that he had to suspect the Germans had bumped into something we didn't know about. And his conversations with Werner [*sic*] von Braun and Willy Ley at Alamogordo in the days after the crash confirmed this. They didn't want to be thought of as *verruckt* [crazy] but intimated that there was a deeper story about what the Germans had engineered. No, the similarity between the Horten wing and the craft they had pulled out of the arroyo was no accident. We always wondered how the Germans were able to incorporate such advanced technology into their weapons development in so short a time and during the Great Depression. Did they have help? Maybe we were now as lucky as the Germans and broke off a piece of this technology for ourselves." [10]

Corso may have stood by the extraterrestrial hypothesis from the time his book *The Day After Roswell* was published in 1997 until his death in 1998, but it is a telling fact that he maintained—in a fashion *very* similar to the testimony that we have already examined— that there *was* a connection between the vehicles recovered in New Mexico in 1947 and the various aircraft designed by the Horten brothers. Were Corso's claims those of an unwitting dupe in a disinformation exercise that began within the Army's Foreign Technology Division in the early 1960s? Or, as the Colonel offers as a possibility, was Corso, as a loyal soldier to the very end, continuing to perpetrate that same operation for reasons that possibly relate to the ongoing and deliberate obfuscation of the true nature of the Roswell events?

For many years, rumors have circulated to the effect that in the early 1950s a UFO crashed on the island of Spitzbergen, Norway, and, under circumstances similar to those that allegedly occurred at both Aztec and Roswell, was recovered along with its deceased alien crew. On March 22, 1968, the State Department forwarded to a host of official bodies within the American intelligence community (including the CIA, the National Security Agency, and Army Intelligence) a translation of a March 12, 1968, news article titled "Flying Saucers? They're a Myth!" that had been written by Viillen Lyustiberg, science editor of the Novosti Press Agency in Russia, that included a small mention of the Spitzbergen allegations. The relevant section of the article stated: "An abandoned silvery disc was found in the deep rock coal seams in Norwegian coal mines on Spitzbergen. It was pierced and marked by micrometeor impacts and bore all traces of having performed a long space voyage. It was sent for analysis to the Pentagon and disappeared there."

The CIA, Army, State Department, and the NSA have all declassified their files pertaining to their apparent interest in Soviet news articles on UFOs in general and the Spitzbergen event in particular. However, the NSA's copy of the document differs significantly from those of its allied agencies. On the NSA's copy, someone had circled the specific section of the article that referred to the Spitzbergen crash with the word "PLANT." This, again, would seem to suggest that this was a faked crashed UFO story, purposefully planted by persons currently unknown but known to the all-powerful National Security Agency.[11]

And spurious UFO stories continue to be spread for psychological warfare purposes. According to testimony from Richard Tomlinson, a former agent with Britain's MI6 (the British equivalent of the CIA): "[D]uring the run-up to the 1992 [United Nations] Secretary General elections, [MI6] mounted a smear operation against the Egyptian candidate, Boutros Boutros-Ghali, who was regarded as dangerously Francophile by the CIA. The CIA are constitutionally prevented from manipulating the press so they asked MI6 to help. Using their contacts in the British and American media, [MI6] planted a series of stories to portray Boutros-Ghali as unbalanced, claiming that he was a believer in the existence of UFOs and extraterrestrial life. The operation was eventually unsuccessful, however, and Boutros-Ghali was elected." [12]

Though unsuccessful, the operation is prime evidence of the way in which spurious UFO data has been spread for psychological warfare purposes. But there is perhaps no better example of the way in which spurious data has been used to confuse the true nature of the Roswell events than the strange saga that began in the early 1980s and involved tales of shadowy informants, supposedly classified documents on crashed alien spacecraft, and the inner sanctuary of an allegedly ultrasecret government project.

FiFTEEN

MAJESTiC

One of the biggest problems surrounding the Roswell case is the almost complete lack of documentation to support the claims that *anything*—Mogul balloon or UFO—crashed or landed there in 1947. Forty years later, however, the situation changed dramatically. In 1987, UFO investigator Timothy Good's bestselling book *Above Top Secret* discussed a document that allegedly originated with a classified research and development group established by the U.S. government in 1947 to deal with the incident at Roswell. It was known variously as Majestic 12 or MJ12.[1]

Classified "Top Secret/Majic Eyes Only," the document can be broken down into two parts: the first is a 1952 briefing prepared by Adm. Roscoe H. Hillenkoetter, the first director of the CIA, for President-elect Eisenhower, informing him that an alien spacecraft was recovered at Roswell and briefing him on the MJ12 group, its activities and membership (which supposedly included Rear Adm. Sidney Souers, the first director of Central Intelligence; Dr. Vannevar Bush, head of the Joint Research and Development Board; and Gen. Nathan Twining, commanding general of Air Materiel Command). The second is a 1947 memorandum from President

Harry Truman to Secretary of Defense James Forrestal, authorizing the establishment of MJ12.[2]

Shortly after Timothy Good published copies of the MJ12 documents in May 1987, additional copies surfaced, this time in the United States, having been released by the research team of William Moore, Stanton Friedman, and television producer Jaime Shandera. Moore had been working quietly with a number of intelligence "insiders" who had contacted him in the wake of the publication of the 1980 book he coauthored with Charles Berlitz, *The Roswell Incident,* and from time to time Moore would receive, under distinctly cloak-and-dagger circumstances, official-looking papers from his "Deep Throat"–like sources, the implication being that someone in the government wished to make available to the UFO research community material—including pro-UFO data on Roswell—that would otherwise have remained forever outside of the public domain.[3]

Needless to say, controversy raged with regard to the nature of the documents and the circumstances under which they surfaced. Some favored the idea that they were official documents, secretly leaked by insider sources connected to the intelligence community. Others cried "Hoax!" amid dark murmurings that Moore himself was responsible for the creation of the papers, while some suspected that the documentation was government-orchestrated disinformation designed to muddy the already dark waters of Roswell even further.

In the almost twenty years that have now passed since the documents emerged, the MJ12 saga continues to flourish. In the mid to late 1990s, a huge batch of MJ12 documents surfaced from a California investigator named Timothy Cooper, who had been delving deeply into the early years of the government's UFO research and particularly UFO activity in the vicinity of New Mexico's White Sands Proving Ground in the late 1940s. Amounting to hundreds of pages, the official-looking papers—purportedly leaked to Cooper by government insiders—once more reinforced the idea that an alien spacecraft had crashed near Roswell and that a supersecret organization had been established to deal with the fraught situation.

Some suspected Cooper had forged the documents, either for money or for fame, and systematically attacked him, just as they had William Moore. And after years of such attacks, Cooper, like Moore in 1989, dropped out of UFO research, sold his files and vanished back into the shadows.[4] The MJ12 controversy, however, continues to flourish: during the course of my interviews with the Colonel, he revealed how, in 1988, he received an enigmatic visit from two FBI agents who were investigating the so-called MJ12 documents. But first some background on just how the FBI became embroiled in the MJ12 affair in the first place.

Howard Blum is an award-winning author and former *New York Times* journalist twice nominated for the Pulitzer prize for investigative reporting. In 1990, Blum's book *Out There* detailed his investigation of U.S. military and governmental involvement in the UFO subject. According to Blum, on June 4, 1987, UFO skeptic Philip J. Klass wrote to William Baker, assistant director at the Office of Congressional and Public Affairs: "I am enclosing what purport to be Top Secret/Eyes Only documents, which have not been properly declassified, now being circulated by William L. Moore, Burbank, California, 91505. . . ."[5] Immediately the FBI swung into action.

According to Jacques Vallee, the UFO author and investigator, and former principal investigator on Department of Defense computer networking projects, the FBI turned away from the MJ12 documents in "disgust" and professed no interest in the matter.[6] But papers and comments made to me by the FBI and the Air Force Office of Special Investigations reflect a totally different scenario. Indeed, the FBI may have launched (or were at least involved in) several MJ12-linked investigations during the late 1980s.

One definitely began in the latter part of 1988. Howard Blum has stated that of those approached by the FBI "in the fall of 1988," one was a "Working Group" established under the auspices of the Defense Intelligence Agency tasked with looking at the UFO subject. In 1990, Blum was interviewed by *UFO* magazine and was asked if the Working Group could have been a "front" for another even more covert investigative body within the government. Blum's response aptly sums up one of the major problems faced by both those inside and outside of government when trying to determine exactly who knows what.

"Interestingly," said Blum, "members of [the Working Group] aired that possibility themselves. When looking into the MJ12 papers, some members of the group said—and not in jest—'Perhaps we're just a front organization for some sort of MJ12. Suppose, in effect, we conclude the MJ12 papers are phony, are counterfeit. Then we've solved the entire mystery for the government, relieving them of the burden in dealing with it, and at the same time, we allow the real secret to remain held by a higher source.' An FBI agent told me there are so many secret levels within the government that even the government isn't aware of it!" [7]

A separate investigation was conducted by the FBI's Counterintelligence Division in the fall of 1988 and operated out of Washington and New York. Some input into the investigation also came from the FBI office in Dallas, Texas, according to Oliver B. Revell, special agent in charge at Dallas FBI. On September 15, 1988, an agent of the Air Force Office of Special Investigations (AFOSI) contacted Dallas FBI and supplied the Bureau with another copy of the MJ12 papers. This set was obtained from a source whose identity, according to documentation released to me by the Bureau, the AFOSI has deemed must remain classified to this day.

On October 25, 1988, the Dallas office transmitted a two-page "Secret Airtel" to headquarters that read:

Enclosed for the Bureau is an envelope which contains a possible classified document. Dallas notes that within the last six weeks, there has been local publicity regarding "OPERATION

MAJESTIC-12" with at least two appearances on a local radio talk show, discussing the MAJESTIC-12 OPERATION, the individuals involved, and the Government's attempt to keep it all secret. It is unknown if this is all part of a publicity campaign. [Censored] from OSI, advises that "OPERATION BLUE BOOK," mentioned in the document on page 4 did exist. Dallas realizes that the purported document is over 35 years old, but does not know if it has been properly declassified. The Bureau is requested to discern if the document is still classified. Dallas will hold any investigation in abeyance until further direction from FBIHQ.

Partly as a result of the actions of the Dallas FBI Office and partly as a result of the investigation undertaken by the FBI's Counterintelligence Division people, on November 30, 1988, a meeting took place in Washington, D.C., between agents of the Bureau and those of AFOSI. If the AFOSI had information on MJ12, said the Bureau, they would like to know.

A memo back to the Dallas office from Washington on December 2, 1988, read: "This communication is classified Secret in its entirety. Reference Dallas Airtel dated October 25 1988. Reference Airtel requested that FBIHQ determine if the document enclosed by referenced Airtel was classified or not. The Office of Special Investigations, US Air Force, advised on November 30, 1988, that the document was fabricated. Copies of that document have been distributed to various parts of the United States. The document is completely bogus. Dallas is to close captioned investigation."

That response would seem to lay matters to rest once and for all. Unfortunately, it does not. There can be no dispute that the Air Force has played quite a strange game with respect to MJ12. The FBI was assured by AFOSI that the MJ12 papers were a "fabricated hoax" and were not leaked, official documents. However, Special Agent Frank Batten Jr., chief of the Information Release Division at the Investigative Operations Center with the USAF, admitted to me on April 30, 1993, that AFOSI is not now maintaining (nor ever has maintained) any records pertaining to either MJ12, or any investigation thereof. This begs an important question. How was AFOSI able to determine that the papers were faked if no investigation on their part was undertaken? Batten has also advised me that while AFOSI did "discuss" the MJ12 documents with the FBI, they made absolutely no written reference to that November 1988 meeting in any shape or form. This is most odd, as government and military agencies are methodical when it comes to documenting possible breaches of security.

Similarly, Richard L. Weaver, formerly the deputy for security and investigative programs with the U.S. Air Force and the author of the U.S. Air Force's 1995 report *The Roswell Report: Fact vs. Fiction in the New Mexico Desert*, advised me on October 12, 1993, that "The Air Force considers the MJ12 (both the group described and the purported documents) to be bogus." Weaver also conceded, however, that there were "no documents responsive" to my request for Air Force files on how just such a determination was reached. Stanton Friedman has also stated that, based on his correspondence with Weaver on the issue of MJ12, he, too, is dissatisfied with the responses he received after filing similar Freedom of Information Act (FOIA) requests relating to the way in which the Air Force made its "bogus" determination.

Moreover, there is the fact that AFOSI informed the FBI that "copies of that document have been distributed to various parts of the United States." To make such a statement AFOSI simply must have conducted some form of investigation or have been in receipt of data from yet another agency with knowledge of the affair.

If the Bureau learned anything more about MJ12 in the post-1989 period, then that information has not surfaced under the terms of the FOIA. Perhaps the Bureau, unable to get satisfactory answers from the military and the intelligence community, simply gave up the chase. Thanks to Richard L. Huff, Bureau codirector within the Office of Information and Privacy, we know that MJ12 remains the subject of an FBI headquarters main file that is titled "Espionage." Today, that file is in "closed status." But why would the MJ12 documents be linked with a FBI HQ main file titled "Espionage?"

An answer to that question comes from the FBI's Counterintelligence Division. In the wake of the publication of my book *The FBI Files: The FBI's UFO Top Secrets Exposed,* I was contacted by a man who served with the FBI when it was investigating MJ12 and had knowledge of the official interest shown in the documents. This man told me that the FBI had actually been aware of the intricacies of the MJ12 saga for two years or so before Timothy Good published the documents in *Above Top Secret.* However, I was advised, the investigation was intensified after the documents were publicized in the United States.

I was also told that initially there was a fear on the part of the Air Force and the FBI's counterintelligence people that the MJ12 papers had been fabricated by Soviet intelligence personnel who intended using them as "bait." That bait was to be used on American citizens who had a personal interest in UFOs but who were also working on sensitive defense-related projects— including the stealth fighter. The Soviets hoped—or so the FBI and AFOSI suspected—that by offering the MJ12 papers to those targeted sources within the American defense industry, the Soviets would receive something of value of a defense nature in return. The man was unsure precisely how the investigation concluded. He did know, however, that no charges were brought against anyone.

This is an ingenious scenario, but my source stressed that the Soviet theory was simply that—a theory and nothing more. It's worth noting, however, that Gerald Haines, historian of the National Reconnaissance Office, made a similar comment in his controversial paper "CIA's Role in the Study of UFOs 1947–1990." In a section of the report dealing specifically with CIA involvement in UFO investigations in the 1980s, Haines commented that "Agency analysts from the Life Science Division of OSI and OSWR officially devoted a small amount of their time to issues relating to UFOs. These included counterintelligence concerns that the Soviets and the KGB were using U.S. citizens and UFO groups to obtain information on sensitive U.S. weapons development programs (such as the Stealth aircraft)."[8]

But my source went on to say that this "Soviet theory" was only one of several avenues being actively pursued by the FBI at the time—including, interestingly enough, the possibility that the MJ12 documents had been created as disinformation by the U.S. government to hide the facts concerning secret "human experiments" undertaken by the military in the immediate postwar period.

There is further evidence, too, that the FBI has in its archives more information pertaining to MJ12 than has surfaced thus far in the public domain. On November 16, 1988, UFO researcher Larry Bryant wrote to Hope Nakamura of the Center for National Security Studies and advised her of William Moore's efforts to secure the release of his FBI file. The bulk of the FBI's dossier on Moore, which amounted to no fewer than fifty-five pages at the time, was being withheld for reasons directly affecting the national security of the United States of America.

Bryant went on to explain that Moore was attempting to find legal assistance in challenging the nondisclosure of the majority of the FBI's file. In a determined effort to assist Moore, Bryant drafted a lengthy and detailed advertisement that he proposed submitting to a number of military newspapers for future publication. Titled "UFO SECRECY/CONGRESS-WATCH," the ad specifically addressed the eye-opening fact that the Bureau's file on Moore was classified as secret and that at least one other (unnamed) U.S. government agency was also keeping tabs on Moore and his UFO pursuits. In particular, those pursuits related to certain "whistle-blower testimony" which Moore had acquired from a variety of sources within the American military and government. Bryant signed off urging those reading the advertisement to contact their local congressperson and to press for nothing less than a full-scale inquiry into the issue of UFOs.

Bryant's advertisement was ultimately published in the November 23, 1988, issue of *The Pentagram*, a publication of the Army. Yet, as spirited as it was, it failed to force the FBI to relinquish its files on Moore. By 1993, the FBI's dossier on Moore ran to sixty-one pages, of which Moore had succeeded in gaining access to a mere six.[9]

Mindful of the FBI's surveillance of William Moore, Bryant in 1989 attempted to force the Bureau to release any or all records on Stanton Friedman. Bryant's efforts on Friedman's behalf came after Friedman had filed FOIA requests with both the Bureau and the CIA. The response from the CIA was that it had no responsive files—except for a "negative" name check from the FBI, who subsequently refused to reveal details of either the size of the file or its security classification. On August 2, 1989, Bryant received the following response from the FBI's Richard L. Huff: "Mr. Friedman is the subject of one Headquarters main file. This file is classified in its entirety and I am affirming the denial of access to it."

So on August 28, 1989, Bryant filed suit in the District Court for the Eastern District of Columbia. "My complaint," explained Bryant, "seeks full disclosure of the UFO-related content of the FBI dossier on Stan Friedman. Neither Stan not I have been able to convince the U.S. Federal Bureau of Investigation to loosen its grasp on that dossier, which Bureau officials assert bears a security classification." Fortunately, in Friedman's case, a "small portion" of his FBI's file was eventually released on November 13, 1989, as a result of Bryant's actions. The remainder of his FBI file has never surfaced, however.

What are we to make of this situation? Consider the following. The FBI conducted several investigations of MJ12 (via its Dallas Office, its headquarters at Washington, D.C., and its Counterintelligence Division). It had close liaison with the Air Force Office of

Special Investigations on an MJ12-related operation that may also have involved the CIA in an attempt to crack either a) a Soviet intelligence operation that may or may not have existed or b) as numerous sources cited thus far have claimed, a domestic disinformation operation designed to act as a smoke screen behind which certain "human experiments" could be hidden.

Whether or not the FBI was ever fully satisfied by its investigations into MJ12 or what it was told by the AFOSI is debatable. But one thing is certain. "All we're finding out is that the government doesn't know what it knows," an FBI source told Howard Blum. "There are too many secret levels." [10]

Now we can return to the Colonel's links to the FBI-MJ12 controversy. "Back in 1988," he told me, "just after the MJ12 controversy kicked off, I get a knock on the door from the FBI, at home on a Friday night. Two guys, early forties, clean-cut, typical Bureau. They identify themselves and say they are looking into the [MJ12] documents and speaking with everyone: NSA, the Company, DIA—even some of their own people. They're trying to understand what these papers are. Are they classified documents that have been compromised, if you will? Are they someone's private joke or is it a disinformation game: the Russians or even us, maybe? Well, they say to me they think I know something of this based on, as they say, 'files you read at DIA that one of your friends on the Hill told us about.' Do I know anything about it? Well, I tell them I don't know a damned thing about any MJ12 documents—which is true. Now, I followed the Roswell story after *The Roswell Incident* [was published] and I bought the magazines and all the books and got into it all pretty deep because of what I knew from back in 1969, so I know what MJ12 was supposed to be, the allegations. But not through official channels, though—just magazines and the UFO books, right?

"I say to the Bureau boys, 'Wait a minute. Are you saying you're investigating Roswell?' They say: 'No. We're just looking into the

MJ12 files. This is a specific investigation. All we want to know is are the documents genuine or not, and if they are, who put them out there.'

"This kind of puzzles me because that suggested there were areas they weren't wanting to pursue that might have opened doors. Well, I tell them, 'Okay. I can't help you with MJ12 but I can help with Roswell, which is the crux of the documents anyway.' They then say something like: 'Don't worry about it. We're categorically not looking into Roswell. If we need to speak to you again, we'll call.' They say thank you very much and I guess go on their way and knocking on the next door in Washington.

"Now, I never heard from them again, but I would have [spoken with them again] if they had asked. And I never do find out who from the Hill sold me out to them or why." [11]

Although Al Barker is loath to go into too much detail lest doing so "identifies players that I don't want identifying," he claims to know the origin of the term "Majestic 12" as it appears in the controversial documents made available by William Moore and Jaime Shandera in the 1980s and the similar material provided in the 1990s by Timothy Cooper. According to Barker, the word *Majestic* was in reality an "inside joke with the intel boys" that was inspired by a newspaper account from 1947 that hit the headlines and that, interestingly, referenced crashed UFOs, Japanese saucers, and even incorporated the word *Majestic* in the account.

As evidence of this, Barker supplied a copy of the following newspaper report from the July 14, 1947, edition of the (Yonkers, N.Y.) *Herald Statesman* newspaper. Titled "Eastchester Style 'Flying Disc' Bears Radio Parts of Jap Make", it reads:

. . . Eastchester came up with its own version of a flying disc on Saturday night, but whether the gadget flew into town under its own power or was placed here by a practical prankster was still being investigated today by Eastchester Police.

On his evening constitutional on Saturday, Lawrence Castellucci of 69 Homestead Avenue, noticed a shiny metal object stuck in the hedge bordering his front lawn. This "what's it" has since been described by various persons as (1) "a cookie can cover," (2) a "pie plate" (3) a "cracker tin cover."

Equipped With Tube

Flying or otherwise, the disc carries on its surface a clutter of mechanical contrivances including a radio tube, a transformer, a condenser and another gadget, which police describe as a "radio speaker unit." If that adds up to a flying machine, Eastchester may have a flying disc.

The disc is about ten inches in diameter and is surrounded by a rim about one inch high. The condenser and the transformer have Japanese markings and are unquestionably of Japanese origin. The radio tube is a "Majestic G-38."

The joker on the contraption is a white label with red trimming on top of the disc. It bears the admonition in English, "Finder, please return to Tokyo Rose, Japan." [12]

According to Barker, the Japanese link to this account caught the attention of those in charge of hiding the White Sands incidents, and there was an initial flurry of major concern that this press report was evidence that the truth was leaking out. Ultimately, however, after a series of frantic phone calls "from the Washington boys," the fact that the newspaper had made a Japanese connection to crashed saucer accounts in the crucial month of July 1947 was determined to be nothing more than a bizarre coincidence based upon the case being a good-natured prank. Nevertheless, states Barker, this incident was never forgotten: nearly forty years later and "with a kind of cruel humor in mind," the word *Majestic* was lifted from the story and employed in the documents that surfaced from Moore, Good, and Cooper as an in-house "cruel, spook joke."

"Intel had one goal and it worked perfectly," said Barker. "The plan was to give the space alien writers something to believe in and use to support their theories and to give their opponents something to fight against. So, while both are fighting [for] years and spending money researching over if these are real files, no one is looking where they should be looking: the human experiments. A wonderful plan that still works today." [13]

SiXTEEN

PROGERiA

The whistle-blowers whose testimony is presented in this book have asserted that the unusual bodies recovered at Roswell and elsewhere in the mid to late 1940s were taken from Unit 731 laboratories in Japan and that at least some of them displayed evidence of conditions such as progeria, Werner's syndrome, and Ellis-van Creveld syndrome. But accounts positing links between strange bodies allegedly recovered from the New Mexico desert in the summer of 1947 that seemed to display symptoms of progeria and Werner's-style syndromes have surfaced on other occasions as well—and in particular with regard to a notorious piece of film footage that was publicized amid a flurry of media interest in 1995 and has come to be known as the Alien Autopsy film.

On January 13, 1995, Reg Presley, lead singer with the British rock band The Troggs, was interviewed on the BBC television show *Good Morning with Anne and Nick*. He disclosed that he had recently viewed a sensational piece of film that purportedly displayed the autopsy of an unusual body recovered from the wreckage of an equally unusual aircraft found near White Sands in the early summer of 1947. Allegedly, a now elderly cameraman who served in the Army Air Forces at the time had filmed it.[1]

In the weeks that followed, when it became clear that the film would receive a public airing, we learned that a man named Ray Santilli, who was described by the London *Daily Mail* newspaper as "an English entrepreneur whose business is making videos," held the footage.

"As a result of research into film material for a music documentary," Santilli later explained, "I was in Cleveland, Ohio, USA in the summer of 1993. [While] there I had identified some old film material taken by Universal News in the summer of 1955. As Universal News no longer existed I needed the film to investigate the source of the film and was able to determine that the film was shot by a then local freelance cameraman. He had been employed by Universal News because of a Film Union strike in the summer of 1955. The cameraman was located, following which a very straightforward negotiation took place for his small piece of film, i.e. cash for three minutes of film. Upon completion of this the cameraman asked if I would be interested in purchasing outright very valuable footage taken during his time in the forces. He explained that the footage in question came from the Roswell crash; that it included debris and recovery footage and, of most importance, autopsy footage."[2]

Since later pronouncements from Ray Santilli contradicted his original account of how he came to acquire the film, he conceded: "I still maintain that the story of the film's acquisition is true. Certain nonrelevant details were only changed to stop people getting to the cameraman."[3] Interestingly, Santilli would assert that the location of the crash site was the Mescalero Reservation, near White Sands.[4]

Nick Pope of the British Ministry of Defense provided additional details about the film. "I'd heard rumors for some time, over a matter of months, I think," he told me, "that there was this film doing the rounds that purported to show an autopsy, or a number of autopsies, from the so-called Roswell crash. I'd had a number of discussions with Philip Mantle [the first researcher and author to view the film during a private screening arranged by Ray Santilli], and I believe it was Philip who invited me to the British premiere at the Museum of London on May 5, 1995.

"I went along not really knowing what to expect, but I suppose with a feeling of excitement that I might be about to witness something important. And I knew that whether it was real or whether it was fake, this was going to be a big story; I certainly had no doubts about that.

"I won't say that I was keeping a low profile at the Museum of London, but I was certainly not advertising my presence. I wasn't, like a number of people, wearing a name badge or going out of my way to speak to the media. Well, I turned up; there was a lectern at the front of the auditorium and there was a kind of expectant atmosphere. I was expecting Ray Santilli, whom I'd heard about but not met, to introduce the film in some way. But to my surprise, and I think to the surprise and disgust of just about everyone there, there was no introduction: the film simply started and then stopped.

"I don't have a particularly strong constitution, and I would say there was a kind of awkward atmosphere. I could smell the sweat and the distaste at one point. Everyone had gone in a lighthearted mood, particularly the journalists. They were thinking: this is a Friday; there's a little bit of a party atmosphere.

"But that mood didn't last long; a rather shocked hush fell over the auditorium. Afterwards, the lights went out and people were expecting an announcement. That announcement didn't come. Now, one or two of the journalists recognized Ray Santilli at the back, and in a fairly aggressive and angry way, they surrounded him and started firing questions. I recall he was almost physically picked up and escorted from the room by his minders or his commercial backers, whoever they were. There were certainly some people there who didn't want him placed in a position where he had to answer the questions that were being fired at him: Where did you get this? Who took it? Can we speak to the cameraman?"

Pope described what he saw in the film. "There was something lying on the autopsy table, and it wasn't human . . . probably around five feet, perhaps a little less. It was essentially humanoid, with a bulbous, hairless head. The eyes seemed slightly larger than ours . . . the nose and mouth were basically humanoid . . . and the mouth was frozen in an expression of terror. The torso looked muscular, especially the upper arms and thighs. It had six fingers on its hands and six toes on its feet. The upper [right] leg appeared to be seriously injured, and the [right] hand almost severed at the wrist. These, presumably, were injuries sustained in the crash."

Pope was not convinced that the film was genuine: "I'm certain as I can be that it's a fake, for a number of reasons. Primarily, the story that we're supposed to be believing simply doesn't make sense. If this really was the most highly classified operation in the world, classified higher than the hydrogen bomb, it's inconceivable that this cameraman would have been left to his own devices to develop these films, and that bits of them would simply not have been recovered from him and that he would have sat on it for nigh on fifty years. The story is more full of holes than a piece of Swiss cheese." [5]

There are, however, those who remain open-minded about the subject—including the respected investigator Jenny Randles, who has made an intriguing comment with regard to the offer of alleged top-secret documents on crashed UFOs from a British Army source, "Robert." Randles told me that within the files Robert described to her in 1986 were photographs, the description of which as if they were images lifted directly from the film. "Bear in mind," Randles told me, "1986 was years before the autopsy film surfaced. In fact, the connections with the autopsy film and with what Robert told me are chillingly similar. One of the impressions that you get from viewing the alien autopsy footage is that the body is very humanlike and is around five foot in height. I have to say, it struck me as soon as I saw the footage that this was very similar to what Robert had described." [6]

There is also the little-known fact that Philip Mantle had the opportunity on April 28, 1995, to view a piece of film footage at Ray Santilli's London office that was strikingly similar in nature to the widely publicized film, but that related to the autopsy of *another* unusual body. "The alien is humanoid," stated Mantle, "almost human looking with an enlarged abdomen. Two arms, two legs, but it has six digits on each of its hands and feet. There is no hair visible anywhere; the head is slightly enlarged but it has a nose, mouth, ears and two dark eyes. Female genitals are also visible.

"The alien's body is cut open and various organs are removed and placed in various receptacles. The people conducting the autopsy are completely covered in protection suits of some kind and unfortunately the faces of these individuals are not visible." Ray Santilli would later state that this second piece of footage was not released due to the graphic dissection of the creature's genitalia.[7]

The controversy continues to this day over the nature of the film and whether it represents a real event, an outrageous hoax, or a piece of government-sponsored disinformation. But comments on the film made by dermatologist Thomas Jansen of the Ludwig-Maximilians University, Germany, at the time of its public airing support the whistle-blower testimony revealed in this book. Speaking with *Der Spiegel* magazine in April 1996, Jansen stated that in his opinion the film showed a female: " . . . about 13 years old, she had unmistakable Progeria — everything fits together."

And, as *Der Spiegel* added: "People sick with Progeria age with remarkable swiftness. Even as children they look old. They suffer dwarfism, hair and teeth that fall out, and clogged arteries. Most of them die before puberty from heart attacks or strokes. Also, it's not unusual that the dead girl has six toes and fingers. Polydactylysm, said the dermatologist, is often seen accompanying rare deformities. Jansen considers his circumstantial evidence to be 'one hundred percent watertight.' Professors around the Ludwig-Maximilians University agree with this judgment, the findings being published in the *Munich Weekly Medical Journal*. So far Jansen has found no indication of cause of death or which doctors did the dissection.

However, he stands firm that the autopsy was 'expertly carried out.'"[8]

Perhaps most controversial of all was the way in which the film footage surfaced. Skeptics scoffed at the idea that someone—even an ex-military source—could successfully hide such monumental material from officials and not suffer the consequences of court-martial or worse. Why was the footage not handed over to the cameraman's superiors immediately after the filming was completed? ask the skeptics, quite correctly.

The cameraman himself, whose identity has been carefully concealed to this day, has explained the circumstances of the filming: "I remember I got a call telling me to immediately report to [Major] General [Clements] McMullen. When I got to McMullen, I was told that a plane had come down just outside Soccoro, New Mexico. A flight was being laid on to go down there and I was to be on it. I was told to film the crash site and stay with the team, nothing else. I flew out of Andrews with the team, mainly medical I think. We stopped at Wright Field to pick up other officers and men, changing planes and flew down to Roswell air base. [W]e had a lot of equipment with us. After the flight we traveled by road and dirt track to the site.

"I filmed the crash site, also the poor freaks and we were told to keep back. I filmed the vehicle itself and the area around it. I felt nervous of something I could not understand or explain. There were injured creatures lying around, obviously in pain, but the men at the site were too scared to get close. Oh, there was a great deal of confusion until we arrived. My authority allowed me to operate as an independent as long as I didn't interfere with the clean up. When I arrived, I set up my tent and equipment and once I had light, I started shooting. How did I feel about it? I was concerned about potential contamination, but I had no choice.

"Most of the processing took place around August, by the time the military as we knew it, ceased to be, the Air Force and the Army were about to split and my unit was about to be disbanded for a time anyway. In fact, you could say I was in a strange position for a time of not belonging to either one service. Then eventually they found a home for us.

"I took all the film because I had no one to report to. My orders were not to discuss the situation with anyone unless they brought up the subject first. The first batch had been delivered, then the department folded and I had no one to deliver to. I tried to contact McMullen, but I couldn't get through. In the end I couldn't leave it laying around, so I took it home which is where it stayed."[9]

By the cameraman's own admission, the event that he filmed did not relate to the July 1947 event at Roswell but to an earlier May 1947 crash in the vicinity of White Sands. In some ways this tallies with the data provided by Bill Salter, who asserted that several vehicles had been involved in high-altitude, radiation, and biological experiments at White Sands in the period from May to August 1947. Similarly, the Black Widow was certain that the strange bodies she had seen at Oak Ridge "were very badly damaged from one of several White Sands crashes. I was told that there were several classified balloon flights in May and July 1947 and at least two were disasters."

And the story does not end there. Bill Salter and Al Barker have no personal or direct knowledge of the film, but they both consider it to be genuine, government-originated material for a specific reason. At one point in the film, the medical team performs a highly unusual procedure on the eyes of the strange body that involves the careful removal of a pair of stereotypical alien "black eye lenses" that reveal distinctly human-looking eyes below.

According to both Salter and Barker, this directly relates to a short-lived project that was undertaken at Randolph Field Air Force Base, Texas, in 1947. It was aimed at trying to better understand the way in which military personnel might be adversely affected by "flash blindness" from atomic bomb detonations. This particularly novel project, stated Barker, was conducted from February to July of that year by people who were "associated with [Hubertus]

Strughold" and involved the use of at least three "handicapped citi-zens" who were fitted with experimental, lightweight and very thin black-tinted eye lenses similar to—but larger than—today's contact lenses.

"The idea," stated Barker, "was to learn if these lenses could be comfortably fitted to a person's eyes and how they might give pro-tection on the battlefield against atomic flash blindness. The prob-lem was that although this was a wonderful plan, it caused nothing but pain, severe eye infections and problems for the person the lenses were fitted to and the project was stopped. But I can tell you that this is why I believe the film to be real: because I am in no doubt that the eye lenses removed from the body in the footage were very similar to those used in the flash blindness tests. So, *some-where* at least, this [film] represents *something* connected with the 1947 experiments." [10]

That extensive research into flash blindness in relation to atomic bomb detonations was undertaken in the immediate postwar period and at the height of the Cold War is not in dispute. For example, a document dated March 8, 1995, from the Advisory Committee Staff to the Members of the Advisory Committee on Human Radia-tion Experiments titled "Debates between the Atomic Energy Com-mission (AEC) and Department of Defense (DOD); Secrecy Policy Revealed" includes a section titled "The Debate over Flashblindess Studies." It reveals that several such projects, including Operation Buster Jangle and Operation Tumbler-Snapper, were initiated to try and better determine the effects of flash blindness on human sub-jects.[11] Notably, the document also demonstrates that much of that work was indeed undertaken at Randolph Field Air Force Base, Texas, and specifically within its School of Aviation Medicine, just as Salter and Barker maintain.[12]

One other critical bit of evidence officially links such conditions as progeria and dwarfism with the activities at the Oak Ridge Na-tional Laboratory and elsewhere in the summer of 1947. Contained within the pages of the November 3, 1947, issue of the *Biology Di-*

vision Bulletin of the Clinton National Laboratory at Oak Ridge is a section titled "Current Journal Articles of Interest in the Biology Library." One of those "articles of interest" happened to be a four-page paper titled "Uptake of Radioactive Iodine by the Normal and Disordered Thyroid Gland in Children." Written by Edith H. Quimby and Donovan McCune, M.D., in August 1947, the paper focused on a series of studies undertaken midway through that year that involved administering radioactive iodine to a particular group of physically and mentally handicapped children in an effort to try and better understand disorders of the thyroid gland.

More specifically, the report focused on the results of a whole range of radiation-related experiments undertaken in mid-1947 on no fewer than "fifty-four test subjects," of whom "Fifteen were between one and four years of age; 7 were controls; 2 were classic cretins; 1 showed some features of hypothyroidism which were not modified by treatment; 2 were dwarfs; in 1 the diagnosis was 'gargoylism;' 1 was suspected of Progeria, a disorder associated with some of the features of hypothyroidism; and the last exhibited features of moderate sexual precocity. Twenty-seven were more than four but less than fifteen years of age. Of these 2 had unmistakable hypothyroidism, 2 Graves disease, [and] four were dwarfs."

It is, of course, decidedly interesting that barely a month after a number of sources have stated that bodies displaying evidence of both dwarfism and progeria were recovered from the New Mexico desert after a series of nuclear- and high-altitude-based experiments and transferred to Oak Ridge, personnel at Oak Ridge's Biology Division were officially expressing "interest" in radiation-related experimentation undertaken on dwarfs and those afflicted with progeria.[13]

And there is yet another document that may give us an indication of the nature of the New Mexico events that predated the Nuremberg clampdown on much human experimentation. A 1949 report titled "Tabulation of Available Data Relative to Radiation Biology" prepared by the NEPA Medical Advisory Panel focuses much of its attention on the ever-vexing problem of trying to avoid bombarding the crew of a nuclear-powered aircraft with hostile radiation. While this report was written in early 1949 and at a time when NEPA was actively lobbying to get official sanction to use human beings in its nuclear experimentation, it makes a brief and enigmatic reference to events that had apparently occurred previously: "While some data on the effects of whole-body radiation on man have been obtained, these are few and fragmentary, and, for the most part, have been obtained on sick individuals. Some information of questionable value has been obtained as a result of occasional accidents and mass exposures, such as occurred at Hiroshima and Nagasaki." Curiously, the authors stated that "Such data has not been included in the present compilation."

This passage speaks volumes. Although the report was written in early 1949, it refers to experimentation that had apparently already been undertaken in the field of "whole-body radiation" at some point previous to the publication of the report—and at a time when NEPA had, supposedly, not even begun human trials. It also alludes to "questionable data" on this subject that had been acquired "as a result of occasional accidents." One might ask, What sort of accident would result in a human body being exposed to whole-body radiation in such a fashion? Indeed, the reference to this in the context of an accident or accidents is significant; so is the fact that the report deliberately avoids any further reference to this brief aside.[14]

One last official document provides support for the whistle-blower testimony that Japanese individuals, many of whom displayed severe physical handicaps, were involved in the Roswell events, all of which occurred in a specific period from May to July 1947. A document found in the files of Maj. Gen. Curtis E. LeMay, U.S. Army, deputy chief of air staff for research and development, states that " . . . a letter contract effective as of July 1, 1947 . . . was entered into between the [Atomic Energy] Commission and the [National Academy of Sciences], in which it was agreed that negotiations should be undertaken for the execution of a definitive contract [to] . . . make studies and conduct research and experimental investigations, primarily in Japan, in accordance with general programs from time to time approved by the Commission. This shall include investigations of the physiological and biological effects of radiation. . . ."[15]

How curious that only days after this July 1, 1947, approval was given to proceed with biological and radiation-related "research and experimental investigations, primarily in Japan," small Oriental and Asian-looking bodies were recovered from the New Mexico desert.

CONCLUSiONS

Forget flying saucers. Roswell had *nothing* to do with the crash of an extraterrestrial space vehicle. The truth is much darker and far more disturbing and has been covered up for more than half a century.

What happened, in short, is this: in May 1947, an experimental aircraft that was borne out of the revolutionary aviation research of the Horten brothers of Germany was test-flown from White Sands, New Mexico. The flight was part of a larger project begun in 1946 to examine the feasibility of both constructing and flying a nuclear-powered aircraft. On board the vehicle were a number of physically handicapped people who had been found in the remnants of the Japanese military's Unit 731 laboratories and who were used in this dark and disturbing experiment—the purpose of which was to try to better understand the effects of nuclear-powered flight on an aircrew. The experiment ended in disaster when the aircraft crash-landed at White Sands, killing some of the crew.

Two months later, in early July 1947, a second and similar vehicle was, once again, flown from White Sands. In this particular instance, the aircraft was affixed to a huge balloon array that was based upon advanced Fugo balloon designs developed in the closing stages of World War II by Japanese forces. The aircraft was piloted by a crew of Japanese personnel who had been specifically trained for the task and crashed near the Foster Ranch after being catastrophically struck by lightning. The lifting-body-style aircraft, the balloon materials, and the bodies of the crew were retrieved under cover of overwhelming secrecy and—either deliberately or unintentionally—hidden behind a smoke screen of crashed flying saucer stories. It is these two incidents (and, as the whistle-blower testimony provided in these pages suggests, possibly several others in the vicinity of White Sands in the early to late summer of 1947) that led to the legend of the Roswell incident.

It is unlikely that this book will cause the Air Force to retract its position on Roswell and admit to the truth. After completing the original manuscript to this book, I made a call to the Pentagon and spoke with a man in the Air Force Office of Public Affairs. I laid my cards on the table—to an extent, at least—and related some of the information I had uncovered. The man listened quietly and after I had finished said: "Mr. Redfern, let me get back to you on this."

Two days later, my call was returned: "Mr. Redfern," began a voice that clearly belonged to another man, "the Air Force considers *any* theory for the Roswell Incident that is not supported by our two reports of 1995 and 1997 to be incorrect. And that is the Air Force's official position and our only comment—except to say we recommend to people they read our reports for the facts. Good luck with your book."

And I say, Good luck with your cover stories.

APPENDIX:

DOCUMENTS

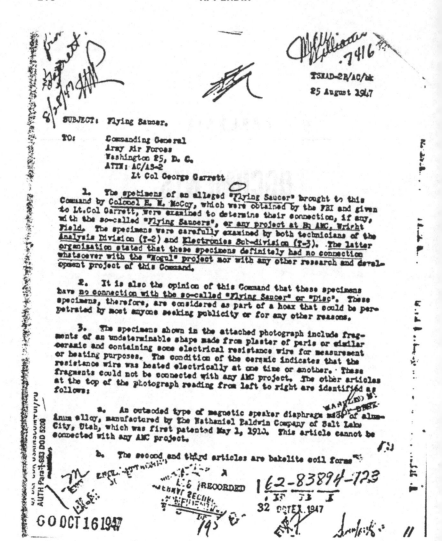

TSEAD-2B/AC/bk

25 August 1947

SUBJECT: Flying Saucer.

TO: Commanding General
        Army Air Forces
        Washington 25, D. C.
        ATTN: AC/AS-2
        Lt Col George Garrett

1. The specimens of an alleged "Flying Saucer" brought to this Command by Colonel H. M. McCoy, which were obtained by the FBI and given to Lt.Col Garrett, were examined to determine their connection, if any, with the so-called "Flying Saucers", or any project at Eh AMC, Wright Field. The specimens were carefully examined by both technicians of the Analysis Division (T-2) and Electronics Sub-division (T-3). The latter organization stated that these specimens definitely had no connection whatsoever with the "Mogul" project nor with any other research and development project of this Command.

2. It is also the opinion of this Command that these specimens have no connection with the so-called "Flying Saucer" or "Disc". These specimens, therefore, are considered as part of a hoax that could be perpetrated by most anyone seeking publicity or for any other reasons.

3. The specimens shown in the attached photograph include fragments of an undeterminable shape made from plaster of paris or similar ceramic and containing some electrical resistance wire for measurement or heating purposes. The condition of the ceramic indicates that the resistance wire was heated electrically at one time or another. These fragments could not be connected with any AMC project. The other articles at the top of the photograph reading from left to right are identified as follows:

     a. An outmoded type of magnetic speaker diaphragm made of aluminum alloy, manufactured by The Nathaniel Baldwin Company of Salt Lake City, Utah, which was first patented May 1, 1910. This article cannot be connected with any AMC project.

     b. The second and third articles are bakelite coil forms

RECORDED   162-83894-123

32 OCT 24 1947

CO OCT 16 1947

A two-page FBI document dated August 25, 1947, relating to an event at an Illinois ranch in which debris initially believed to have originated with a Mogul balloon was recovered. The routine procedures put in place to handle this recovery were in stark contrast to the high security that existed at Roswell and offer demonstrable evidence that the Roswell

Ltr, CO,AAF, Wash. DC
Subject: Flying Saucers

25 & 1st 1947

wrapped with ordinary thin enameled copper wire. These coils indicate that they were skillfully made at one time but were crudely rewrapped by one not familiar with the art of making a coil. These coils also have no connection with any AMC project.

    c. The fourth article is a metallic box which is the remains of an electronic filter condenser made by the Polymet Manufacturing Company of New York, N. Y. This article also has no connection with any AMC project.

    d. The fifth article is the remains of a metallic magnetic ring that could not be identified as any part of any device used at this command.

    4. This information and attached photograph may be transmitted to the FBI to inform various agencies throughout the United States as to what action to take in the event other similar specimens are found.

    FOR THE COMMANDING GENERAL:

1 Incl:
  1 Photo 8-1/2x11
    "Flying Saucer"

    H. M. McCOY
    Colonel, Air Corps
    Deputy Commanding General
    Intelligence (T-2)

REGRADED UNCLASSIFIED
ON · NOV 0 6 1978
BY DEP CDR US/INSCOM FOI/PO
AUTH Para 1-603 DOD 5200

CONFIDENTIAL

event involved the recovery of something more exotic than a Mogul balloon.

TOP SECRET

HEADQUARTERS, ARMY AIR FORCES
WASHINGTON

1 4 JUL 1947

SUBJECT: Employment of German Scientists - Atmosphere Heat-Energy Project.

TO   :   Commanding General
           Air Materiel Command
           Wright Field, Dayton, Ohio.
           Attention: Intelligence, T-2.

1. On 1 June 1947, Headquarters, European Command informed the War Department that three Germans, Fritz Morhard, a mechanical and electrical engineer, August Reis, a physician, and Max Ostenrieder, a biochemist, claim to have invented a revolutionary method of converting heat energy from atmospheric and other sources such as atomic pile directly into electrical energy at high power levels.

2. At General Clay's instigation these scientists divulged a portion of their claim to Dr. H. K. Stephenson. They plan to pass air through a "heat generator" (design undisclosed), similar in principle to units used for heating buildings in Switzerland. The hot air passes thence to a "tube" (design undisclosed), where it is converted directly into electrical energy.

3. General LeMay, Deputy Chief of Air Staff for Research and Development, evinced an immediate interest in the project and agreed to contract the scientists for the Army Air Forces.

4. Since there were no other terms upon which the scientists would divulge their discovery, the War Department agreed to hire them under Paperclip and use their existing inventions for experimental purposes but not publish information relating to these inventions in order to allow the inventors the opportunity to exploit them later commercially at their own risk. Additional resulting inventions during the period of War Department employment are still to be retained by the War Department.

5. The War Department also agreed to pay the German scientists a fixed sum annually, the amount to be determined by both parties after the scientists have arrived in the United States, for the use of their invention or discovery for as long as the government may wish to keep the discovery secret.

A top-secret Headquarters Army Air Forces document dated July 14, 1947, on the subject of advanced research undertaken by Paperclip scientists for the AAF on an "Atmosphere Heat-Energy Project."

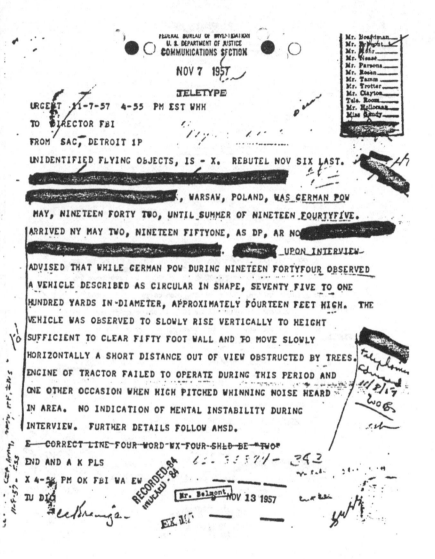

An FBI document dated November 7, 1957, that describes a circular-
shaped aircraft developed by the Nazis during World War II.

DEPARTMENT OF THE AIR FORCE
HEADQUARTERS UNITED STATES AIR FORCE
WASHINGTON

A I R   M A I L

INSPECTOR GENERAL USAF
13TH DISTRICT OFFICE OF SPECIAL INVESTIGATION
Offutt Air Force Base, Omaha, Nebraska

MT/EES/dmb
16 January 1950

CLASSIFICATION CANCELLED TO NOT OFFICIAL ASSEMBLY
BY AUTHORITY OF THE DIRECTOR OF SPEC INV

BY _____ RT X KUNZE, Capt, USAF
Historian
DATE _____ 4 DEC 1975

SPOT INTELLIGENCE REPORT

SUBJECT: Flying Saucers from Venus Come to Earth

TO: Director of Special Investigations
         Headquarters USAF
         Washington 25, D. C.

UNCLASSIFIED

1. SYNOPSIS: Article in Wyandotte Echo, Kansas City, Kansas,
6 January 1950, stated Kansas City auto dealer, ▇▇▇▇▇▇▇, while in
Denver, met an engineer named ▇▇▇▇▇▇▇, who claimed to have seen two
"flying saucers" which had crashed at a radar station near the New
Mexico and Arizona border. These craft, each carrying a crew of two,
were constructed of some unknown metal, and were stocked with food in
tablet form. ▇▇▇▇▇ said about fifty (50) of these craft had been
found in the United States in a two year period—forty (40) of them
being presently in the United States Research Bureau in Los Angeles.
▇▇▇▇▇ stated it was assumed the craft had come from the planet Venus.
Evaluation – unknown.

2. DETAILS: A newspaper article appearing in the Wyandotte Echo,
Kansas City, Kansas, January 1950, stated that two weeks ago he ▇▇▇▇▇▇▇
well known Kansas City auto dealer, stopped in Denver where he called on
the manager of the Ford Agency. Their conversation was interrupted by
some engineers arriving for a meeting. One of these arrivals, a man
named ▇▇▇▇▇▇ revealed the following information:

He, ▇▇▇▇▇▇ "crashed the gate" at a radar station near the
New Mexico and Arizona border. While there he saw two of the highly
secret flying saucers which had crashed near that site. One was badly

Classification cancelled or changed to
▇▇▇▇▇▇

By authority of Chief of Staff, USAF UNCLASSIFIED
By: _____
Date: 24 JAN 1950

3763

A two-page Air Force document dated January 16, 1950, that focuses its
attention on rumors that UFOs had crashed in the United States and
had been recovered by the military. These "crashed UFO rumors" were
spread officially to confuse the truth surrounding the Roswell event.

Subj: Flying Saucers from Venus Come to Earth   16 January 1950

damaged, the other almost perfectly intact. These craft consisted of two parts: the cockpit or cabin, approximately six (6) ft. in diameter; and a ring, 18 ft. across, and about 2 ft. thick, surrounding the cabin. These craft were constructed of a metal resembling aluminum but the actual components of the metal could not be defined. ▓▓▓▓▓▓ had a small piece of this metal in his possession and gave it to the Ford man to send to the Ford Dearborn Plant for analysis. Each of the two craft had a crew of two. In the damaged ship the bodies were charred. The occupants of the other ship were in a perfect state of preservation, although dead. They were almost identical with human beings, were of a uniform height of 3 ft, uniformly blonde, beardless, and their teeth were completely free of fillings or cavities. The bodies were dressed in a blue material, the threads in the cloth seemingly a sort of wire. They did not wear under-garments but the bodies were taped. There was a quantity of food in the ship in tablet form and water found in the craft had a weight double that of water here on earth. ▓▓▓▓▓▓ showed the group, including ▓▓▓▓ a clock or automatic calendar taken from one of the craft, consisting of two pieces of metal. On the face of one piece of this metal appeared an indentation which rotated around the disk, completing a cycle each twenty-eight (28) days. According to information given ▓▓▓▓▓▓ there have been fifty (50) of these craft found in the United States in a two year period. Forty (40) of these are in the United States Research Bureau in Los Angeles. It was assumed the craft came from the planet Venus because that is the only planet having an atmosphere in any way similar to ours, and also Venus seems to have magnetic properties which would make it the logical home base for these space ships. Mr. ▓▓▓▓ assumed the reason behind the apparent lack of security is that the Government desired this information to be spread from unofficial sources until people are more or less familiar with the facts. He feels that the security department of the military fears that the sudden shock of a surprise announcement that interplanetary travel is possible might cause mass hysteria. Editor of the Kansas City Star, Kansas City, Missouri, stated that while his newspaper was aware of this story, they did not dare put it into their paper because it was too fantastic. Reputation of ▓▓ is that he is well known locally and has a number of friends on the Kansas City Star. COULTER was not otherwise identified but apparently can be readily located through the Ford Agency in Denver, Colorado.

3. ACTION: Initial "Spot Report" transmitted to Headquarters, OSI, and to DO #14 and #17 by TWX on 13 January 1950. DO #13 will interfiew FHCK and make additional inquiries in Kansas City. Copies of this report are being sent to DO #14 for locating and interviewing COULTER, and to DO #17 for inquiry as to the radar station on the New Mexico and Arizona border, the possible site of craft from the planet Venus.

Copies furnished:
   DO #14
   DO #17

Earl E. Sparks
MATTHEW THOMPSON Capt
Lt Colonel, USAF
District Commander

S E C R E T

APPENDIX "E"

TECHNOLOGICAL ESTIMATE ON DEVELOPMENT OF
VARIOUS NEW TECHNIQUES, REVOLUTIONARY DE-
SIGNS OR CONFIGURATIONS, REVOLUTIONARY
PROPULSIVE MEANS, ETC.

NEW WEAPONS AND COUNTERMEASURES

ITEM: NUCLEAR ENERGY FOR PROPULSION OF AIRCRAFT (NEPA PROJECT)

SUMMARY STATEMENT: Shortly after the dropping of the atomic bombs in Japan,
Air Force officers approached Manhattan Engineering District, which was then
in charge of all nuclear projects, with respect to utilizing this new source
of energy for the propulsion of aircraft. It was fully recognized that
tremendous problems would be presented, but the potential reward justified
the effort required for the solution of the problems.

The Manhattan Engineering District permitted the Air Force to consider
the project on the basis that personnel would not be hired from the District;
one agency would be the point of contact with the project and all research
and development projects would be coordinated with the District prior to their
initiation. On this basis, the Air Force selected the Fairchild Engine and
Airplane Corporation as the monitoring agency with a Board of Consultants
representing each contractor engaged in the manufacture of tactical engines
for the Army and Navy; the Bureau of Aeronautics, Navy Department, and the
National Advisory Committee for Aeronautics. This Board was to meet at
regular intervals, having now had five meetings, to advise the NEPA organization established by Fairchild and become informed on the problems involved
in the application of nuclear energy to aircraft propulsion.

It is the ultimate intention that if and when nuclear power plants have
been demonstrated as feasible, the NEPA Division will no longer exist and
the various engine manufacturers will be placed in the same competitive
position they occupy with respect to the more conventional engine types.

The NEPA Division functions through subcontracts, not only to the member
companies that have formed the Board of Consultants, but also to universities,
non-profit organizations and other industrial organizations. In addition,
the NEPA Division has at Oak Ridge a small staff of scientists and engineers
investigating the problem on a full-time basis, and a large group of consultants that have had long and intensive experience with the nuclear project.

The nuclear reactor should be considered as a heat source, to be made
available at a temperature which can be utilized in some type of heat engine.
Because of the nature of the reaction, this heat source may be available for
several hundred hours without additional fuel. With this heat source is
presented many new problems of heat transfer and high temperature materials.

*A two-page Research and Development Board, Committee on
Aeronautics, document of 1948 detailing the background on the
Nuclear Energy for Propulsion of Aircraft program.*

APPENDIX "E" (continued)

Encompassed in this problem of aircraft propulsion are, because of weight limitations, many problems new to the Atomic Energy Commission and its contractors. At opposite ends of the spectrum of nuclear science and engineering are the slow, or thermal neutron piles, used for plutonium conversion and isotope manufacture and the atomic bomb, or fast neutron reactor. It is in the more or less unexplored intermediate ground in which aircraft propulsion reactors will automatically be oriented. The problem is the selection of the desirable features of each type of reactor to obtain the smallest overall reactor mass and volume. To evaluate this area will require the closest cooperation between the Atomic Energy Commission and the Air Force in extending the knowledge and in conducting the feasibility experiments which will require fissionable material. The shielding problems, so readily solved in stationary reactors by large quantities of concrete which is obviously impossible for aircraft, presents one of the most serious problems. This problem in itself encourages the use of the smallest possible reactor.

The problems of maintenance, repair, storage, and general operation of nuclear powered aircraft present problems, the solution of which are quite uncertain. It is probable that nuclear powered aircraft will be used for special missions and will not be of the type normally collected into squadrons and groups for operation as tactical aircraft are now utilized.

There is no positive assurance that nuclear powered aircraft will be successful; but the possibility of aircraft of unlimited range is so attractive that extensive research and engineering effort is warranted. No estimate can be made as to when nuclear powered aircraft will be available because of the enormous amount of research and development required, but it will probably be of the order of 10 to 15 years with the projected rate of fund expenditure. It is anticipated that funds to the amount of twelve to fifteen million dollars per year will be required after Fiscal Year 1950 when the program will be fully under way and provided funds to this extent are made available.

U. S. Department of Justice

Washington, D.C. 20530

Mr. Nicholas Redfern   A3

                                    Re: Appeal No. 93-0886
                                           RLH:MAP:KJM

Dear Mr. Redfern:

     You appealed from the action of the Federal Bureau of
Investigation on your request for access to records pertaining to
the MJ-12.

     After careful consideration of your appeal, I have decided
to affirm the initial action in this case. The MJ-12 is the
subject of a Headquarters main file entitled Espionage. Certain
information was properly withheld from you pursuant to 5 U.S.C.
§ 552(b)(7)(C) and (7)(D). These provisions pertain to records
or information compiled for law enforcement purposes, the release
of which could reasonably be expected to constitute an unwar-
ranted invasion of the personal privacy of third parties and to
disclose the identities of confidential sources. Names of FBI
agents and employees and other government personnel were among
the items excised on the basis of 5 U.S.C. § 552(b)(7)(C). This
material is not appropriate for discretionary release.

     Judicial review of my action on this appeal is available to
you in the United States District Court for the judicial district
in which you reside or have your principal place of business, or
in the District of Columbia, which is also where the records you
seek are located.

                          Sincerely,

                          Richard L. Huff, Co-Director
                          Office of Information and Privacy

*A July 22, 1993, letter to the author from the FBI stating that the
controversial MJ12 documents are the subject of an HQ main file titled
"Espionage."*

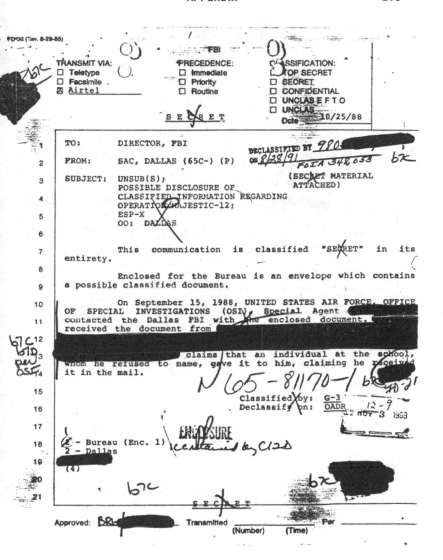

FD-36 (Rev. 8-29-85)

FBI

TRANSMIT VIA: PRECEDENCE: CLASSIFICATION:
☐ Teletype   ☐ Immediate   ☐ TOP SECRET
☐ Facsimile   ☐ Priority   ☐ SECRET
☒ Airtel   ☐ Routine   ☐ CONFIDENTIAL
                                            ☐ UNCLAS E F T O
                                            ☐ UNCLAS
S E C R E T   Date   10/25/88

TO: DIRECTOR, FBI   DECLASSIFIED BY 980
FROM: SAC, DALLAS (65C-) (P) On 8/28/91   FOIA 348,053
SUBJECT: UNSUB(S);   (SECRET MATERIAL
         POSSIBLE DISCLOSURE OF   ATTACHED)
         CLASSIFIED INFORMATION REGARDING
         OPERATION MAJESTIC-12;
         ESP-X
         OO: DALLAS

         This communication is classified "SECRET" in its
entirety.

         Enclosed for the Bureau is an envelope which contains
a possible classified document.

         On September 15, 1988, UNITED STATES AIR FORCE, OFFICE
OF SPECIAL INVESTIGATIONS (OSI), Special Agent
contacted the Dallas FBI with the enclosed document.
received the document from

                          claims that an individual at the school,
whom he refused to name, gave it to him, claiming he received
it in the mail.

                          N 65 - 81170 - 1

                          Classified by: G-3
                          Declassify on: OADR   12-9
                                                    12 NOV 3 1988

( ) - Bureau (Enc. 1)   ENCLOSURE
  2 - Dallas
  (4)

S E C R E T

Approved: Transmitted   Per
                          (Number)   (Time)

A two-page extract from the FBI's files of 1988 on their investigation of the MJ12 documents.

SE C R E T

DL 65C-

Dallas notes that within the last six weeks, there has been local publicity regarding "OPERATION MAJESTIC-12" with at least two appearances on a local radio talk show, discussing the MAJESTIC-12 OPERATION, the individuals involved, and the Government's attempt to keep it all secret. It is unknown if this is all part of a publicity campaign.

b7C
per
OSI

██████████ from OSI, advises that "OPERATION BLUE BOOK," mentioned in the document on page 4 did exist.

Dallas realizes that the purported document is over 35 years old, but does not know if it has been properly declassified.

REQUEST OF THE BUREAU

The Bureau is requested to discern if the document is still classified. Dallas will hold any investigation in abeyance until further direction from FBIHQ.

S E C R E T

2*

SUMMARY REPORT
Report No. F-SU-1110-ND
Date   10 January 1946

HEADQUARTERS
AIR MATERIEL COMMAND
WRIGHT FIELD, DAYTON, OHIO

GERMAN FLYING WINGS DESIGNED
BY HORTEN BROTHERS

By

N. LeBlanc, Captain, Air Corps

Approved By:

Walter F. Nyblade

Walter F. Nyblade, Major, Air Corps
Chief, Aircraft Branch
Technical Section
Analysis Division
Intelligence (T-2)

For the Commanding General:

M. E. Goll

M. E. Goll, Lt Colonel, Air Corps
Acting Chief, Analysis Division
Intelligence (T-2)

1595

WF-(A)-O-5 JULY 46 800

The cover page of a January 10, 1946, document titled German Flying
Wings Designed by Horten Brothers *and written by Capt. N. Leblanc,
United States Air Corps.*

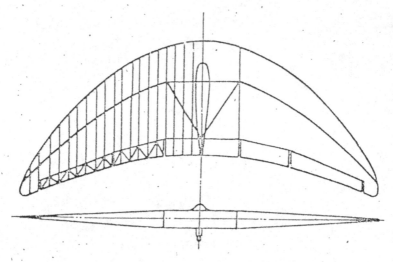

HORTEN PARABOLA

SPAN	12·0 m (39·4 ft.)
AREA	33·0 m² (355 ft²)
ASPECT RATIO	4·37
WEIGHT, EMPTY	90 kg (196 lb)
WEIGHT, LOADED	170 kg (375 lb)
WING LOADING	5·05 kg/m² (1·0 lb/ft²)
GLIDING ANGLE	19·0°
SINKING SPEED	0·65 m/sec (2·13 fps)

A drawing of one of the Flying Wing designs of the Horten brothers (extracted from German Flying Wings Designed by Horten Brothers and written by Capt. N. Leblanc, United States Air Corps).

TO   :   D. M. LADD   DATE: August 19, 1947

FROM   :   E. G. FITCH

SUBJECT: FLYING DISCS

S.W. Reynolds

        Special Agent ~~~~~~~ of the Liaison Section, while dis-
cussing the above captioned phenomena with Lieutenant Colonel ~~~~~
of the Air Forces Intelligence, expressed the possibility that flying
discs were, in fact, a very highly classified experiment of the Army or
Navy. Mr. ~~~~~ was very much surprised when Colonel ~~~~~ not only
agreed that this was a possibility, but confidentially stated it was his
personal opinion that such was a probability. Colonel ~~~~~ indicated
confidentially that a Mr. ~~~~~ who is a scientist attached to the Air
Forces Intelligence, was of the same opinion.

        Colonel ~~~~~ stated that he based his assumption on the
following: He pointed out that when flying objects were reported seen over
Sweden, the "high brass" of the War Department exerted tremendous pressure
on the Air Forces Intelligence to conduct research and collect information
in an effort to identify these sightings. Colonel ~~~~~ stated that, in
contrast to this, we have reported sightings of unknown objects over the
United States, and the "high brass" appeared to be totally unconcerned.
He indicated this led him to believe that they knew enough about these
objects to express no concern. Colonel ~~~~~ pointed out further that the
objects in question have been seen by many individuals who are what he
terms "trained observers," such as airplane pilots. He indicated also that
several of the individuals are reliable members of the community. He stated
it is his conclusion that these individuals saw something. He stated the
above has led him to come to the conclusion that there were objects seen
which somebody in the Government knows all about.

        Mr. ~~~~~ pointed out to Colonel ~~~~~ that if it is a fact
experimentations are being conducted by the United States Government, then it
does not appear reasonable to request the FBI to spend money and precious
time conducting inquiries with respect to this matter. Colonel ~~~~~ stated
that he agreed with Mr. ~~~~~ in this regard and indicated that it would be
extremely embarrassing to the Air Forces Intelligence if it later is learned
that these flying discs are, in fact, an experiment of the United States
Government.

        Mr. ~~~~~ subsequently discussed this matter with Colonel L. R.
Forney of the Intelligence Division of the War Department. Colonel Forney
stated that he had discussed the matter previously with General Chamberlin.
Colonel Forney indicated to Mr. ~~~~~ that he has the assurance of General

SWR:LL   RECORDED
                        EX-64   INDEXED   1 - 83894 -

5 1 SEP 29 1947 COPIES DESTROYED   1 4   34 SEP 20 1947
                  270 NOV 18 1954

*A two-page FBI document dated August 19, 1947, that refers to sources
in Air Force Intelligence who were of the opinion that flying saucers
were "a very highly classified experiment of the Army."*

MEMORANDUM FOR MR. LADD

Chamberlin and General Todd that the Army is conducting no experimentations with anything which could possibly be mistaken for a flying disc.

Colonel ████ of the Air Forces Intelligence subsequently contact Mr. ████ and indicated that he had discussed this matter with General Schulgen of the Army Air Forces. General Schulgen had previously assured bot Mr. ████ and Colonel ████ that to the best of his knowledge and information no experiments were being undertaken by the Government which could mistaken for flying discs. Colonel ████ indicated to Mr. ████ that he had pointed out his beliefs to General Schulgen and had mentioned the possibility of an embarrassing situation arising between the Air Forces Intelligence and the FBI. General Schulgen agreed with Colonel ████ that a memorandum would be prepared for the signature of General McDonald, A2, to General LeMay, who is in charge of Research and Development in the Air Corps. Colonel ████ indicated that this memorandum will set forth the characteristics of the objects seen by various reliable individuals. The memorandum will then request General LeMay to indicate whether or not any experiments are being undertaken by the Air Forces which could possibly be connected with any of the observed phenomena. Colonel ████ stated that when a reply is received from General LeMay, a communication will be addressed to the Bureau.

Mr. ████ will follow this matter closely with Colonel ████ and General Schulgen so that the Bureau will be promptly advised of all information regarding the flying discs, especially any information indicating that they are, in fact, an experiment of some Governmental agency.

A 1947 document from the Office of the Air Surgeon concerning
"experiments on mutations in extreme altitudes."

[retyped from original]
Restricted

Transmittal of Copy of Correspondence

AC/AS-1, The Air Surgeon   DATE: 28 May 1947
Attn: Maj. V. [Illegible]

AC/AS-2, Collection Branch   COMMENT NO. 3
    Air Intelligence Requirements Division   Capt. Hacken/rn/6282

1. In accordance with telephone communication 20 May 1947, between Major Downey of your office and Captain Hacken of this office, correspondence returned herewith.
2. There is also attached correspondence from the Chief of Ordnance, inclosing a letter from Dr. Werner von Braun, dealing with Dr. Generales and his experiments.

                      ROBERT TAYLOR
                      Colonel, Air Corps
                      Chief, Collection Branch
                      Air Intelligence Requirements Div.
                      AC/AS-2

3 Incls
1 & 2 n/c
3. Added ltr dtd
   18 Apr 47 w/incls.

Guided Missiles and Air Defense Division AC/AS-3   DATE: 6 June 1947

Medical Research Division, Office of the Air Surgeon, AC/AS-1   COMMENT NO. 4

                            Maj.Downey/rad/71834

1. The inclosed correspondence concerning Dr. Constantine Generales is Forwarded for your information and whatever action you may deem is indicated.
2. The Air Surgeon is not interested in the services of Dr. Generales unless it is desired to carry forward these experiments on mutations in extreme altitudes.

                      Otis O. Benson
                      [Illegible] Medical Corps
                      Chief, Medical Research Division
                      Office of the Air Surgeon

REFERENCES

1: THE OAK RIDGE SECRET

1. Interview, July 28, 2001.
2. www.ornl.gov
3. Interview, July 28, 2001.
4. Army Air Forces, May 14, 1946.
5. Maj. Gen. Curtis LeMay to the commanding general, Air Transport Command, Washington, D.C., September 27, 1946.
6. Interview, July 28, 2001.

2: DARKNESS IN THE DESERT

1. 2nd Lt. Walter Haut, press information officer, in a press release for the Roswell Army Air Field, July 8, 1947.
2. Information provided to the author by Stanton T. Friedman, December 19, 1993.
3. Friedman, Stanton T., and William L. Moore. *The Roswell Incident: Beginning of the Cosmic Watergate.* Proceedings, MUFON Symposium, Cambridge, Mass., 1981.
4. Berlitz, Charles, and William L. Moore. *The Roswell Incident.* London: Granada Publishing, 1980.
5. Moore, William L. *The Roswell Investigation.* Burbank, CA: William L. Moore Publications and Research, 1982.
6. Ibid.
7. Friedman, Stanton T., and Don Berliner. *Crash at Corona: The U.S. Military Retrieval and Cover-up of a UFO.* New York: Paragon House, 1992.

8. Berlitz, Charles, and William L. Moore. *The Roswell Incident.* London: Granada Publishing, 1980.

9. Moore, William L. *Crashed Saucers: Evidence in the Search for Proof.* Proceedings, MUFON Symposium. St. Louis, 1985.

10. Randle, Kevin D., and Donald R. Schmitt. *The Truth About the UFO Crash at Roswell.* New York: M. Evans, 1994.

Randle, Kevin D., and Donald R. Schmitt. *UFO Crash at Roswell.* New York: Avon, 1991.

11. Ibid.

Berlitz, Charles, and William L. Moore. *The Roswell Incident.* London: Granada Publishing, 1980.

12. www.math.ohio-state.edu/history/biographies/lapaz

13. Randle, Kevin D., and Donald R. Schmitt. *The Truth About the UFO Crash at Roswell.* New York: M. Evans, 1994.

Randle, Kevin D., and Donald R. Schmitt. *UFO Crash at Roswell.* New York: Avon, 1991.

14. Ibid.

Good, Timothy. *Alien Contact.* New York, William Morrow, 1992.

15. Randle, Kevin D., and Donald R. Schmitt. *The Truth About the UFO Crash at Roswell.* New York: M. Evans, 1994.

Randle, Kevin D., and Donald R. Schmitt. *UFO Crash at Roswell.* New York: Avon, 1991.

16. Ibid.

17. Pflock, Karl. *Roswell in Perspective.* Mt. Rainier, MD: The Fund for UFO Research, 1994.

18. Pflock, Karl. *Roswell in Perspective.* Mt. Rainier, MD: The Fund for UFO Research, 1994.

Randle, Kevin D., and Donald R. Schmitt. *The Truth About the UFO Crash at Roswell.* New York: M. Evans, 1994.

Randle, Kevin D., and Donald R. Schmitt. *UFO Crash at Roswell.* New York: Avon, 1991.

Berlitz, Charles, and William L. Moore. *The Roswell Incident.* London: Granada Publishing, 1980.

Friedman, Stanton T., and Don Berliner. *Crash at Corona: The U.S. Military Retrieval and Cover-up of a UFO.* New York: Paragon House, 1992.

19. Federal Bureau of Investigation, July 8, 1947.

20. William Moore lecture, July 1988.

3: THE SECOND COVER-UP

1. Claiborne, William. "GAO Turns to Alien Turf in Probe." *Washington Post,* January 14, 1994, p. 21.

2. *Results of a Search for Records Concerning the 1947 Crash Near Roswell, New Mexico,* General Accounting Office, July 28, 1995.

3. Weaver, Col. Richard L. *Report of Air Force Research Regarding the Roswell Incident.* United States Air Force, 1994.

Weaver, Col. Richard L. *The Roswell Report: Fact vs. Fiction in the New Mexico Desert.* United States Air Force, 1995.

4. Carey, Thomas J., and Donald R. Schmitt. "You and I Never Saw This," *The Roswell Report.* www.scifi.com/ufo/roswell/articles/013.html

5. Carey, Thomas J., and Donald R. Schmitt. "We Both Know What Really Happened Out There," *The Roswell Report.* www.scifi.com/ufo/roswell/articles/009.html

6. Weaver, Col. Richard L. *Report of Air Force Research Regarding the Roswell Incident.* United States Air Force, 1994.

Weaver, Col. Richard L. *The Roswell Report: Fact vs. Fiction in the New Mexico Desert.* United States Air Force, 1995.

7. www.roswellproof.com

8. Weaver, Col. Richard L. *Report of Air Force Research Regarding the Roswell Incident.* United States Air Force, 1994.

Weaver, Col. Richard L. *The Roswell Report: Fact vs. Fiction in the New Mexico Desert.* United States Air Force, 1995.

9. McAndrew, Cap. James. *The Roswell Report: Case Closed.* United States Air Force, 1997.

10. United States Air Force Press Conference. The Pentagon, Washington D.C., July 4, 1997.

11. "Dummies Weren't Classified, Says Retired Colonel." Associated Press, July 5, 1997.

12. Friedman, Stanton. "Scientist Challenges Air Force Regarding UFOs." www.v-j-enterprises.com/sfchlgaf.html

13. www.more.abcnews.go.com/dispatches/bureaus/roswell702/roswell702.html

4: BALLOONS AND BOMBS

1. Mikesh, Robert C. *Japan's World War II Balloon Bomb Attacks on North America.* Washington D.C., Smithsonian Institution Press, 1997.

Arakawa, H. *Basic Principles of the Balloon Bomb.* Meteorological Research Institute, Tokyo, Japan, January 1956.

Rhodes, Richard. *The Making of the Atomic Bomb.* New York: Simon & Schuster, 1986.

Webber, Bert. *Silent Siege III: Japanese Attacks on North America in World War II.* Medford, OR: Webb Research Group Publishers, 1997.

2. Associated Press, June 5, 1945.

3. "No Need to Worry Over Jap Balloons." *Tacoma News-Times,* June 6, 1945.

4. "Jap Balloons Fell in Sixteen States." *Tacoma News Tribune,* August 15, 1945.

5. Ibid.
6. Brines, Russell. "Japanese Abandoned Paper Balloon Weapon." *Tacoma News-Times*, October 2, 1945.
7. Ibid.
8. Williams, Peter, and David Wallace. *Unit 731: Japan's Secret Biological Warfare in World War II*. New York: The Free Press, 1989.
9. Ibid.
10. Mikesh, Robert C. *Japan's World War II Balloon Bomb Attacks on North America*. Washington D.C., Smithsonian Institution Press, 1997.

5: MEDICAL MADNESS

1. Gold, Hal. *Unit 731 Testimony*. Yenbooks, 1996.
Harris, Sheldon H. *Factories of Death*. New York: Routledge, 1994.
Williams, Peter, and David Wallace. *Unit 731: Japan's Secret Biological Warfare in World War II*. London: Hodder & Stoughton Ltd., 1989.
Materials on the Trial of Former Servicemen of the Japanese Army Charged with Manufacturing and Employing Bacteriological Weapons, Moscow: Foreign Languages Publishing House, 1950.
Daws, Gavan. *Prisoners of the Japanese: POWs of World War II in the Pacific*. New York: William Morrow, 1994.
2. *History of AAF Participation in Project Paperclip, May 1945–March 1947*. Air Materiel Command, Wright Air Force Base, 1948.
Bower, Tom. *The Paperclip Conspiracy: The Hunt for Nazi Scientists*. Boston: Little, Brown, 1987.
Nazi Conspiracy and Aggression. Washington D.C.: U.S. Government Printing Office, 1946.
Shirer, William L. *The Rise and Fall of the Third Reich*. New York: Fawcett Crest, 1962.
3. Shirer, William L. *The Rise and Fall of the Third Reich*. New York: Fawcett Crest, 1962.
4. *Nazi Conspiracy and Aggression*. Washington, D.C.: U.S. Government Printing Office, 1946.
Shirer, William L. *The Rise and Fall of the Third Reich*. New York: Fawcett Crest, 1962.
5. Ibid.
6. *Advisory Committee on Human Radiation Experiments: Final Report*. Washington, D.C.: Department of Energy, 1995.
Human Radiation Experiments Associated with the U.S. Department of Energy and Its Predecessors. Washington, D.C.: U.S. Department of Energy, 1995.
Human Radiation Experiments: The Department of Energy Roadmap to the Story and Records. Washington, D.C.: U.S. Department of Energy, 1995.

6: PAPERCLIP

1. *History of AAF Participation in Project Paperclip*, May 1945–March 1947, Air Materiel Command, Wright Air Force Base, 1948.

Bower, Tom. *The Paperclip Conspiracy*. Boston: Little, Brown, 1987.

2. Hunt, Linda. *Secret Agenda: The United States Government, Nazi Scientists, and Project Paperclip, 1945–1990*. New York: St. Martin's Press, 1991.

3. Advisory Committee Staff, Advisory Committee on Human Radiation Experiments. Memorandum, April 5, 1995.

4. Ibid.

5. Ibid.

6. Ibid.

7: WHITE SANDS AND THE NUCLEAR AGE

1. Karman, Dr. Theodore von. *Where We Stand: A Report for the AAF Scientific Advisory Group*. Headquarters Air Material Command, 1946. http://www-groups.dcs.st-and.ac.uk/~history/Mathematicians/Karm an.html

2. www.Ornl.gov/ORNLReview/rev25–34/chapter3.shtml.

3. *Brief History of the Aircraft Nuclear Propulsion Project at ORNL*. Oak Ridge, TN: June 16, 1950.

4. www.wsmr.army.mil

5. *Advisory Committee Staff, Advisory Committee on Human Radiation Experiments*. Memorandum, April 5, 1995.

6. www.wsmr.army.mil

8: THE BRITISH CONNECTION

1. *Out of This World*, BBC Television, July 1996.

2. Redfern, Nick. "Tales from the Station." Published privately, 2001.

3. Berlitz, Charles, and William L. Moore. *The Roswell Incident*. London: Granada Publishing, 1980.

Good, Timothy. *Alien Liaison: The Ultimate Secret*. London: Random Century, 1991.

4. Greg Bishop wrote at length about the Bennewitz saga in his book *Project Beta*, and a truly bizarre story it is. Bishop, Greg. *Project Beta: The Story of Paul Bennewitz, National Security, and the Creation of a Modern UFO Myth*. New York: Paraview Pocket Books, 2005.

5. Interview, March 28, 1997.

9: INSIDER INFORMATION

1. Interview, December 6, 2003.

2. Interview, December 9, 2003.

3. www.ncbi.nlm.nih.gov/disease/EVC.html

4. www.Progeriaresearch.org

5. Interview, December 9, 2003.

6. www.soc.mil/swcs/museum/Macmemo.shtml

7. Redfern, Nick, and Andy Roberts. *Strange Secrets: Real Government Files on the Unknown.* New York: Paraview Pocket Books, 2003.

8. Interview, December 9, 2003.

9. "Early Cloud Penetration." Air Research and Development Command, Kirtland Air Force Base, New Mexico, January 27, 1956.

10. Interview, December 9, 2003.

10: DESERT SECRETS

1. Interview, January 12, 2004.

2. Scully, Frank. *Behind the Flying Saucers.* New York: Henry Holt, 1950.

3. Interview, January 12, 2004.

4. Interview, January 12, 2004.

11: CORROBORATION

1. Carey, Thomas J., and Donald R. Schmitt, *Mack Brazel Reconsidered.* www.nicap.dabsol.co.uk/rosbraz.htm and *International UFO Reporter*, Winter 1999.

2. Ibid.

3. Cooper, Timothy. *The White Sands Proving Ground UFO Incidents of 1947: A Preliminary Report.*

4. Ibid.

5. Interview, January 12, 2004.

6. *The Grizzly*, January 10, 1991.

7. Stringfield, Leonard. *UFO Crash Retrievals: The Inner Sanctum.* Cincinnati, OH: 1994 (published privately).

8. Cooper, op. cit.

9. *UFO*, Vol. 9, No. 2, 1994.

10. Vallee, Jacques. *Revelations.* New York: Ballantine, 1991.

11. Cannon, Martin. "The Lost Files of the Controllers: Roswell, Part 1, Truth and Consequences," *The Lighthouse Report*, www.redshift.com/~damason/lhreport/articles/roswell.html

12. Pflock, Karl. *Roswell In Perspective.* Mt. Rainier, MD: Fund for UFO Research, 1994.

13. Secret memorandum. *Holloman Air Force Base Range Safety, 1947–1959.* National Archives and Records Administration, Holloman Air Force Base: July 14, 1960.

14. www.af.mil/bios/bio.asp?bioID=4669

15. Memorandum to Air Surgeon's Office from Deputy Chief of the Air Staff, May 20, 1947.

16. Memorandum. Medical Research Division, Air Surgeon's Office, July 1, 1947.

17. Memorandum. Office of the Air Surgeon, September 22, 1947.

18. Wilson, Jim. "Roswell Plus 50." *Popular Mechanics*, July 1997. www.popularmechanics.com/science/space/1282456.html

19. Wilson, Jim. "The Dummies of Roswell." *Popular Mechanics*, September 1997. www.popularmechanics.com/science/space/1282461.html

20. Interview, February 10, 2004.

21. Redfern, Nick. *The FBI Files: The FBI's UFO Top Secrets Exposed.* New York: Simon & Schuster, 1998.

22. "New Mexican Had Lookout Job For 'Japanese Germs.'" Press release, University of New Mexico, 1945.

23. "No Jap Balloon, Light in the Sky was a Meteorite." Press release, University of New Mexico Press Release, 1945.

12: HITLER'S DISKS

1. Interview, February 12, 2004.

2. U.S. Air Force Intelligence Memorandum, January 3, 1952, from Brigadier General W. M. Garland to General John Samford, Air Force Director of Intelligence. National Archives and Records Administration, MD.

3. Central Intelligence Agency Intelligence Report. May 27, 1954. www.cia.gov

4. Federal Bureau of Investigation. Memorandum dated November 7, 1957. National Archives and Records Administration, MD.

5. Federal Bureau of Investigation. Memorandum dated June 8, 1967. National Archives and Records Administration, MD.

6. The National Archives: AIR 20/9321. Crown copyright exists.

7. The National Archives: DEFE 41/117 and DEFE 41/118. Crown copyright exists.

8. Interview, February 12, 2004.

9. Federal Bureau of Investigation. Memorandum dated August 15, 1947. National Archives and Records Administration, MD.

10. Federal Bureau of Investigation. Memorandum dated August 19, 1947. National Archives and Records Administration, MD.

11. Ibid.

Redfern, Nick. *The FBI Files: The FBI's UFO Top Secrets Exposed.* New York: Simon & Schuster, 1998.

13: BODY SNATCHERS

1. Nuclear Energy for Propulsion of Aircraft (NEPA) Medical Advisory Committee files 1950–1952.

2. M. C. Leverett, technical director, to Dr. Shields Warren, director of medicine and biology, Atomic Energy Commission, February 12, 1951.

3. *Advisory Committee on Human Radiation Experiments: Final Report.* Washington, D.C.: Department of Energy, 1995.

Human Radiation Experiments Associated with the U.S. Department of Energy and its predecessors. Washington, D.C.: U.S. Department of Energy, 1995.

Human Radiation Experiments: The Department of Energy Roadmap to the Story and Records. Washington, D.C.: U.S. Department of Energy, 1995.

4. "Documentary Update on Project Sunshine 'Body Snatching.'" Memorandum. Advisory Committee on Human Radiation Experiments, Advisory Committee Staff, June 9, 1995.

5. Lynn, Tan Ee. "Pressure Mounts on H.K. for Probe of Nuclear Baby Tests." Reuters, June 8, 2001.

6. *Western Australian Newspapers.*, June 12, 2001.

14: THE CRASHED UFOS THAT NEVER WERE

1. Newman, Bernard. *The Flying Saucer.* London: Gollancz, 1948. Taylor, Phillip. "The Mystic and the Spy: Two Early British UFO Writers." *Magonia* 61 (November 1997) and www.magonia.demon.co.uk.

New York Times, January 9, 1945.

Times, February 27, 1968.

2. Lt. H. W. Smith and Mr. G. W. Towles. Project Grudge Technical Report No. 102-AC 49/15-100. Air Materiel Command, August 1949. National Archives and Records Administration, MD.

3. *JCS Pub 1,* Joint Chiefs of Staff. August 16, 1980.

4. Haines, Gerald K. *CIA's Role in the Study of UFOs 1947–90.* Studies in Intelligence, Vol. 1, No. 1, Central Intelligence Agency, 1997. www.cia.gov

5. *The Day After Aztec,* Karl Pflock, self-published.

Scully, Frank. *Behind the Flying Saucers.* New York: Henry Holt Publishers, 1950.

Steinman, Williams, and Wendelle Stevens. *UFO Crash at Aztec.* UFO Photo Archives, 1987.

Clearwater Sun, October 27, 1974.

Official UFO, December 1975.

Fate, February 1988.

Berlitz, Charles and William Moore. *The Roswell Incident.* London: Granada, 1980.

Good, Timothy. *Beyond Top Secret: The Worldwide UFO Security Threat.* London: Sidgwick and Jackson, 1996. http://www.aztecufo.com

6. Ibid.

7. Moore, William. "The Crown of St. Stephens and Crashed UFOs." *Far Out,* No. 1, 1992.

Clarke, Dr. David, and Andy Roberts. *Out of the Shadows: UFO's, the Establishment, and the Official Cover-up.* London: Piatkus, 2002.

8. Interview, February 20, 2004.

9. Corso, Col. (ret) Philip J. and William J. Birnes. *The Day After Roswell.* New York: Simon & Schuster, 1997.

Lin, Richard. "Shape Memory Alloys and Their Applications." www.stanford.edu/~richlin1/sma/sma.html

10. Corso, Col. (ret) Philip J. and William J. Birnes. *The Day After Roswell.* New York: Simon & Schuster, 1997.

11. Lyustiberg, Viillen. "Flying Saucers? They're a Myth!" Moscow: Novosti Press Agency, March 12, 1969.

12. *Independent,* June 1, 2001.

15: MAJESTIC

1. Good, Timothy. *Above Top Secret: The Worldwide UFO Cover-up.* London: Sidgwick & Jackson, 1987.

2. Friedman, Stanton T. *Top Secret: Majic.* New York: Marlowe and Company, 1996.

3. Moore, William L., and Jaime H. Shandera. *The MJ-12 Documents: An Analytical Report.* Burbank, CA: The Fair Witness Project, 1990.

4. www.majesticdocuments.com

5. Blum, Howard. *Out There.* New York: Simon & Schuster, 1990.

6. Vallee, Jacques. *Revelations.* New York: Ballantine, 1991.

7. *UFO,* Vol. 5, No. 5.

Haines, Gerald K. *The FBI Files: The FBI's UFO Top Secrets Exposed.* London: Simon & Schuster, 1998.

8. "CIA's Role in the Study of UFOs 1947–90." *Studies in Intelligence,* Vol. 1, No. 1, 1997. Central Intelligence Agency, www.cia.gov

9. *Pentagram,* November 23, 1988.

10. Blum, Howard. *Out There.* New York: Simon & Schuster, 1990. See also: Redfern, Nick. "The FBI Connection." www.nickredfern.com/news/htm

11. Interviews, January 26 and February 20, 2004.

12. "Eastchester Style 'Flying Disc' Bears Radio Parts of Jap Make." The (Yonkers, N.Y.) *Herald Statesman,* July 14, 1947.

13. Interview, February 12, 2004.

16: PROGERIA

1. *Good Morning with Anne and Nick,* BBC Television, January 13, 1995.

2. Easton, James. "Alien Autopsy: FAQ."
www.darkconspiracy.com/alienufo/autopsy/faw/txt September 21, 1996.

3. Hesemann, Michael, and Philip Mantle. *Beyond Roswell: The Alien Autopsy Film, Area 51, and the U.S. Government Coverup of UFOs.* New York: Marlowe, 1997.
www.beyondroswell.com/roswell/autopsy.html

4. Ibid.

5. Interview, January 22, 1997.

Pope, Nick. *Open Skies, Closed Minds.* New York: Simon & Schuster, 1996.

6. Interview, March 28, 1997.

7. Hesemann, Michael, and Philip Mantle, op/ cit/.

8. "Wie Im Lehrbuch." *Der Spiegel*, April 23, 1996.

9. www.beyondroswell.com/roswell/autopsy.html

10. Interview, February 12, 2004.

11. Committee Staff, Advisory Committee on Human Radiation Experiments, March 8, 1995. National Archives and Records Administration, MD.

12. Memorandum. Project 4.5, Atomic Energy Commission, March 5, 1952.
National Archives and Records Administration, MD.

13. Quimby, Edith H., and Donovan McCune, M.D. "Uptake of Radioactive Iodine by the Normal and Disordered Thyroid Gland in Children." *Biology Division Bulletin* of the Clinton National Laboratory, November 3, 1947.

14. *Tabulation of Available Data Relative to Radiation Biology*, NEPA Medical Advisory Panel, 1949.

15. U.S. Army, memorandum, Deputy Chief of Air Staff for Research and Development, July 5, 1947.

INDEX

Printed in the United States
By Bookmasters